BEYOND THE HIGHLAND LINE

BEYOND THE HIGHLAND LINE

Highland History and Culture

CAROLINE BINGHAM

CONSTABLE · LONDON

First published in Great Britain 1991
by Constable and Company Limited
3 The Lanchesters, 162 Fulham Palace Road
London W6 9ER
Copyright © 1991 Caroline Bingham
The right of Caroline Bingham to be
identified as the author of this work
has been asserted by her in accordance
with the Copyright, Designs and Patents Act 1988
ISBN 09 468790 0
Set in Monophoto Caledonia
by Servis Filmsetting Limited, Manchester
Printed in Great Britain
by St Edmundsbury Press Limited
Bury St Edmunds, Suffolk

A CIP catalogue record for this book
is available from the British Library

To my godfather,
KEVEN MEREDITH

CONTENTS

ILLUSTRATIONS

James V, who voyaged to Orkney and the Western Isles. (*National Galleries of Scotland*)

James VI, who promulgated the Statutes of Iona. (*National Galleries of Scotland*)

John Grahame of Claverhouse, Viscount Dundee, the victor of Killiecrankie. (*National Galleries of Scotland*)

Prince James Francis Edward Stuart, to the Jacobites 'King James VIII and III'. (*National Gallery*)

Prince Charles Edward Stuart in 1745. (*National Galleries of Scotland*)

An unknown Highland Chief, wearing the *feileadh mor*, the version of highland dress which was the forerunner of the kilt. (*National Galleries of Scotland*)

A young woman of the Clan Matheson. McIan's rendering of the traditional highland woman's dress described by Martin Martin. The boy is shown wearing *cuarans* or buskins of red deerskin.

Tartan clothes:
Flora MacDonald wearing a tartan dress of fashionable cut. (*National Galleries of Scotland*)
Neil Gow, the Highland fiddler, wearing tartan breeches and stockings. He is shown similarly dressed, playing the fiddle in David Allan's painting 'The Highland Wedding'.

The harsh conditions of crofting life in the nineteenth century:
Crofters planting potatoes in Skye. The men are using the *Cas Chrom*. (*Aberdeen City Arts: libraries*)
Crofters outside their houses in Cromarty. (*Edinburgh City libraries*)

Tourism in the Highlands:
A nineteenth century deerstalker at rest. (*Edinburgh City libraries*)
Winter sports:
Skiers on the Glenshee ski-lift. (*D.C. Thomson and Co Ltd*)

Maps

All maps drawn by John Mitchell

ACKNOWLEDGEMENTS

Readers will notice that the Kings of Scots from Robert II to James V are 'Stewarts' and thenceforward 'Stuarts'. The change in spelling comes with Mary Queen of Scots, whose French upbringing led to the adoption of the form 'Stuart'. Her second husband, Lord Darnley, appears as Stewart, Steuart and Stuart, but with their son James VI of Scotland and I of England the spelling 'Stuart' becomes established. There is a well-known saying 'Not all Stewarts are sib[related] to the King'; but a great many are – of either spelling.

My debt to a number of historians is acknowledged in the 'Notes and References'. I am grateful to be able to rely on the resources of the London Library and the Institute of Historical Research. I should also like to thank Professor Donald MacRae of the London School of Economics for his immensely interesting discourse on the Gaels.

Finally I should like to thank a number of people for whose care and kindness I owe particular gratitude: Frances Bingham, Liz Mathews, Dr Denis Couchman, Mrs Aileen Horne, Mr John Hale and Dr Anne Folkes. I am always indebted to my parents, Cedric and Muriel Worsdell, and I am always aware of how much I owe to CDL and SC.

Regrettably I cannot thank the late Mrs Nonie Ison for the bequest of her collection of books on Scottish History, but I should like to put on record my gratitude for it.

C.B.

PROLOGUE

HIGHLANDS AND ISLANDS

No natural geographical barrier divides Scotland from England. The wandering frontier which extends from the Tweed to the Solway was defined by centuries of warfare and diplomacy. It is sufficiently illogical to include the town of Berwick-on-Tweed in England and the old county of Berwickshire in Scotland. Paradoxically, Scotland is bisected by a natural division, the 'Highland Line', which has never served as a political frontier. It has been, and to some extent remains, a line of division between the societies and the cultures of Highland and Lowland Scotland. An account of life beyond the Highland Line requires a definition of the area as a preliminary.

North of the border between Scotland and England the Scottish border country extends to the Southern Uplands, an area which contains its own ranges of hills, the Pentlands, Moorfoots and Lammermuirs. Beyond them the land falls away again to the plain of the Central Lowlands, where the estuaries of the Clyde and Forth stretch far inland to form a narrow isthmus, now highly industrialized. North of the isthmus the central mass of the Scottish mainland is bisected diagonally on a north-east to sourth-west line by a geological fault which runs from near Stonehaven to Helensburgh, the 'Highland Boundary Fault' to which the Highland Line adheres closely but stops short of the east coast, so that the eastern seaboard is lowland throughout its length. Beyond Stonehaven a broader wedge of lowland country extends as far as Nairn on the Moray Firth. In the far north, Caithness, the north-eastern promontory of the Scottish mainland, is lowland in character but its remoteness from the main lowland area has linked it historically with the Highlands and the Northern Isles.

The Highland Line is thus a continuous division which extends from a point on the Clyde to a point near the centre of the north coast. If this meandering line is traced on a map of Scotland it shows a nearer approximation to a division between east and west than to one between north and south. Beyond the Highland Line the Highlands themselves are intricately fragmented. The division between east and west is reinforced by the mountain range which in early times was named *Druim Alban* – the 'Ridge of Scotland'. Marked by a line of high peaks it runs from Ben Lomond at the head of Loch Lomond, by way of Ben Nevis and Ben More Assynt, to Ben Hope in Sutherland. To the east of Druim Alban lies the mountain massif of the Central Highlands, known as the Grampians. Some writers on Scottish toponymy object to the name Grampians because it is a corruption of the Latin *Mons Graupius* but it has been established by usage and made official by the naming of the modern Grampian Region, so there seems little point in rejecting it. Other names have been given at different times to the central mountain mass of the Grampian range, which for centuries created an effective barrier between the Lowlands and the far north: in Gaelic it was called *Monadliath* – the Grey Mountain – and in the Middle Ages this was corrupted in Lowland speech to the 'Mounth'. The courses of several rivers, forcing their way down from the mountains to the east coast, formed a series of gateways to and from the Highlands: Spey, Don, Dee, Esk and Tay formed routes of communication between the Central Highlands and the Lowlands before man-made transport systems.

On a north-east to south-west line parallel with the Highland Boundary Fault and sixty to seventy miles beyond it on the further side of the Grampians, another great geological fault cuts off the remote northern Highlands. The *Glen Mor nan Alban*, or 'Great Glen of Scotland', with its string of lochs – Loch Linnhe, Loch Lochy, Loch Oich and Loch Ness – links the Firth of Lorne to the Moray Firth, and since the completion of the Caledonian Canal in 1822 has formed a continuous waterway. But long before the canal was cut the Great Glen formed an important route of communication, the easiest way of crossing Druim Alban. Beyond the Great Glen the north-west Highlands contain the wildest country in Great Britain, seen at its most dramatic in the savage landscape of Sutherland, with its bare peaks of Torridonian sandstone, some of them capped with glittering white quartzite which looks from a distance like snow, a region inhospitable to humanity and, in the present century, very sparsely populated.

The west coast of Scotland has a far more complex coastline than the east. From north to south it is fretted by a series of spectacular inlets, the mouths of the tapering sea-lochs which run many miles inland. Throughout the greater part of its length the west coast belongs to the Highlands, and the sharp slant of the Highland Line is well illustrated by the fact that the Highland town of Campbeltown in Kintyre on the west coast lies south of the English town of Berwick-on-Tweed on the east coast. Galloway, the extreme south-western area of the Scottish mainland, which lies between the Firths of Clyde and Solway, is Lowland in character, but its remoteness from the south-eastern Lowlands, which became the seat of the Scottish government, enabled it for centuries to maintain its separateness from both Highlands and Lowlands.

Off the west coast of Scotland lie the Western Isles, which are linked with the Highlands both geographically and historically. These islands collectively are called the Hebrides, a beautiful name which few would wish to reject, even though it is a corruption resulting from a mis-reading of the Latin *Ebudae*. The Inner Hebrides fall into three groups centred upon the large islands of Skye, Mull and Islay. Westward of them lies the broken chain of the Outer Hebrides, Lewis (or 'The Lews'), Harris, North Uist, South Uist and Barra. They are sometimes called the 'Long Island', a name which recalls what was once a fact. Both the main groups of islands are surrounded by a multitude of islets and rocky skerries. Far out in the Atlantic lies the small archipelago of St Kilda and beyond it the furthest outlier of Scottish territory, the uninhabitable crag of Rockall.

From the earliest times of human habitation the sea was a means of communication, not a cause of division. The sea linked the Highlands and the Western Isles and offered easy contact with Ireland, for the channel between Northern Ireland and the Mull of Kintyre is only twelve miles wide. The seaways also gave easy access to the islands of the Firth of Clyde. For centuries the whole area shared a common culture based on the Gaelic language.

Ease of passage, even though longer voyages were involved, similarly led to close relations between Scandinavia and the Northern Isles, which lie beyond the north coast of Caithness. The Northern Isles consist of two archipelagos, Orkney and Shetland, and in each instance the largest island of the group is called the Mainland. Orkney is separated from Caithness by the Pentland Firth, and the islands with their dividing firths and sounds follow the north-east south-west alignment of the faults and mountains of the Scottish mainland. The Shetland Islands lie north-east of Orkney, some two hundred miles equidistant from Aberdeen and Bergen, and at 60° north on the same latitude as the southern tip of Greenland.

In the ninth century, when the political kingdom of Scotland was taking shape, both the Western and the Northern Isles fell under

Scandinavian rule, from which the Western Isles were recovered in 1266, and the Northern Isles in 1469. In the Western Isles the Gaelic culture absorbed the Norse, but in the Northern Isles the Scandinavian influence remained so strong that a Scandinavian dialect, the Norn, was current until the eighteenth century.

The subject of this book is the area of Gaelic culture, but it cannot be examined without reference to its neighbours, Ireland and the Northern Isles. Throughout the historical period its context is the history of Scotland.

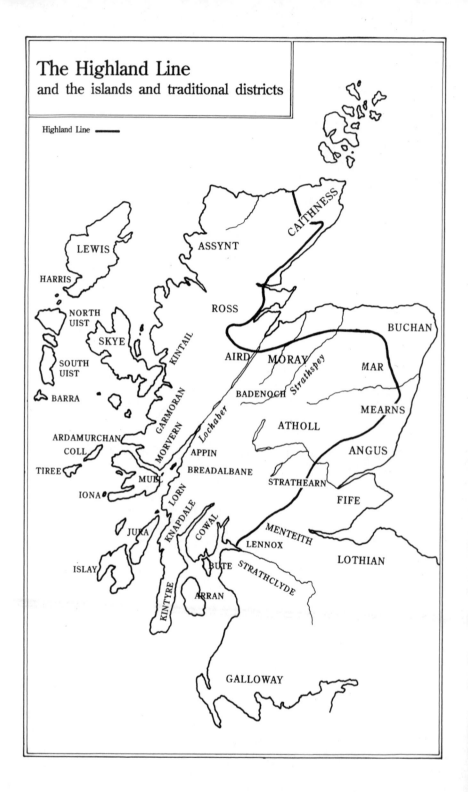

The Highland Line
and the islands and traditional districts

Highland Line ━━━

LEWIS

HARRIS

NORTH
UIST

SKYE

SOUTH
UIST

BARRA

ARDAMURCHAN

COLL

TIREE

IONA

JURA

ISLAY

ASSYNT

CAITHNESS

ROSS

KINTAIL

AIRD MORAY

BUCHAN

MAR

Strathspey

BADENOCH

GARMORAN

MORVERN

Lochaber

APPIN

BREADALBANE

ATHOLL

MEARNS

ANGUS

STRATHEARN

FIFE

MULL

LORN

KNAPDALE

COWAL

MENTEITH

LENNOX

LOTHIAN

BUTE STRATHCLYDE

KINTYRE

ARRAN

GALLOWAY

1

THE HIGHLANDS AND ISLANDS IN PREHISTORY

> The ruins of houses, settlements, strongholds, places
> of forgotten ceremonial, tombs and graves – and the
> relics found in them – can be translated into history
> by inference and comparison, and only thus can any
> contact at all be made with the nameless gene-
> rations who opened up the land.[1]

Eighteen thousand years ago the whole of Scotland was covered by a
vast ice sheet which extended as far south as the English Midlands.
Slowly the temperature rose and the ice retreated, until some thirteen
thousand years ago Scotland was ice-free, with a climate similar to the
present. Then the ice flowed south again in a movement which
geologists call the 'Loch Lomond Advance'. It is possible that in the
temperate period between these two ice ages men of the Upper
Palaeolithic period may have reached Scotland, for at this time Britain
was still a promontory of Europe, with no Straits of Dover to impede
the passage of wandering bands of hunters, who certainly reached
southern England and Wales. But if Old Stone Age men ever entered
Scotland every trace of their presence was expunged by the Loch
Lomond Advance.

The last ice age was brief. Some ten thousand years ago Scotland
was ice-free once more, and about two thousand years later the first
people to have left a record of their lives began to arrive in the
Highlands. These people saw a Highland landscape different from that
of the present day. The severity of glacial action had left sharp
landforms which time and frost would soften and crumble. The lochs
were larger, the areas of bog were more widespread and the sea lochs
stretched further inland. The rivers were more powerful watercourses
which thundered down from the heights deepening their beds with

19

meltwater from the rapidly disappearing snowfields. No areas of permanent snow now remain in the Highlands, though it would be a rare summer in which patches of the previous winter's drifts could not be found in a few high places and, as all walkers and climbers know, the sunniest day can produce a sudden snowstorm.

The small groups of Mesolithic hunters who penetrated the Highlands as advance parties of human occupation were encouraged by a kinder climate. They were living in the Boreal period, during which the summers were drier and warmer than they are now. Forests of oak and Scots pine, interspersed with hazel, birch and rowan, spread rapidly over the Highlands and the Western Isles, with alders and willows growing beside the watercourses. The north-east mainland and the Northern Isles remained always bare of trees. Their windy grasslands were grazed by herds of reindeer, wild cattle and small wild horses. The forest fringes were the habitat of elk and red deer. Wild boar rooted in the oak-woods. The depth of the forest was the home of wolves, brown bears and lynx and the numerous small animals which provided their prey.

The earliest people entered the Great Caledonian Forest fearful of the predators but determinedly seeking edible plants and easy game. Possibly, being men, they already possessed the human desire to dominate their environment rather than the animal instinct to adapt to it, for layers of wood ash beneath later deposits of peat suggest that they burned clearings, either to flush out the game or to make safe encampments for themselves.[2]

They preferred to live on the coast, building temporary shelters of turf and branches or finding more comfortable lodgings in caves. Mesolithic cave-dwellings were found at Oban, during building works in the late nineteenth century. But hunters and gatherers did not stay long in one place; they followed the movements of animals and the seasonal availability of plants. Sometimes, on the shoreline, they might find a stranded whale to provide an impromptu feast. Without such luck they faced the tedious work of knocking limpets off the rocks and gouging them out of their shells, or catching and cleaning other kinds of edible shellfish. Some of their enormous middens, sifted by archaeologists from the late nineteenth century onwards, have proved to contain several millions of shells, which bear witness to the hours these wandering groups had to spend in the effort to keep themselves alive.

The invention of boats made available the greater variety of fish which could be caught at sea, types which are still eaten today, including haddock, skate, grey mullet, wrasse and sea-bream. The earliest surviving boats are dug-outs, tree-trunks laboriously hollowed with small stone tools, assisted by careful burning. These would have been unwieldy craft in dangerous currents or tidal waters. A more seaworthy type of boat was the currach, a timber or wickerwork frame covered with skins, which was probably the type used by the earliest Highlanders to colonize the Western Isles and cross to Ireland, or by Irish colonists to reach the Western Isles. There is much to be discovered about the routes and patterns of settlement.

The earliest inhabitants of the Highlands and Isles, who remained nomadic hunters and gatherers, were joined around 4000 BC by seaborne immigrants from Europe, who brought domestic animals and knowledge of the farming techniques which are thought to have been developed in the Near East as early as 9000 BC. Wild dogs had been tamed by Palaeolithic and Mesolithic men and used for hunting. The Neolithic incomers brought new breeds of dogs, to guard their settlements and help control their flocks and herds of cattle, sheep, goats and pigs. They brought seed corn to establish crops of barley and a primitive form of wheat, and agricultural implements of stone for ploughing and harvest.

At first they farmed on fertile raised beaches near the coast which had formed as the land lifted in response to its release from the pressure of the ice. As new land was required for farming and grazing they set about systematic forest clearance, for which they needed constantly available supplies of good axe-blades. The quest for suitable stone took them to the Western Isles, where they found pitchstone on Arran and bloodstone on Rum. But Neolithic axe-blades which have been found in the Highlands have been traced to sites in Wales, Ireland and the English Lake District. Flint is in short supply in Scotland, except in the form of beach pebbles. From these were chipped the sharp microliths which were used for small tools, while large flint implements must have been acquired through trade with fairly distant areas. A series of jadeite axe-blades is presumed to have come from a European source, so far undiscovered. Axes made from such a rare and precious substance would probably have been used for ceremonial purposes: for sacrifice, or in the instance of blades which have never been used, as religious symbols.[3] But what were the ceremonies and who were the gods of these farmers and herdsmen remains unknown.

The ceremonies connected with death and burial were clearly of great importance to them, for over a thousand of their tombs remain, scattered over the Western Isles and the West Coast of Scotland, in the Great Glen, and in Orkney and Shetland. These are the earliest monumental remains in the landscape. They were not tombs of the illustrious dead, but community graves which remained in use over long periods and were often reused and enlarged. The original inhabitants did not always remain undisturbed. Sometimes disarticulated bones and cremated fragments were pushed aside to make way for new burials. These communal graves were of two basic designs: gallery graves and passage graves. A gallery grave consisted of an oblong chamber divided into stalls like a stable, the whole covered by a long cairn. A passage grave had a circular chamber entered through a passageway and covered by a round cairn. Several varieties of each type have been classified, but no two are exactly alike; they vary just as the churches of the Middle Ages vary.[4]

It is not surprising that in the course of some two thousand years the tomb-builders changed their ideas about burial rites. Sometimes they favoured inhumation and sometimes cremation, followed by the burial of the remains. Some archaeologists have discerned excarnation – exposing the body until the flesh had rotted, and then burying the bones. In Neolithic societies, whatever the chosen method of disposing of the dead, the purpose was always to ensure their welfare in the afterlife. Burials with accompanying grave goods and food offerings suggest that an afterlife was imagined in which material possessions would continue to be required.

The fact that so many tombs have survivied while of the houses of their builders there remains scarcely a trace, suggests that the Neolithic communities may have regarded the afterlife as more important than life in this world. But this impression may be mistaken. Tombs are seldom destroyed while the dead are protected by reverence or superstition, but houses are always being pulled down and rebuilt with a view to improvement. The evidence of the daily lives of Neolithic people in the Highlands and Islands might have been lost altogether had it not been for the survival of some houses in an area where timber was so scarce that everything, including furniture, had to be made of stone, and chance preserved the stone from being reused.

In Orkney, at Skara Brae on Mainland, there remains the best preserved Neolithic settlement in Northern Europe. In this village a small community lived from about 3500 to 2000 BC. The houses may belong to two or more periods of occupation, with no more than six occupied at any one time. They were built in a compact group, their doors opening off connecting covered passageways. To help exclude the northern gales a packing of dung, ash, sand and rubbish was heaped around the walls, so that the whole place must have been pervaded by a continuous stench.

Each house was a one-roomed dwelling with rounded corners and corbelled walls which curved inwards to support the roof, which was probably of turf resting on rafters of driftwood or whalebone. Within the thickness of the walls were cells, probably for storage. In each house there was a central hearth, two stone bed-boxes, a dresser made of stone shelves, and ingeniously constructed stone tanks let into the floor and made watertight with clay, in which live seafood could have been kept, to be eaten in stormy weather.

The enormous numbers of sheep and cattle bones in the midden material at Skara Brae suggest that pastoralism was the basis of the economy. The people seem to have bothered little about hunting, for the deer antlers which they made into tools have been identified as cast ones. Limpet-gathering, typical of earlier times, continued, but there was little evidence of deep-sea fishing. Professor V. Gordon Childe, whose excavation between the two World Wars unlocked the secrets of Skara Brae, reckoned that two stranded whales could have provided all the whalebone remnants which were found.

The villagers made whales' vertebrae into small vessels; larger containers they made from sandstone and pottery. There is no evidence that their ingenuity extended to making textiles. They still relied on the primitive materials of skin and fur, scraped clean of flesh with stone flakes, for their clothes and bed coverings.[5] Some of the shells they collected contain traces of pigments, which suggest that the shells were used as palettes for mixing facial and body paints. Adornments such as bead and bone necklaces were worn, and curiously carved stone balls have been found, which have no obvious use. Perhaps they were used for some kind of divination, perhaps not. It is always tempting to imagine that non-functional objects must have some religious or magical significance.

The archaeological detective work done at Skara Brae by Professor Childe and his successors has made it possible to imagine the daily life of a hard-working, self-sufficient community, living in conditions of cosy squalor. This isolated and circumscribed daily round was brought to an end in a dramatic fashion which almost miraculously preserved its minutiae. In about 2000 BC the village was engulfed by a sandstorm and the people fled in such haste that a woman who broke her necklace as she ran from her house left a scatter of beads in the passage outside her door. The buried village remained hidden until another exceptionally violent storm exposed it again in the mid-nineteenth century, by which time fashionable interest in antiquities ensured its preservation for later scientific study.

A natural disaster which paradoxically destroys and preserves recalls the destruction of Pompeii; but the end of Skara Brae was apparently less tragic, for no victims of the disaster were found when the village was excavated. The villagers escaped, but where they began their new life has never been discovered.

While Skara Brae lived out its last centuries the West Coast of Scotland received a new group of European settlers who have been called the 'Beaker Folk' after their characteristic handleless pottery. There may not have been many of them. At present archaeologists are less inclined to visualize a large invasion than to see a contagion of new ideas and fashions from small numbers of settlers to the existing communities. If so, far more important to future generations than a fashion for attractive red pottery or for individual burial in stone 'cists' instead of communal graves, was the introduction of the first objects of metal and the earliest knowledge of metallurgy. That working in metal suggested divine or magic power is illustrated by the metalworking gods and magical smiths of Classical, Norse and Celtic mythology. The earliest metal objects found in the Highlands were small implements of copper, gold and bronze, but these must have been in short supply because stone weapons and edge-tools continued to be made and widely used. A further indication that metal objects were rare is that they were seldom buried as grave goods, no doubt because they were too precious to be allowed to go out of circulation.

Meanwhile great social changes must have been taking place, which are suggested by the building of greater monuments than could have been produced by small autonomous communities. The authority of powerful tribal chiefs would have been required to command the building of the henges and stone circles which were raised all over Britain and to direct the large labour forces required. The purpose of these monuments remains controversial and the difference between the two types does not make questions concerning them any easier to answer. Henges are surrounded by a bank and a ditch and stone circles are not, but both are associated with burial pits and with cairns which stand within them or close to them. In the Highlands and Isles there are over thirty henges and circles, of which the most impressive of the former is the Ring of Brodgar on the Orkney mainland, and of the latter the circle and associated avenues at Callanish on Lewis.

The most obvious explanation of the henges and circles is that they were centres of religious observance, and that, as would be expected of the religion of farming people, their rituals were connected with the seasons, especially with festivals celebrating the equinoxes and solstices. A more elaborate theory has been propounded, that they were 'megalithic observatories' from which sophisticated calculations of the movements of heavenly bodies could be made. Great skills were required to design these monuments and to transport and raise the stones; whether their builders possessed the even greater skills of aligning them to observe the heavens will continue to fuel controversy.[6] The megalithic circles seem to have begun to fall out of use again by about 1500 BC, to judge by the dating of their associated tombs. The reason is unknown, but a possible explanation may be the decline of the religion with which they were associated, and this in turn could have had a climatic cause. The warm sub-Boreal period in which the Neolithic cultures had flourished gave way about 2000 BC to the colder and wetter sub-Atlantic period, which has continued with some variation to the present day. Cloudier skies would have made observation of the stars more difficult and, if this was the purpose of the megalithic circles, it might have suggested the anger of the gods. So might the encroachment of deep layers of peat around the feet of the standing stones. Perhaps these natural phenomena led to a crisis of faith. At all events, megalithic circles were survivals of a forgotten past before the beginning of history.

In the course of a single chapter in which many social changes are mentioned it is easy to forget that over so long a period the rate of change was extremely slow. Many lifetimes might elapse before an innovation spread very far. The introduction of metals is an obvious example. It was as late as 600 BC that the first metalworker arrived in Shetland and set up his workshop in the settlement which was later named Jarlshof, but as early as 2000 BC that the use of bronze was spreading across the Highlands and the Western Isles, and leading to the development of much more effective tools and weapons.

The spread of bronze was accompanied by increasing warfare, for which various explanations have been offered. Possibly growth of population led communities to stake territorial claims. Agriculturalists may have found that they could no longer convert woodland to farmland as they required without encountering their neighbours attempting to do the same. Pastoralists may have met the same problem when driving their beasts to new pastures. Climatic deterioration may have enhanced the problem. The sub-Atlantic climate causing the metamorphosis of grassland into peat-bog may have increased competition for the possession of good grazing. At the same time the techniques of metal production themselves may have encouraged strife. Bronze is an alloy of copper and tin. Copper ore is found in Scotland, but for supplies of tin Highland metalworkers relied upon sources in Cornwall and Europe. Fighting for commodities is probably as old as trading in them. Hoards of bronze swords, perhaps the stock in trade of early arms dealers, found in the Highlands, have been dated to between 1100 and 1000 BC. At this period swords were the latest type of offensive weapon, and the appalling gashes which they could inflict led to the development of sheet-bronze body armour.

The remains of buildings dating from the first millennium BC show a shift of emphasis from the religious and monumental to the secular. As the Megalithic circles were abandoned burial customs changed. Communal and individual graves above ground were no longer built. The dead were cremated, their ashes were packed in cinerary urns no different from domestic storage jars, and they were buried in urn-fields. From time to time these burial places are discovered by chance, for there are no visible monuments. Perhaps this was the first result of mass-produced death.

The most impressive remains from the later centuries of prehistory are those of fortified dwellings, or fortifications which provided shelter for short periods in times of danger. Most of the larger hilltop forts so far identified have been found in southern Scotland. The remarkable 'vitrified' forts are mostly in the Lowlands, though some have been found in the Highland foothills. These forts have drystone cavity walls filled in with rubble and tied with transverse timbers to stabilize the filling and to prevent pressure from causing the supporting walls to bulge. The curious feature shared by all these forts so far discovered is that the timber lacing within the walls has been burned, causing the drystone walling to become fused or vitrified. The most likely explanation of the vitrification is that the forts were fired by their inhabitants' enemies, for the timber-laced walls would catch fire all too easily. But the forts may have been burned accidentally by their own inhabitants, who sometimes built wooden lean-to's against the insides of their own fortifications, thus greatly increasing the fire hazard. At all events, the vitrified walls are far stronger than the original drystone walls would have been, for they have proved almost indestructible.

A very different type of defensible place, constructed all over Scotland, was the crannog, a lake-dwelling built on timber piles, or on an existing islet strengthened by the sinking of piles, on which a round wooden house was built, approached by a timber gangway from the land. Crannog platforms naturally attracted silt, which helped to strengthen them. As a result, in some places the site of a crannog has become indistinguishable from a natural islet and only archaeological investigation has revealed the true origin. In some instances the site was so well chosen for defence that the original structure was later replaced by a stone castle. Loch an Eilean, Invernessshire, is an impressive example.[7]

North-west of the Highland Line other types of fortifications were developed which are seldom found in the Lowlands. Duns are round or D-shaped enclosures with high, thick drystone walls, sometimes built with internal galleries. Like the chambered tombs of earlier millennia they are classified by their common features, but are as variable in their details. Duns seem to have been the Highland equivalent of the hillforts of the Lowlands; they are much smaller, and were doubtless built to serve the needs of smaller communities.

Characteristic defences of the north-western Highlands, the Western Isles and Orkney and Shetland are brochs, which are much more consistent in design. These drystone towers were developed several centuries after the vitrified forts and the duns, for they date from the last century BC and the early centuries of the Christian era. They were so well built they continued to be occupied by squatters for many centuries thereafter, and though their stones were gradually reused for other buildings they proved none too easy to dismantle. An almost intact example is the Broch of Mousa, Shetland. Brochs are cylindrical in outline, narrowing towards the top and then straightening again; the walls are hollow in construction, with internal stairways and galleries. Whether they were lookout towers or temporary refuges against sudden raids, their cramped quarters make it obvious that they could not have housed many people for long periods.

Unfortified homesteads were also built. Typical of the Western Isles was the round stone 'wheel-house', so called from its spoke-like partition walls radiating from a central roof support. Souterrains, or tunnel-like earth houses, were probably storage-places rather than dwellings, though they could have served as refuges for people and animals against sudden attack. A souterrain is the earliest surviving structure on Hirta, the main island of the St Kilda group, but it may not have been built by the island's earliest inhabitants. St Kilda may have been visited by Mesolithic explorers who bivouacked without trace.

The development of a great variety of fortified or defensible places all over Scotland suggests a long troubled period. It was also a period of technological advance. The introduction of iron in the middle of the first millennium BC would have been an immense help to all fortification builders. The vast numbers of tree-trunks required for the construction of a timber-laced fort or a crannog is perhaps easier to imagine than to estimate, but the advantage of possessing iron axes for such an enterprise can scarcely be exaggerated.

The introduction of iron raises the controversial question of the arrival of the Celts. The metalwork (not only of iron, but also of gold and bronze) associated with the Celtic 'Hallstatt Culture' of *c.* 800 to 450 BC* could have reached Scotland through trade with Europe, but the manufacture in Scotland of metalwork typical of the Celtic 'La Tène Culture'† which lasted from *c.* 450 BC to the Roman conquest of Gaul, presupposed a strong Celtic element in the population. Probably trade with the continental Celts was followed by the arrival of Celtic immigrants, perhaps bands of warriors who established settlements by force of arms. Later, when the Celts in Europe and southern Britain were experiencing the pressure of Roman expansion, more groups may have arrived as refugees. When the Romans discovered Scotland they found a Celtic warrior aristocracy akin to that of southern Britain and of Gaul.

The name Celts – Keltoi – had been given by the Greeks to a group of European tribes which they recognized as possessing a common

* So named from a site in Austria associated with objects of this style and period.
† So named from a site in Switzerland and applied to associated objects.

language and culture and a typical appearance. The Celts were taller than the Mediterranean Europeans and were imagined as being universally fair-haired, which they were not. The impression of general similarity was enhanced by a fashion among Celtic warriors for bleaching and spiking their hair with limewash, shaving their cheeks and chins and cultivating their moustaches. The typical appearance of a Celtic warrior is exemplified by a famous Roman statue, copied from a Pergamene bronze, the *Dying Gaul*. The Gaul had stripped for the battle in which he received his death wound. When dressed the Celtic warrior sometimes wore *brakai* or trousers, sometimes a long shirt or tunic, in either instance covered by a large rectangular cloak, held in place by a brooch. Women's costume was a longer tunic and a similar cloak. The brightly striped or checked textiles of the Celts have been seen by some students of costume as the precursors of tartan.

The Celts impressed the Classical world as being so much obsessed with war that if they had no external enemies they fought among themselves. This probably explains why, when there were Celtic settlements from Ireland to Galatia in Asia Minor, there was never a Celtic Empire. They never developed political cohesion and in consequence lacked the power to resist the organized expansion of Rome.

Celtic society was tribal and hierarchical. The tribal leader was the king or occasionally the queen: the famous examples of Boudicca and Cartimandua witness that women could hold supreme power among the Celts.[8] Julius Caesar identified three classes in tribal society: *equites*, *druides* and *plebs*, or warriors, priests and people. The equites were the aristocracy who formed the King's immediate following. Probably from this class also were drawn the immensely powerful druids, whose entry to the priesthood followed a long noviciate during which druidic learning was memorized in vast quantities of verse. The *plebs* were freemen in a client relationship to the aristocracy, warriors themselves, whose livelihood was derived from cattle-breeding and agriculture, of which the former possessed the higher status. From this class probably came the highly respected craftsmen: makers of decorative metalwork, weaponsmiths, armourers and sculptors. Below the freemen in the social scale lay an unfree class by whom perhaps most of the agricultural work was done. Most wretched of all was a substratum of slaves, who were probably prisoners of war and their families.

Despite the myths of high druidic wisdom which were invented in

29

later centuries, the religion of the Celts was bloodthirsty. The cult of the human head as the seat of power led Celtic warriors to collect the heads of their slaughtered enemies. Sanctuaries were decorated with skulls and sculptures of severed heads. Human sacrifice was practised by ritual burning, drowning or hanging, in accordance with the supposed taste of the god to whom the sacrifice was offered, or by a sword-cut followed by the sprinkling of the sacrificial blood on altars, images or sacred trees.[9] The Celtic *nemeton* or sacred grove near Marseilles, with its burdened altars and bloody trees disgusted Caesar who ordered its destruction, as a shrine of barbarism and as a focus of Gallic resistance. There was a sacred grove, doubtless of similar character, called Medionemeton at an unidentified site in southern Scotland.[10]

A more attractive aspect of Celtic society was the aristocracy's delight in personal display, in massive gold torcs, armlets, brooches and rings, which were copied by less wealthy members of society in bronze. Love of adornment was not expressed in vulgar opulence. Graceful and imaginative patterns, incorporating human, animal, foliate and geometrical forms characterize Celtic metalwork. Reluctance to leave a surface undecorated and ability to cover it with intricate and beautifully laid out designs is shown in jewellery, weapons, shield ornaments, horse harness, mirrors and vessels of all kinds, from great cauldrons to small vases. Many objects of Celtic art in the La Tène style have been found in Scotland. They show that the Celtic population kept alive the traditions brought from Europe and continued to employ them with vigour long after the Romanized Gauls had absorbed classical influences, a fusion of traditions which contributed to the development of Romanesque art.

The Romans' discovery of Scotland followed their conquest of southern Britain and was inspired by the need to establish a frontier for their province of Britannia. Fortunately for our knowledge of this period, the Roman historian Tacitus wrote a eulogy of his father-in-law, Gnaeus Julius Agricola, Governor of Britannia from AD 78 to 84, the earliest historical narrative which deals with Scotland.

Agricola evidently intended a conquest of northern Britain, for artificial frontiers played no part in his plans. In 80 he led his army as far as the Tay, advancing through the territories of tribes hitherto unknown to the Romans. The following year he secured the country as far as the Forth-Clyde line under Roman occupation, and in 82 he sailed his fleet up the West Coast. In the summer of 83 he entered Caledonia, the area north of the Forth, occupied by the Caledonii, whose territory extended as far as the Great Glen. It was from the Caledonii and their neighbours that Agricola encountered serious resistance, the short-lived 'Caledonian Confederacy' which according to Tacitus brought together an army of 30,000 men. Their leaders were drawn from the Celtic warrior aristocracy, who still went to war in chariots, a practice long abandoned by the continental Celts. The Celtic war chariot did not require the existence of roads. It was a light-bodied two-wheeled vehicle designed to bounce easily over rough open ground, drawn by two horses, harnessed one each side of a central pole, and carrying a spear-wielding warrior and his charioteer. The paramount leader of the Caledonians was Calgacus, the first man in Scottish history to be named, whose name means 'Swordsman', but who must have possessed more than soldierly qualities to bring the tribes together to resist the Roman advance.

Precisely where the Caledonians offered battle to Agricola is unknown. Mons Graupius which gave its name to the battle (and was later misread as 'Mons Grampius') could be the name of the Grampian range, as is 'Mons Apenninus' of the Apennines. But since Agricola had already constructed a legionary base near Inchtuthil, in Perth-shire, and a substantial camp is mentioned by Tacitus, possibly it was in this area that the battle was fought. In his account of it Tacitus imputes a battle oration to Calgacus, who addresses to the assembled tribes a famous condemnation of Roman imperialism: 'They are the only people on earth to whose covetousness both riches and poverty are equally tempting. To robbery, butchery and rapine they give the lying name of government; they create a desolation and call it peace.' The words are imaginary, but their value lies in Tacitus' effort to represent the Caledonian viewpoint.[11]

The battle was a heavy defeat for the Caledonians, whose impetuous courage was no match for Roman discipline. After the battle the survivors dispersed into the Highlands, where Agricola's troops were unable to pursue them among the roadless mountains. Calgacus, like Vercingetorix, was defeated as much by the fissile inclinations of his own people as by the might of Rome. However, the defeat of the tribes proved to be a victory for the terrain. The Roman army, foiled of pursuit, went into winter quarters south of the Forth. The Roman fleet, which had sailed up the east coast in support, was sent round the north of Scotland on a voyage which may have been intended to intimidate, but which also served the purpose of exploration. Tacitus himself named few tribes but by the next century the Alexandrian geographer Ptolemy knew the names of seventeen tribes in northern Britain and some of his information is likely to have been derived from the voyage of Agricola's supporting fleet. Part of the territory of the Brigantes, one of the most turbulent tribes which occupied the Roman province, extended into the Border region. The Selgovae and the Votadini occupied the east and central Lowlands. Galloway was the country of the Novantae, and Ayrshire and Lanarkshire of the Damnonii. Fife was the land of the Venicones, and the east coast Lowlands were the lands of the Vacomagi and the Taezali. Apart from the Caledonii of central Scotland, the Highland tribes were the Epidii of Kintyre, the Creones of the West Coast, the Carnonacae of Wester Ross and the Decantae of Easter Ross, the Caereni, Smertae and Lugi of Sutherland and the Cornovii of Caithness. The names of the inhabitants of the Western Isles are not known; but the Orci gave their name to Orkney. Not all these tribal names are identifiably Celtic, but some of them are cognate with the names of Celtic deities and sacred animals. For example the Epidii may have worshipped Epona, a Celtic horse or mare goddess, and the deity of the Smertae may have been Rosmerta 'the Exceedingly Smeared One' – smeared presumably with sacrificial blood. The Lugi – 'Raven Folk' – and the Orci – 'Boar Folk' – may have venerated these creatures as their totems.

Shortly after the battle of Mons Graupius Agricola was recalled to Rome, and his plan for the complete conquest of Britain was never readopted. The Emperor Hadrian visited Britain in AD 120 or 122, and ordered the construction of the wall which bears his name. It took the Tyne-Solway line as the frontier of the province and bisected the territory of the troublesome Brigantes. A later experiment was the construction of the Antonine wall across the Forth-Clyde isthmus, during the governorship of Lollius Urbicus, following a northern campaign of 142–3. The relevance of later Roman activity to the history of the Highlands is very slight. Agricola had approached the Highlands but not entered them and the later Roman fortifications were constructed for the purpose of preventing the Highland tribes from threatening the Roman province. A few Roman objects have been found in Highland duns and brochs; probably they were bartered by tribesmen who had never seen the Romans, but admired their artefacts.

Passing reference to the northern tribes by later Roman writers provides glimpses of how society in northern Britain was changing. The area between Hadrian's Wall and the Antonine Wall became a Roman protectorate, but north of the Antonine Wall hostility to Rome continued unyielding. In 209 the Emperor Severus decided on a punitive expedition, and the historian Dio Cassius, who knew him personally, wrote of this period: 'The two most important tribes are the Caledonians and the Meatae, the names of the other tribes having been included in these. The Meatae dwell close by the wall that divides the island into two parts [the Antonine Wall], the Caledonians beyond them.'

Severus 'bought peace' from the Meatae, and marched as far as the Moray Firth without bringing the Caledonians to battle, though he suffered heavy losses from continual harassment. He retired south again, to die at York in 211.

Almost a century later, in 306, Eumenius wrote that Constantius Chlorus was obliged to invade Caledonia, in order to drive back 'the Caledonians and other Picts'. This name occurs again in 360 when, according to Ammianus Marcellinus, 'the fierce nations of the Picts and Scots' had broken the peace which the Emperor Constans had formerly concluded with them. Ammianus Marcellinus wrote that the Picts were divided into Dicalydones and Verturiones, who stood in the same relationship to each other as Dio Cassius' Caledonians and Meatae. Since Caledonii and Dicalydones are obviously related names it has been suggested that Dicalydones meant 'double Caledonians', implying that the Caledonians were divided into two parts, living north and south of the Mounth. Verturiones is a more problematical name, but since they were obviously the same people as the Meatae, perhaps the names were simply alternatives.

In 367 the Picts and Scots formed the 'Barbarian Conspiracy', overran Hadrian's Wall and, joined by Teutonic mercenaries of the Romans who chose this moment to revolt, attacked the Roman province with a ferocity from which it did not recover. Though a restoration of the frontier was attempted by Theodosius, the years of the Roman occupation were numbered, for the chaos into which the Empire itself was falling demanded the withdrawal of Roman troops from outlying provinces. The occupying forces dwindled as one crisis followed another and the last of them departed early in the fifth century.

The encounter of the Highland tribes with the Romans had not been close, but in the brief notices given of them by Roman writers, they passed from prehistory into history.

2

PICTS AND SCOTS

The three sons of Erc, son of
                            pleasant Eochu,
three who got the blessing of Patrick,
took Alba, high was their vigour,
Loarn, Ferghus, and Aonghus.[1]

In the centuries which followed the departure of the Romans, the
British tribes in the areas which later became southern Scotland and
northern England formed themselves into little kingdoms. In the
south-west of Scotland the kingdom of Strathclyde stretched as far as
the head of Loch Lomond, and its capital was Dumbarton (which
means 'Dun of the Britons'). The smaller kingdom of Rheged centred
on Carlisle and extended along the Eden Valley, and Manaw
Goddodin covered the old territory of the Votadini, with its fortresses
on the rocks which later became the sites of Stirling and Edinburgh. In
the north-east of England the Angles from Frisia, encouraged by
existing settlements of their kinsmen, who had first arrived as
mercenaries of the Romans, established themselves at York, which
became the capital of Bernicia, and Bamburgh, which became the
capital of Deira. These two small kingdoms were absorbed into the
powerful kingdom of Northumbria, whose warrior kings overran both
Rheged and Manaw Goddodin, in the course of the seventh century.
These southern kingdoms require to be mentioned because of their
relations with their northern neighbours.

North of Strathclyde and Manaw Goddodin lay the kingdom of the
Picts, which extended as far as Shetland and included the Highlands
and the Western Isles, with the exception of Argyll and its adjacent
islands. This area had been colonized by the Scots, Celtic immigrants
from Northern Ireland, who had been mentioned by the later Roman
writers as allies of the Picts in the 'Barbarian Conspiracy' of AD 367.
The Picts, who entered history in the almost casual references of these

writers, left scarcely any written records of their own, and the gap between archaeological remains and the first literary references has led to a great deal of hypothesizing about their ancestry. It seems obvious that the Picts must have been descended from the northern tribes whose names were recorded by Ptolemy and who were later described as having fused into those larger groups, the Caledonians and Meatae or Dicalydones and Verturiones. The question which has preoccupied historians of the Picts is whether or not they were Celts.

A Celtic people is identifiable by its language, and in this the name 'Picts' is no help because it is not what the tribes called themselves. The Latin word 'Picti' meaning 'painted men' probably originated as military slang, and was used to describe the northern tribesmen because they used warpaint or tattooing. By their Celtic-speaking Welsh and British neighbours, and probably by themselves, they were called 'Priteni' or 'Pritani', which means 'the People of the Designs' – a more dignified way of describing their self-decoration. At the time the name must have had a wider application, because the Romans also gave their version of it – Britanni – to the inhabitants of their province. Caesar notoriously commented on the southern Britons' use of blue body paint. In its Roman form the name of the people and the province is still current, but it is the Celtic form which gives a clue to the identity of the Picts.

The Celtic languages belong to the Indo-European group of languages. A common Celtic tongue, spoken by the prehistoric European Celts, underwent divergent changes as they migrated from the continent and settled on its fringes. Those who settled in Wales and southern Britain spoke 'P-Celtic', while those who settled in Ireland spoke 'Q-Celtic' (substituting 'qu' or 'k' for 'p'). The most familiar illustration of the difference is that the word for 'son' is 'ap' in Welsh and 'mac' in Gaelic. Q-Celtic speakers called the Picts 'Cruithni', which was the nearest they could get to 'Priteni'.

Professor Kenneth Jackson studied the evidence for the Celtic language in tribal names, personal names, place names and inscriptions, and concluded that the Picts spoke a form of P-Celtic akin to, but not the same as, the language of the southern Britons, and also similar to that of the Gauls, and therefore to be described as 'Gallo-Brittonic'. This seems conclusive evidence that the Picts were descendants of the Celtic immigrants of the Iron Age. But it is possible that Gallo-Brittonic was the language of a Celtic warrior aristocracy superimposed on a pre-Celtic population.

As previously mentioned, not all Ptolemy's tribal names are Celtic and there are survivals of a non-Celtic language, which has been presumed to be that of the earlier inhabitants, in a small number of Pictish inscriptions, which hitherto have defied translation. These inscriptions are few, very weather-worn, and to add to the difficulty of deciphering them, are carved in ogham, a writing system of Irish origin, which the Picts are most likely to have learned from their neighbours, the Scots. It is a kind of cipher in which the letters are represented by short strokes incised at angles to a base line. It has been suggested that the Picts revered the non-Celtic language as an ancient and perhaps a sacred tongue, and used it for monumental purposes, as Latin is still used on war memorials and tombstones in the late twentieth century. But all languages die at last, and though people still understand 'Pro Patria Mori' and 'Requiescat in Pace', if they know no other Latin, in a few generations these words may have become as incomprehensible as

CRROSCC: NAHHTVVDDADDS: DATTRR: ANN BENNISES: MEQQDDRROANN

This inscription comes from a stone in the island of Bressay, Shetland. It belongs to the Christian period of Pictish history and it has been suggested that 'CRROSCC' means 'cross' and 'MEQQ' means 'son of', both borrowed from Gaelic, and that 'DATTRR' means 'daughter' and is borrowed from Norse, as are the punctuating dots, which occur in Norse runic inscriptions. But without the discovery of some northern equivalent of the Rosetta stone, bearing inscriptions in all three languages, it seems improbable that the surviving fragments of the unknown language will be translated.[2]

In addition to believing that the Celtic-speaking Picts took over, even to a limited extent, the language of the earlier inhabitants, some historians believe that they also took over from them the custom of matrilinearism, which certainly would have set them apart from other Celtic societies. There is not a great deal of evidence on which to base this belief. In the Pictish king-lists fathers are not succeeded by their sons, but matrilinearism is not necessarily the explanation. The Picts appear to have had a high king and a number of subsidiary kings, who were either the chiefs of kindreds or the rulers of provinces.[3] It is possible that the high king of the Picts was chosen from these ruling families in turn, which would explain why fathers were not succeeded by their sons. In a few instances Pictish kings are known to have been the sons of foreign kings or princes, and the matrilinear school of thought explains this by the exogamy, or marriage outside their own people, of Pictish princesses and a strict application of matrilinear principles. Yet this seems inherently unlikely because it would so obviously have weakened the kingdom of the Picts. A more likely explanation is that the kings in question were imposed on the Picts when the neighbouring kingdoms were strong enough to exert their power. Talorgen son of Eanfrith a Northumbrian prince (deposed 657) and Bridei son of Beli King of the Strathclyde Britons (d. 693) were probably set on the throne by a powerful Northumbria and Strathclyde respectively; and Gartnait, son of Gabrán King of Scots, could have become king of an area of the Pictish kingdom through the influence of his brother Áedán, a particularly powerful Scottish king. Of course, in a true matrilinear society the names of the fathers would be either unknown or considered unimportant and the fact that the names of the fathers of Pictish kings are always recorded is in itself an argument against matrilinearism. Finally, a well known statement by the English ecclesiastical historian Bede (d. 735) that 'when the matter was in doubt' the royal succession was chosen from the female line is not a description of matrilinearism, though it has been quoted as an argument for it. A more likely explanation is that the Picts usually chose their kings from certain families or kindreds and that Bede's statement means exactly what it says. If this is so, Pictish kingship would have been similar to Irish and Scottish kingship, and this similarity would be an indication that the Picts were predominantly Celtic.[4]

The Picts would be a very shadowy people if they had left nothing but controversy behind them. Fortunately they also left their accomplished and highly individual sculptures, even though these are themselves regrettably mysterious. The earliest Pictish sculptures are the 'symbol stones', and the symbols carried on them may have been the designs which the Picts had used to decorate their bodies. These stones were boulders selected because they possessed surfaces smooth enough to be used as fields for carving. On such stones the Pictish sculptors incised with beautiful economy of line and sense of movement, the outlines of animals, including boars, bears, wolves, stags, eagles and salmon, and of unidentifiable creatures which have been described as 'mammoths', 'swimming elephants' or, more cautiously, as 'Pictish beasts'. A symbol stone in Rhynie Old Kirkyard shows a saurian-looking beast with flippers and a reptilian head, a representation which has encouraged some believers in the Loch Ness monster. Besides their animals and zoomorphs the Picts carved geometrical symbols known as the 'V-rod' and the 'Z-rod', patterned crescents and rectangles and a design which looks like a comb and a hand-mirror. Some of the symbols also appear on the small quantities of surviving Pictish silverware, which is of high quality.

The purpose of the symbol stones is as mysterious as the symbols themselves. It has been suggested that they could have marked the boundaries of tribal territories; or since the symbols frequently occur in pairs, that they could have been set up to commemorate royal or noble marriages (in this context the 'comb and mirror' symbol could have represented the bride). Other possibilities are that they could have been cenotaphs or grave-stones. Theories abound but conclusions are lacking.[5]

After the Picts became Christian, which was a gradual process during the seventh century, their style of sculpture changed, under Hiberno-Scottish or Northumbrian influence. The symbols were not abandoned, which suggests that they must have had a social and non-religious significance, since they were not considered inappropriate on Christian monuments. The Christian Pictish sculptures were in low relief instead of being incised, and were carved on stones dressed in the form of rectangular slabs. On one side of the slab was a cross, usually of interlace pattern and never bearing the figure of Christ, and in the four spaces between the arms of the cross were carvings of scenes among which episodes from the life of Christ and the story of King David have been identified. The scenes were usually biblical, but not always. For example, the Glamis Manse symbol stone bears a very elaborate interlace cross, with a representation of two men fighting with axes in the lower left-hand space, and in the upper right-hand space a centaur bearing an axe in each hand. On the reverse side of the Pictish cross-slabs the old Pictish symbols appear, sometimes accompanied by scenes of hunting, or of war. A stone from Birsay, Orkney, shows a procession of three Pictish warriors, wearing long tunics and carrying small square shields and spears with leaf-shaped blades. The leading figure has a more elaborately decorated shield than the others, a fringe on his tunic, and curled hair. Another fine stone, from Hilton of Cadboll, Ross-shire, bears a hunting scene which shows a woman riding side-saddle, two mounted men, and two hounds attacking a hind. These reliefs offer us the only glimpses we possess of a vanished

39

people. The last of the Pictish carvings are in high relief, and are no longer accompanied by the symbols. Dating the sculptures has proved as controversial as everything else concerning the Picts, but it seems likely that the disappearance of the symbols followed the unification of the Picts and the Scots, which had taken place by *c.* 850.[6]

That the union took place under a Scottish and not a Pictish king might have seemed an unlikely outcome when the Scots first established their colony on the fringe of the Western Highlands. They had probably begun to settle there as early as the 'Barbarian Conspiracy' of 367. As allies of the Picts they would not have been unwelcome, and the areas which Ptolemy had shown as inhabited by only two tribes, the Epidii and the Creones, may have been very thinly populated.

The Scots were descendants of prehistoric Celtic migrants from Europe, who settled in Ireland and spoke the form of Q-Celtic which became known as Gaelic. They called themselves *Gaidheal*, or Gaels, and their name for northern Britain was Alba. When they had ceased to think of themselves as Irish settlers in Alba they called themselves *Albannach*. But to Roman writers *Scotia* was Ireland and the *Scotti* were Irish. Scotti they remained in later Latin writings, and the kingdom of the Scots took its name from them as a natural historical process when they became its politically dominant people.

The Irish society, of which the Scots were representative, had a structure similar to that observed by Julius Caesar in Gaul, for its Celtic character had survived in Ireland unmodified by Roman influence. Essentially recognisable under other names were the tribal kings, the *equites*, *druides* and *plebs*. The basic social unit in Ireland was the *tuath* or *cenel*, a tribe which was regarded as a kindred. It was ruled in peace and commanded in war by the *ri*, or king. His companions were the *flaithi*, warrior nobles who were patrons of the *oes dana* ('men of art'), who were regarded as being ennobled by their skill. The greatest of the *oes dana* were the *filid*, the poets, who had probably been druids in pagan society, and with the coming of Christianity still retained something of the druids' power and prestige. Of lower status than the noble was the ordinary free man, the *cele*, or client, of the nobleman, who in return was his protector. This ancient social structure survived in the Highlands, at least, in a recognizable form, until the sixteenth century.[7]

The dress of the Irish and the Scots of the sixth century was identical, and still similar to that of the Iron Age Celts. Both men and women wore the *léine*, a long linen shirt, and the *inar*, a shorter tunic worn over it, and, as an outer garment the *brat*, a square or rectangular woollen cloak, fastened with a *delg* or brooch, which might be an elaborate jewel. Bright dyes and gold embroidery characterized the clothes of the nobility. Torcs, bracelets and rings of gold, silver, electrum and bronze were worn by both sexes.[8] The warrior carried a shield and was armed with a sword and a spear. His code of honour required him to utter or accept the challenge to single combat and, even in the Christian era, did not forbid him to collect the head of his enemy.

In Ireland the Scots had established a small kingdom in the coastal area of the present County Antrim, which they named *Dál Riata* ('Riata's portion') or Dalriada. The same name was given to their colony in Argyll, where one of their chief centres of power was the rock of Dunadd, a naturally defensible rocky mound, rising out of flat agricultural land in mid-Argyll, which in former times was a great moss or bog. On the summit of Dunadd is a bare table of rock on which is incised the outline of a boar, which may be Pictish, thus signifying previous possession of the place. There is also an ogham inscription, a hollowed-out basin or stoup, and the outline of a large footprint. It is believed that the stoup and the footprint were used in the inauguration ritual of the Kings of Dalriada.

By *c.* 500 the Scottish Dalriada had outstripped the Irish in size and prosperity, and the King, Fergus Mór mac Eirc (Fergus the Great, son of Erc), removed his seat of government from Dunseverick in Ireland to Argyll, bringing with him his brothers, Loarn and Óengus.

Each of the brothers founded a kindred which occupied a specific area. The descendants of Fergus himself took the name of his grandson Gabrán. The *Cenel nGabráin* (kindred of Gabrán) occupied Kintyre, Gigha, Jura, Cowal and its adjacent islands, Bute and probably Arran. The *Cenel Loairn* (kindred of Loarn) occupied Lorne, which takes its name from them, Colonsay, Mull and Ardnamurchan, and the *Cenel nÓengusa* (kindred of Óengus) occupied Islay. The frontier with the Picts was marked by the northern coastline of the Ardnamurchan peninsula and the mountain range of Druim Alban, but Scots may have crossed the mountains and settled in Pictish territory from an early period. The head of each kindred continued to be regarded as a *rí* ('king') and his successor had to be a mature male kinsman who was regarded as *rígdomnae* ('the material of a king'). The group from which the king's successor was chosen was the *derbfine* ('certain kin'), which consisted of four generations descended from a common ancestor who had been a king. Thus a king could be succeeded by his son, but since life expectancy was short, a mature heir would be more likely to be a brother or a cousin. In an attempt to prevent strife a king's successor, the *tánaise ríg* or tanist ('second to the king') was nominated in his lifetime. The weakness of the system was that the tanist was frequently challenged by an ambitious kinsman. The high kingship of the Scots belonged to the king of the Cenel nGabráin, but during a prolonged period of strife this monopoly was contested by the Cenel Loairn which provided two kings of Scots, Ferchar Fota (d. 697) and Selbach (d. 722).

A source dating from the seventh century, the *Senchus Fer nAlban* ('History of the Men of Alba') indicates how the three kindreds had developed by that period and records their resources and the military service which they owed to the high king. The Cenel nGabráin numbered 560 households, the Ceneal Loairn 420 and the Cenel nÓengusa 430. From these the Cenel nGabráin could muster 800 men, the Cenel Loairn 700 and the Cenel nÓengusa 500. The Cenel Loairn mustered more men from fewer households by recruiting the difference from the *Airgialla* ('the hostage-givers') a people from northern Ireland who had settled in the islands dominated by the Cenel Loairn, and performed military service for them in return. The large numbers cited suggest that all the members of each *cenel* could not possibly have been kinsmen or descendants of Gabran, Loarn and Óengus. Kinship must have been a convenient fiction or convention, and the Airgialla may have been the least easily absorbed recruits, or the least willing to surrender their identity. Each group of twenty households had to provide two seven-benched ships with two oarsmen to each bench. The ships were of great importance because when the kings of Irish Dalriada removed to Argyll they did not relinquish their Irish territories, which they continued to rule for over a century.

Apart from the military obligation to turn out and fight for their lord, *feachd* and *sluagh* 'military expedition' and 'hosting', the men of Dalriada were also subject to two forms of taxation in kind: *cain*, a payment of produce from their land, and *coinmeadh* (or conveth), the obligation to offer their lord hospitality.

* * * *

Perhaps because the Irish connection remained strong the Scots were nostalgic for their homeland. To various places in the Highlands they gave Irish names which now seem so thoroughly Scottish that their origin is generally unsuspected. Glen Elg, for example, is thought to mean 'Glen of Ireland'. Dunyardil or Dun Deirduil means 'the Dun of Deirdre', and the river Avon or A'an may recall the Irish hero Fionn. These last two names illustrate the attachment of the Scots to the myths and sagas of Ireland, which continued to inspire their storytelling and poetry. They loved the epics now known as the 'Ulster Cycle', many of which recount the deeds of the hero Cu Culainn. Dunyardil is a reminder of the famous tale of the fatally beautiful Deirdre, who fled from her ageing suitor King Conchubor of Ulster, to live in the Highlands with her lover, the young warrior Naoise, an idyll which ended when he was treacherously slain, and Deirdre, given by Conchubor to Naiose's killer, leapt from his chariot to her death by dashing her head against a rock. The raw passions and brutal slaughters of these stories are tempered by poetic passages of extraordinary beauty.

More popular in style, and more frequently lightened by touches of humour, were the stories of the 'Fenian Cycle', concerning Fionn or Fingal, his band of warriors, the Feine, and his son, the warrior-bard Oisin or Ossian. These tales, transferred with the passage of time from Irish to Scottish settings, entered Highland folklore and maintained their popularity until the nineteenth century, when David Stewart of Garth recalled how, in his youth, when any stranger visited a Highland community, after he had been welcomed, he would be asked 'Bheil dad agad air an Fhéinn?' ('Can you speak of the days of Fionn?').[9] If he could do so, the inhabitants would gather to hear him tell a tale, perhaps a new one, for the Fenian Cycle continued to grow, and its heroes grew with it, until they were imagined as having been giants.

Poems based on these stories, and verses attributed to Ossian himself, became part of the heritage of Gaelic Scotland. They were handed on by oral tradition and fortunately many of them were written down by James McGregor, Dean of Lismore, early in the sixteenth century. His versions, collected in Perthshire, survived the failure of folk memory, and were published in the nineteenth century as *The Dean of Lismore's Book*.

When Fergus Mór and his brothers came to Dalriada they were already Christians. An eleventh-century Gaelic poem, the *Duan Albanach* ('the Scottish Poem'), calls them 'three who got the blessing of Patrick'. This is possible, because St Patrick died *c.* 461, and Fergus Mór could have been past middle age when he founded his new kingdom, as he died soon afterwards. The Scots found the Christian ethic a difficult contrast to the heroic ideals of pagan society. One of the poems attributed to Ossian collected by the Dean of Lismore consists of a dialogue between Ossian, who has converted to Christianity in old age, and St Patrick. Ossian asks whether the pagan Fionn and his warriors, the Feine, have been admitted to heaven:

> Tell us, O Patrick, what honour is ours,
> Do the Feine of Ireland in heaven now dwell?
> In truth I can tell thee, thou Ossian of fame,
> That no heaven has thy father, Oscar or Gaul.*
> Sad is the tale thou tellest me, Priest,
> I worshipping God, while the Feine have no heaven . . . .
> Better see the face of heaven's son each day,
> Than all the gold on earth, were it thine to possess . . .
> For thy love's sake, Patrick, forsake not the heroes,
> Unknown to heaven's King, bring thou in the Feinn . . .[10]

This poem eloquently expresses the emotional conflict which would have arisen in a period of religious transition, in which it was hard for the Scots to accept that their greatest heroes were denied salvation for the very deeds of prowess, which had made them admired.

The transition from a pagan to a Christian society was not effected in one generation, for Celtic paganism had been established in Scotland since the Iron Age. Some pagan festivals were adopted and Christianized by the Church, and these, in their Christian or more recently secularized forms, continue to be celebrated.

The pagan Celtic year ended and began at *Samain*, 1 November, when the tribe gathered together to slaughter the cattle which could not be fed over the winter and were not required for breeding. The gathering and the slaughter provided an occasion for feasting and the great fires which were kindled for the practical purpose of roasting also served to keep at bay the spirits which were free to move between their own world and that of humanity in the hiatus between one year and the next. Samain was Christianized as the feast of All Souls and All Saints, and retains something of its original character as Hallowe'en.

---

* Gaul is Goll mac Morna, leader of the Feine of Connaught.

The atavistic desire to light bonfires at this time of year has been suggested as an explanation of the continuing popularity of Guy Fawkes Night, a curiously persistent celebration of a non-event.

The pagan Celtic summer began at *Beltainn*, 1 May, possibly the festival of the god Belenos, when fires were kindled again, and cattle were driven between two fires by the druids, a ritual designed to purify and protect the herds before they were driven to their summer pastures. 1 May has retained its character as a celebration of spring or early summer, whether it be celebrated with the pagan ritual of dancing round the maypole, or with the Christian observance of the first day of Our Lady's month or the feast of St Joseph the Worker, or with modern Labour Day processions.

While Samain and Beltainn were the principal festivals of the Celtic year, two others were greatly honoured. *Oimelc*, or *Imbolc* ('Ewe's Milk') sought the favour of the fertility goddess Brigit at the beginning of the lambing season. It was Christianized as the Feast of St Bridget, the converted goddess, and gained additional sanctification from its proximity to Candlemas (2 February). *Lugnasad*, 1 August, was an agrarian festival in honour of the god Lug, and was designed to ensure a good harvest. It was not a harvest festival in the Christian sense, for it preceded the harvest: as the date implies, it was a rite designed to propitiate the god, which if correctly performed would ensure plenty. The idea of offering thanksgiving for a good harvest was a Christian innovation which shifted the festival to the end of summer, when the harvest was brought home. The metamorphosis of the pagan festivals did not occur rapidly following the adoption of Christianity. Beltainn, in particular, retained its original character the longest, with 'Beltainn Fires' being kindled in many parts of the Highlands until the eighteenth century.[11]

Certain attitudes rather than beliefs also long continued to survive from the pagan past. For example, Highlanders retained an animistic reverence for wells, springs, trees and stones, and even for manufactured objects, especially those made of iron. The latent power of natural and manufactured things could be harnessed to do good, or their latent malignity propitiated to prevent evil. The practical result of such attitudes was at worst a high level of unnecessary anxiety, at best what we would now describe as respect for the environment. The former might be illustrated by such a gesture as placing an iron implement beside a baby's cradle, so that the infant could not be stolen by the fairies and a changeling substituted; the latter by the horror and anger which would attend such an act as the pollution of a well.

The Christianity of the Scots was strengthened, perhaps transformed by St Columba, who came to Dalriada *c.* 563, and founded his monastery on Iona. Colum Cille ('Dove of the Church') as he was called, in Gaelic, was a member of the Ui Neill, the most powerful kindred in Ireland. Besides the prestige of high birth, he possessed a forceful character and great personal holiness, though his sanctity was flawed by a vein of misogyny, the negative aspect of clerical celibacy. Columba's biographer Adomnán, ninth abbot of Iona (d. 704) credited him with visionary and miraculous powers. Adomnán's Life of St Columba shows how the saint influenced pagan and semi-Christian kings and warriors. As a Christian thaumaturge he resembled a magic-working druid, and his superior powers were admired before his sanctity was understood. Respect for holiness followed in the wake of awe.

Columba typified the leaders of Celtic Christianity in that he was aristocratic, monastic, ascetic and intellectual. The founders and abbots of Celtic monasteries were frequently members of royal or noble kindreds, whose authority over their monks mirrored that of a king over his warriors. The monastic foundations of St Moluag of Lismore, St Maelrubai of Applecross, and St Donnán of Eigg were inspired by the desire to become exiles from the world for the sake of Christ, and the inevitable austerity of life in remote places encouraged the cultivation of asceticism. Some Celtic monks, like St Brendan of Clonfert, sought holiness in even greater isolation and sailed in their currachs as far as the Faroes, Iceland, and perhaps Greenland. A group of stories called *Immrama* ('voyages') describes their quest for 'The Land of Promise of the Saints'. The legend of St Brendan tells how he made two voyages in search of it, the first unsuccessful, the second successful. After the first voyage St Brendan consults his foster-mother St Ita on the cause of his failure which she imputes to his having sailed in a currach covered with the skins of dead animals. So the saint and his companions build a vessel of wood, in which the blessed destination is reached. But the island is a pilgrimage, not an ultimate goal. The saint returns to found the monastery of Clonfert, and his death is anchored in history with the date 577.[12]

Those who sought God in loneliness turned their backs on intellectual life, but the larger Celtic monasteries were centres of learning and artistic achievement, where manuscripts were collected and copied and original works were written. *The Book of Kells*, the great illuminated Gospel which was described in the Annals of Ulster in 1007 as 'the chief relic of the western world', is believed to have been begun on Iona *c*. 800, and Adomnán described St Columba as copying a psalter on the last day of his life, in 597. Adomnán himself wrote a book of *The Holy Places*, based on a description given him by a bishop named Arculf, who had visited them.[13] Gospels, psalters and liturgical books were regarded as holy objects in themselves and were sometimes kept in book-shrines of exquisite metalwork. The *cumdach* or book-shrine of the Gospels of Bishop Fothad was kept on the high altar of the Cathedral of St Andrews during the later Middle Ages, but neither this nor any other Scottish example appears to have survived the Reformation.

Though the monastery of Iona was a centre of learning it was not a refuge from the world, for it lay midway between Ireland and Scottish Dalriada, and its founder was a statesman as well as a holy man. On Iona in 574 Columba consecrated Áedán mac Gabráin as King of Scots, an action which linked the monarchy to Christianity and claimed for the Church a role in kingmaking. The following year he arbitrated at the Convention of Druim Ceat in Ireland, where Áedán defended his possession of Irish Dalriada against the claims of the Irish high king, Áed mac Ainmerech of the Uí Neill. With the support of Columba, the high king's kinsman, Áedán was able to sustain his claim. The Irish territories continued to be controlled by the Scots, under a vague Irish overlordship, until 637, when they were lost through the defeat of the Scots king Domnall Brecc, who took arms against the Uí Neill at the battle of Mag Rath. Domnall Brecc had been twice defeated by the Picts and was finally slain in a battle against the Strathclyde Britons in 642; but though his reign was a series of disasters the loss of the Irish territories was to the ultimate advantage of the Scots. It concentrated their resources on the side of the Irish Sea where Fergus Mór had decided that their future lay and this concentration reinforced them in their later conflicts with the Picts.

It was probably as an ambassador of Áedán that Columba visited the high king of the Picts, Bridei son of Mailchon (d. 585), a pagan, and according to Bede 'a most powerful king'. Adomnán says that Columba won Bridei's respect but not that he converted him, so presumably he did not as the Pictish king's conversion would have been too important an event to leave unmentioned. Bridei's court was in a fortress near Loch Ness, which may have been Craig Phádraig, near the junction of the Ness and the Moray Firth. Columba reached it by travelling up the Great Glen, the route later followed by the Scottish missionaries by whom the conversion of the Picts was achieved. According to Bede all the monasteries in the Pictish kingdom which existed in his time were daughter houses of Iona and the influence of Hiberno-Scottish art, which reached the Picts by way of Iona, has been remarked in Christian Pictish sculpture.

The conversion of the southern Picts – those who lived south of the Mounth – had been undertaken at the beginning of the sixth century by St Ninian of Whithorn and his successors, though whether the effects of this mission had been lasting is uncertain. Ninian, according to Bede, had been instructed at Rome and consecrated a bishop, but by the second half of the seventh century it was the Celtic Christianity of the Iona pattern which predominated throughout the Pictish kingdom. But this dominance was short-lived because conflict broke out between the Roman and Celtic forms of Christianity, in which the Roman triumphed.

The most famous aspect of this conflict is the 'Easter Controversy'. The Celtic Church, which was long out of touch with Rome, was unaware that the Roman Church had adopted a different system of calculating the date of Easter and in consequence different dates of the movable feast resulted.[14] While paganism was still very much alive, it was an obvious scandal and a possible cause of discredit that two branches of the Church should disagree about the date of the central event of Christianity. It was necessary to synchronize the liturgical years. There were other divergences of which the most important was the status of bishops. The Roman Church, which had developed in the cities of the Roman Empire, had been organized in episcopal sees established in the cities. The Celtic Church, which had grown up in tribal societies, was predominantly monastic and its aristocratic abbots possessed higher authority than its bishops, whose sacramental functions were none the less highly respected. Liturgical and organizational divergences did not, however, make the Celtic Church schismatic. The problems which required solution were far less complex than those which divide the Christian Churches of the twentieth century.

The triumph of Rome in the northern kingdoms spread from Northumbria, where King Oswiu convened the Synod of Whitby in 664 to decide between the merits of the two rites. The Celtic Church had been established in Northumbria, under St Aidan of Lindisfarne, who had been a monk of Iona, in 634 but when Oswiu decided to adopt the Roman rite the Celtic clergy left the kingdom and returned to Iona. A little over twenty years later, Adomnán, who was a friend of the Northumbrian King Aldfrith, was convinced by the Roman arguments in Northumbria. He spent the rest of his life attempting to persuade the Picts and Scots to accept the Roman rite, in which he had failed at his death in 704. The Iona community was split by the controversy, and did not accept the change until 712. In 717 Nechtan son of Derile, King of the Picts, threatened by internal enemies, wooed the support of Northumbria by seeking advice on the Easter question, asking for Northumbrian architects to build him a stone church which he promised to dedicate to St Peter, and banishing the Celtic clergy.

These events did not destroy the Celtic Church, though they ensured that it would yield to change. Yet the change was slow. In the late eighth century it still had the vigour to produce a characteristic movement of monastic reform, the *Celi Dé* ('Clients of God'), or Culdees, an order which maintained its influence in early medieval Scotland until the spread of European monasticism in the twelfth century.

At the height of the Easter Controversy Adomnán succeeded in promulgating his 'Law of Innocents', an agreement to guarantee the humane treatment of noncombatants – women, children and clerics. Pictish, Scottish and Irish kings, tribal rulers and ecclesiastics ratified it at the Synod of Birr in Ireland in 697, and it was re-enacted in 727, which suggests that, as one would expect, though its ideals had been accepted in principle, practice fell far short of them. The promulgation of the Law of Innocents shows that the Church, irrespective of Celtic-Roman controversies, was capable of speaking with one voice on an important moral issue, and that the Celtic rulers could pause in their ceaseless warfare long enough to acknowledge the moral authority of Christianity.[15]

It was through ceaseless warfare not temporary agreement that the unification of the Picts and Scots came about, though the process which led to it is still incompletely understood. In the decade following the Synod of Whitby Northumbria imposed its overlordship on both the Picts and the Scots. The Northumbrian expansion was checked when the Pictish king Bridei son of Bili, defeated Ecgfrith of Northumbria at Dunnichen Moss in 685. The victory was decisive enough to free the Picts and Scots from the control of Northumbria and regain the southern Pictish territory which the Anglians had overrun. Bridei, however, was the son of the King of Strathclyde, and in effect his victory may have been that of the Britons who had been constant enemies of Northumbria. When Bridei died in 693, Adomnán, friend of many kings, lamented him with moving words on the power of death over the most powerful of men:

> It is strange, it is strange,
> That after being in the kingship of the people,
> A block of hollow withered oak
> Should be about the son of the king of Dumbarton.[16]

Not many years had passed before the Pictish king Nechtan son of Derile turned to Northumbria when his own high kingship was threatened. After a period of strife within the Pictish kingdom the high kingship was secured by Óengus I son of Fergus, who went on to defeat the Scots in 741 and become king of Dál Riata.

Initially it seems surprising that after this defeat the Scots should have taken over the kingdom of the Picts within a century and speedily obliterated all traces of Pictish culture. But recent research has shown that this was not a sudden reversal after a century of Pictish domination. By *c.* 750 Teudubr son of Bili, King of Strathclyde, had made himself overlord of the Picts. The first Scottish king to rule over both Picts and Scots appears to have been Constantine son of Fergus, of the Cenel nGabráin (d. 820), who appears in the Pictish king list as Castantin son of Uurguist. He was succeeded by his brother Óengus (d. 834) who appears in the Pictish list as Unuist son of Uurguist. Constantine's son Drest ruled over the Picts only, and died in 837 but Óengus's son Eóganán (Uuen to the Picts) ruled over both peoples. In 839 Eóganán and his brother Bran, together with a great host of Picts and Scots, were killed in battle against a new enemy, the Norsemen.

The slaughter of many members of the Pictish and Scottish royalty apparently cleared the way for the new candidate for the dual monarchy, Cináed mac Alpin – better known as Kenneth mac Alpin – who unified the two peoples. Medieval Scottish historians described Kenneth as a member of the Cenel nGabráin; but if he was so, he may not have belonged to the *derbfine*. He had a struggle to impose his rule on the Scots before he began his task of subjugating the Picts. Evidently he was not a readily acceptable candidate, though he must have been aristocratic enough to possess a strong band of warriors. After almost a decade of strife he had fought his way to both thrones and the ruthlessness of his ambition is captured in the later, perhaps fictitious story, that he owed his final success to a massacre of Pictish nobles at a feast.[17]

What made Kenneth seem different from his predecessors was not that he ruled both Picts and Scots but that the unification of the peoples under his dynasty was lasting. Equally momentous was that he decided, like Fergus Mór before him, to move the Scots' seat of government to the east. Kenneth's move was from the Western Highlands to central Scotland south of the Mounth, where an important centre was Dunkeld, to which he brought relics of St Columba from Iona. The dominance of the Scots over the Picts and their move to the centre of the new kingdom had the effect of relegating the old Dalriada to the periphery, while the Western Isles were soon lost to Norse domination.

3

GAEL, NORSE AND NORMAN

In Lewis Isle with fearful blaze
The house-destroying fire plays;
To hills and rocks the people fly
Fearing all shelter but the sky.
In Uist the king deep crimson made
The lightning of his glancing blade.
The peasant lost his land and life
Who dared to bide the Norseman's strife.[1]

The unification of the Picts and Scots led in the course of a century to
the disappearance of the Picts as a separate people. Two measures,
one legal the other ecclesiastical, marked stages of their submergence.
Donald I, brother and successor of Kenneth mac Alpin, proclaimed
that the laws of Áed Find, King of Dalriada (d. 778), were to be
enforced on both Picts and Scots. In 906 Constantine II and Bishop
Cellach of St Andrews jointly pledged that 'the laws and disciplines of
the Faith . . . should be kept in conformity with /the customs of/ the
Scots'. No doubt the unification of the Picts and Scots was confirmed by
the exceptionally long reign of Constantine II, from 900 to 943, by the
end of which almost a century had elapsed since the victory of Kenneth
mac Alpin. Constantine II abdicated in 943 to join the order of the
Culdees at St Andrews, where he died and was buried in 952. His
choice of St Andrews for his burial place, instead of Iona, where his
predecessors had been buried, may be seen as symbolizing the
completion of the transfer of Scottish power from west to east. It had
been accompanied by the spread of Gaelic culture, which obliterated
all but the visible traces carved in stone of the earlier culture of the
Picts. The Pictish people appear to have yielded to the process, without
suffering genocide or persecution. It has to be assumed that many
present day Scots have Pictish ancestry, but there is no definable
'ethnic minority' of Picts.

52

In the new kingdom, which came to be known as 'Scotia', the kings were accompanied in their move to the east of Druim Alban by the old leading kindreds of Dalriada. The kindred of the ruling house accompanied it to the centre of the kingdom. The Cenel Loairn moved through the Great Glen and settled in Moray. This great province extended from the Mounth to the border of Sutherland, taking in the old county of Ross-shire, and extending from coast to coast. The ruler of Moray, the *Mormaer* ('great steward') was a subject of the king of Scotia but as chief of the Cenel Loairn, from which earlier kings of Dalriada had come, he was scarcely less powerful than the king.

Dalriada itself became the province of Argyll (*Erra Gaidheal*, 'the coast of the Gael'). It was a dangerous coast, exposed to the full fury of the Viking raids. By the end of the eighth century the Scandinavians were the most skilful shipbuilders in the northern hemisphere. They possessed the materials, in abundant supplies of timber and iron, and the encouragement of their long coastlines and multitudes of harbours. In the case of the Norwegians, long fjords and difficult land communications were a compulsion rather than an incentive to put to sea. The causes of the Viking expansion belong to the history of Scandinavia and lie outside the scope of this book but overpopulation of their homelands is thought to have been one of the causes which drove the Scandinavians to seek new lands to colonize. However, it was an extraordinary explosion of energy, which history has recorded but not explained, which drove the Swedes to Russia and Constantinople, the Danes to Europe, England and Ireland, and the Norwegians to the Northern and Western Isles of Scotland, to Ireland, Iceland, Greenland and North America. The activities of the Vikings were varied; exploration, colonization and trade all inspired their voyages. But their first introduction to their neighbours was as raiders.

The long, lean Viking ships look magnificently beautiful when they are lifted from the resting places in which they provided ship-burials for kings and chiefs, restored and displayed in museums, or replicated by modern archaeological techniques from their imprints in the ground. But when they first appeared off the 'coast of the Gael', slid into quiet firths or were beached in island bays, they were objects of terror, premonitions of the brutality and slaughter which swiftly followed. The Norwegian Vikings who sacked Iona in 795 were pagans who acknowledged no Law of Innocents. To them the monastery enriched with gifts of Irish, Scottish and Pictish kings was not a sacred place but a vulnerable treasure-house of loot. They returned in 802 and again in 806. Little treasure can have remained by the third occasion, for they vented their disappointment by murdering sixty-eight monks. This massacre decided Cellach the abbot to leave the island; the following year he began to build a new monastery for his community at Kells, in Ireland. The decision to leave Iona cannot have been easy, for it was one of the greatest spiritual centres of the Celtic world. As a gesture of hope that the retreat was only temporary, the abbots of Kells continued to be styled abbots of Iona. In fact, Iona was not wholly abandoned, for a handful of monks willing to face martyrdom remained as a token community. Martyrdom came in 825 when the Vikings visited Iona for the fourth time. They spared the few monks but tortured to death the head of the community, Blathmac, in an attempt to make him reveal the whereabouts of the by now non-existent treasure. Blathmac was a warrior turned monk, who may have courted martydom to test his vocation against the type of violence which he had abjured.[2] The fate of Iona was but one example among many. There is a terrible pathos in a verse written by an Irish monk, thankful for the temporary protection of stormy weather:

> Bitter is the wind tonight,
> It tosses the ocean's white hair;
> Tonight I fear not the fierce warriors of Norway
> Coursing on the Irish sea.[3]

The Viking raiders in the Isles were advance parties of colonization. Sometimes the same men returned to take possession of lands which they had plundered. The Norwegian Ketil Flatnose, some of whose exploits are recounted in the *Laxdaela Saga*, when forced to leave Norway, said that he would 'go west across the sea to Scotland because . . . the living was good there. He knew the country well, for he had raided there extensively.'[4] He ruled the Hebrides briefly, from about 850 to 857.

The Vikings did not become peaceable landowners overnight. As late as the twelfth century the half-peaceful, half-piratical lifestyle of Svein Asleifarson of Gairsay, Orkney, is thus described in a lively modern translation of the *Orkneyinga Saga*:

This was how Svein used to live. Winter he would spend at home, where he entertained some eighty men at his own expense. His drinking hall was so big, there was nothing in Orkney to compare with it. In the spring he had more than enough to occupy him, with a great deal of seed to sow which he saw to carefully himself. Then, when that job was done, he would go off plundering in the Hebrides and in Ireland on what he called his 'spring trip', then back home just after midsummer, where he stayed till the cornfields had been reaped and the grain was safely in. After that he would go off raiding again, and never come back until the first month of winter was ended. This he used to call his 'autumn trip.'[5]

There was a difference between these two men, even if the victims of their raids might not have appreciated it. Ketil Flatnose, at the beginning of the Viking age, was a freebooter who made himself a local ruler; Svein Asleifarson, at the end of it, was a subject of the earl of Orkney, and more remotely of the king of Norway, essentially a landowner whose spring and autumn trips were undertaken to finance his winter revelry.

In the intervening centuries Norse power was extended over both the Northern and the Western Isles. The Norwegians were the first to arrive, but their supremacy was contested by the Danes. In 841 the Norwegian Viking Turges founded Dublin, which ten years later was seized by the Danes. From such an advantageous position the Danes could have cleared Norwegian settlements out of the Western Isles at their leisure unless Norwegian royal power had been exerted to protect them. In 853 King Olaf of Vestfold, Norway, who was known as Olaf the White, defeated the Danes of Dublin, and ruled there himself until 871. One of Olaf's queens was the daughter of Ketil Flatnose, a remarkable woman nicknamed Aud (or Unn) the Deep-Minded. Olaf repudiated Aud in favour of a new wife, possibly a daughter of Kenneth mac Alpin, and Aud returned to live with her father in the Western Isles. Years later, after the death of her son by Olaf, Aud the Deep-Minded sought new horizons in her old age, and led her kindred to settle in Iceland, a great enterprise which is recorded in the *Laxdaela Saga*. Aud and some of her family had converted to Christianity in the Western Isles; they were the first Norse Christians in Iceland, which did not officially adopt Christianity until 1000, after a resurgence of paganism, and the reintroduction of Christianity from Norway.

The Norse settlers in the Western Isles intermarried with the islanders, and their descendants were a mixed race which the Gaels of the mainland called the *Gall Gaidheal* ('foreign Gael'). A Gaelic contribution to this race was made by the Airgialla, who it may be remembered had come from Ireland, settled in the islands of the Cenel Loairn, and provided a fighting force for them. With the departure of the Cenel Loairn to Moray, the Airgialla remained in possession, and for a time were submerged by the Norse incomers. But their Gaelic heritage was not forgotten, and by the twelfth century Gaelic culture and language had absorbed the Norse influence and become predominant once more. Christianity played an important part in civilizing the Norse settlers, and in this achievement the courage of the monks who had refused to abandon Iona was rewarded; though Iona did not regain its glory as a centre of art and learning, it once again became the spiritual centre of the Western Isles. In 980, Olaf Cuaran, King of Dublin, who ten years previously had looted the monastery of Kells, abdicated his throne and became a monk on Iona.

The Northern Isles, like the Western Isles, were first colonized by Norwegian freebooters, who were threatened by the later arrival of the Danes, until the Norwegian kings of Vestfold acted to protect them. Rognavald of Møer in western Norway was created Earl of Orkney. But, according to the *Orkneyinga Saga*, Rognavald did not want to live in the Northern Isles, so he offered them to his three sons. The offer was accepted by his bastard son Einar who was 'tall and ugly, and though he was one-eyed he was still the most keen sighted of men'.[6] In about 895 he was given the title of earl, and he was also nicknamed 'Turf Einar' because he was the first Norseman who thought of digging peat for fuel. The story may be partly fictitious, but Einar was certainly the first historic Earl of Orkney. He cleared the islands of Danish marauders and founded a long-enduring dynasty which ruled Orkney under the remote authority of Norway.

On occasions, however, that authority made itself felt in a forceful manner. Around 995 Olaf Tryggvason, King of Norway, visited Orkney. After a career of excessive violence, even by Viking standards, he had been converted to Christianity in the Scilly Isles. He was eager to share the benefits of his new faith. Arrived at Osmundwall, Orkney, he summoned Sigurd the earl aboard his ship, and said to him 'I want you and all your subjects to be baptized. If you refuse I'll have you killed on the spot, and I swear I'll ravage every island with fire and steel.'[7] The result was a gratifying mass conversion. Unfortunately for the dramatic effect of this story, the Orcadians may have had a preliminary acquaintance with Christianity. The first Norse settlers in the islands had found them inhabited by *Peti* and *Papae*: Picts and

Christian monks. These monks were Celtic anchorites, and since they did not possess treasures like the great monasteries, they were more likely than the members of rich communities to have been permitted to survive. From them the Norse settlers in Orkney may have received their first impressions of Christianity, which would have been more appealing than the violent proselytization of the Norwegian king. Conversion to Christianity, whether voluntary or enforced, was not always complete or irrevocable. Some converts lapsed into paganism again, as did the descendants of Aud the Deep-Minded, in Iceland. Others hedged their bets by worshipping both the 'White Christ' and the old Norse gods, the latter especially in times of crisis. Their state of mind was no doubt like that of the semi-Christian convert in John Buchan's poem *Wood Magic*: 'For gods are kittle cattle, and a wise man honours them all.'[8]

Scotia lost extensive territories to the Norse settlers. Those in the Northern Isles spread on to the Scottish mainland, the northern counties of which had composed the Pictish province of Cait. From the Norse viewpoint this area was *Sudrland*, the south country, and *Katanes*, the promontory of Cait; they settled in these areas, and their designations survive as Sutherland and Caithness. Earl Thorfinn the Mighty of Orkney (d. 1064) ruled extensive territories in these areas and beyond: 'He won for himself nine Scottish earldoms, along with the whole of the Hebrides and a considerable part of Ireland.'[9] Thorfinn's power deeply impressed his contemporaries. A skald, or Norse praise-poet, wrote of him:

> The bright sun will blacken
> Heaven's bowl break
> asunder, earth sink in dark
> seas, mountains soar
> through ocean ere
> the islands bear another
> like Thorfinn: help him,
> Heaven, this hero.[10]

The claims to territorial possession made on his behalf may have been exaggerated, because not long after his death the Hebrides became subject to the kingdom of the Isles, which was governed from the Isle of Man. The Norse name for the Hebrides was *Suthreyjar*, or Southern Isles, to differentiate them from the Northern archipelagos.

The name of the Manx bishopric 'Sodor and Man' perpetuates this name, and also provides a reminder that the kings of Man were for a time kings of the *Suthreyjar*. Authority over the Western Isles was constantly disputed by the earls of Orkney and the kings of Dublin and Man. In 1093 King Magnus Barelegs of Norway brought a great expedition to assert Norwegian overlordship of the Western Isles, and in 1098 he forced on Edgar, King of Scots, a treaty in which Norwegian sovereignty of the Western Isles was recognized.

Although the kings of Scots were obliged to accept the facts of the Norse conquests both of the Northern Isles and of the Western Isles, which for a time were called *Innse Gall* ('the isles of the foreigners'), they never acknowledged Norse supremacy over any areas of the mainland. Thorfinn's earldoms on the mainland were theoretically held from the King of Scots, and Magnus Barelegs' attempt to claim that Kintyre was one of the isles by having himself dragged in a ship across the Tarbert isthmus was contemptuously ignored. The territory which had fallen under Norse control was regarded as Scottish territory, to be recovered at a later date.

King Magnus owed his sobriquet of Barelegs to his adoption of the Hiberno-Scottish dress. Magnus, copied by many of his followers, took to wearing the *leine* and the *brat*, the shirt and cloak, which left the lower legs bare. The *leine* was often called the *leine chroich*, or 'saffron shirt', because yellow was the favoured colour, though it is unlikely that true saffron, made from the stigmas of the autumn crocus, was often available. Yellow shirts were probably more frequently dyed with common local plants of the Highlands and Isles, such as bird's foot trefoil, bog myrtle, lichens, ragwort, gorse, broom and heather.[11]

A valuable and lasting legacy of Norse influence in the Western Isles was the Norse skill in shipbuilding. Though the skin-covered currach continued to be made for local purposes, the clinker-built *birlinn*, developed from the Norse galley, and improved by the introduction of a rudder in place of a steering-oar, became the islesmen's ship for longer inter-island voyages, and for sea-warfare. The *birlinn* was a symbol of power and status to the chief whose power was reckoned by the number of ships which he could command. It was represented in heraldry and on monuments in later centuries. It figured frequently in Gaelic liturgy and poetry. At the Reformation the blessing of a ship was added by Bishop John Carswell to his Gaelic translation of the *Book of Common Order*. The *iorram*, or Gaelic rowing-song, with which the steersman gave time to the rowers, was a poetic form which survived as long as the *birlinn* survived. As late as the eighteenth century the Gaelic poet Alasdair MacMhaighstir Alasdair included both a blessing and a rowing song in his great sea-poem *Birlinn Chlann Raghnaill* ('The Galley of Clan Ranald'), which tells of a voyage from South Uist to Ireland. A translation by Hugh MacDiarmid contains the following lines from the blessing:

> Father who fashioned the ocean
> And winds that from all points roll,
> Bless our lean ship and her heroes,
> Keep her and her whole crew whole.
>
> Your grace, O Son, on our anchor,
> Our rudder, sails and all graith
> And tackle to her masts attached,
> And guard us as we have faith . . . .
>
> Holy Ghost, be you our helmsman
> To steer the course that is right.
> You know every port under Heaven
> We cast ourselves on your sleight.[12]

The successors of Kenneth mac Alpin, who made Scone their centre of government, were increasingly preoccupied with events south-east of the Highland Line, where they seized opportunities for territorial expansion to compensate for the losses in the north and west.

Before the end of the ninth century Strathclyde, weakened by Viking raids, and finally brought to its knees by the capture of its capital, Dumbarton, fell under the domination of the Scots. During the tenth century Strathclyde underwent the fate which had earlier befallen the kingdom of the Picts: at first it retained its territorial identity, while it was ruled by Scottish kings, later it was absorbed into the kingdom of the Scots. Once Strathclyde had become subject to Scottish overlordship it was used to provide an appanage for the *tanist* of the King of Scotia. Thus, when Constantine II abdicated in 943 he was succeeded by his cousin Malcolm I (d. 954) while his son Indulf ruled Strathclyde; on Malcolm's death Indulf became King of Scotia, and Malcolm's son Dub became King of Strathclyde. This system continued until the reign of Malcolm II (1005–1034) whose grandson

Duncan was King of Strathclyde before he succeeded as King of Scotia and united the two kingdoms.

In the meantime the Scots had been equally successful in expanding to the south-east. In 866 the Northumbrian capital of York had fallen to the Danes. The Danish kingdom based on York occupied the southern area of Northumbria, which had once been the kingdom of Deira; the northern area, the erstwhile kingdom of Bernicia, became an isolated Anglian enclave, which fell gradually under Scottish domination. About 954 Indulf captured the rock of Edinburgh, and thereafter annexed the province of Lothian. In 1018 Malcolm II defeated the Anglians at Carham-on-Tweed, a victory which not only confirmed his possessions north of the Tweed but extended his overlordship of Bernicia at least as far south as Durham. Although the southern boundaries were undefined for more than another century, and were subject to minor variations for longer than that, when Duncan I succeeded his grandfather he became king of a significantly enlarged kingdom, no longer 'Scotia' but Scotland.

Malcolm II was over eighty when he died in 1034, and he was not survived by any male who qualified to succeed as a member of the *derbfine*: there were no surviving sons, grandsons or great-grandsons of a Scottish king in the male line. Duncan I was the son of Malcolm II's daughter Bethoc by her husband Crinan, hereditary abbot of Dunkeld, a great territorial magnate and a member of the kindred of Columba. Duncan was the obvious choice as Malcolm's successor because of the unification of territories which his accession would secure. But once the necessity of succession through a female had been accepted, Duncan was not the only candidate. Malcolm II had a nephew who would have been regarded as having as good a claim to the throne as Duncan. The relationship was probably that Malcolm's sister had married Finlaech *mormaer* of Moray, so that their son Macbeth was the king's nephew. His claim was strengthened by his marriage to Gruoch, who is thought to have been the granddaughter of Kenneth III. By her first marriage to Gillacomgan, Finlaech's successor as *mormaer* of Moray, she had a son named Lulach, who could also be a claimant to the throne when he reached maturity. Gillacomgan was Macbeth's cousin; on his death Macbeth both succeeded him as *mormaer* and married his widow. It is not unrealistic to suppose that Gruoch, the historical 'Lady Macbeth', would have encouraged Macbeth to assert his claim to the throne with an eye to the future claim of her own son.

On Duncan's accession Thorfinn of Orkney refused to pay the tribute which he owed for his Scottish territories, and Duncan mounted a campaign against him, in an attempt to recover them from Orcadian possession. Macbeth allied with Thorfinn and Duncan was defeated and killed in battle in 1040. He was not murdered. Macbeth became King of Scots and Thorfinn was rewarded by retaining his Scottish possessions. Duncan's two sons, Malcolm and Donald Bán, who were still children, survived to contest the throne in later years.

Macbeth ruled for seventeen years, a respected and successful king whose position was strong enough to permit his making a pilgrimage to Rome. Though Macbeth was descended from the Cenel Loairn and was ruler of the province of Moray, it would be mistaken to regard him as a more Celtic king than Duncan, or his victory as a 'Highland' defeat of a 'Lowland' ruler. Macbeth ruled from Scone like his immediate predecessors and, despite his northern origins, acknowledged that the political centre of the kingdom must remain where it had been established. Macbeth was overthrown by Malcolm mac Duncan in 1057, when he was killed in battle in Aberdeenshire. He was succeeded by his stepson Lulach, who was killed in turn by Malcolm the following year. These events were typical examples of the succession struggles which were the great weakness of the system of tanistry. They are recorded appropriately in the *Duan Albanach*:

> Six years of pure wise Donnchadh;
> seventeen years the son of Finnlaoch;
> after MacBeathadh the famed
> seven months in the rule of Lulach.
> Maolcholuin is king now,
> the son of Donnchadh the handsome, of lively aspect;
> his duration no one knows
> but the Learned one who is Learned.*[13]

Malcolm III *Ceann Mór* or Canmore ('great chief') ruled until 1093 and his reign witnessed the first stages in the metamorphosis of the Scottish monarchy from a Celtic into a European institution. Malcolm secured good relations with Orkney by marrying Thorfinn's widow Ingibiorg, by whom he had a son who reigned briefly in 1094, as Duncan II. In about 1068 Malcolm married his second wife, Margaret

---

* i.e. God, who alone knows the future.

61

(canonized 1250), who came to Scotland as a refugee from the Norman Conquest of England. Margaret's father, Edward the Exile, was a prince of the royal house of Wessex, her mother was German, and her childhood was spent at the court of Hungary. She was a cosmopolitan figure who probably regarded herself as a missionary of civilization in Scotland. That she was the 'Celtic hating Margaret' of tradition seems disproved by the fact that she was a benefactress of the Culdees. But she was shocked by some of the characteristics of the Celtic church which still survived: the non-celibacy of many of the clergy, the neglect of the sabbath as a day of rest, which is surprising in view of the later strength of sabbatarianism in Scotland, a 'barbarous rite' in the celebration of the Mass, possibly the use of the vernacular, and the reluctance of the people to receive Holy Communion at Easter, on the grounds that they were not worthy. Margaret's zeal for Catholic uniformity contributed as much as her sanctity to the cause of her canonization.

The marriage of Malcolm and Margaret, and his support of her brother Edgar the Atheling, the dispossessed heir to the English throne, involved Malcolm in bad relations with William the Conqueror. But in the next generation close connections were established between the two royal houses. Edith, the elder daughter of Malcolm and Margaret, married Henry I of England, the Conqueror's youngest son, while Malcolm and Margaret's fifth son, Alexander I of Scotland (d. 1124) married Henry I's illegitimate daughter Sibylla, thereby becoming both brother-in-law and son-in-law to Henry I. The three younger sons of Malcolm and Margaret, Edgar, Alexander I and David I, held the Scottish throne consecutively from 1097 to 1153, a long period of stability, which enabled David I to secure the succession of his twelve-year-old grandson Malcolm IV (d. 1165), the first child to succeed as King of Scots and by no means the last. Malcolm IV, a holy young man who remained celibate and for this reason was known as 'Malcolm the Maiden', was succeeded by his brother William the Lion (d. 1214), and William was followed by his son Alexander II (d. 1249) and his grandson Alexander III (d. 1286). If Malcolm II had intended to establish a single line of succession through his grandson Duncan I this aim had been frustrated by the reversion to tanistry under Macbeth and Lulach. By the time Alexander III succeeded, at the age of eight, the principle of primogeniture had been established, but it was not accepted without a struggle.

The deaths of Malcolm III and Margaret in 1093 were followed by a Celtic reaction. The welcome accorded to an influx of English refugees under the aegis of Margaret, and the intimations of change in Church and State which had characterized the reign, led conservative elements to welcome the accession of Donald Bán, the late king's brother. Under the old system of succession he would have had a better claim than the king's sons, and he had the added appeal of being a thoroughgoing Celt, who had spent his years of exile in Ireland and the Western Isles. However, he was overthrown by Duncan II, son of Malcolm III and Ingibiorg, who had spent some years at the English court and was provided by King William Rufus with an army of Norman knights to help him assert his claim. Duncan II was accepted in Scotland, on condition that he sent home his Norman supporters. Without them he was easily ousted again by Donald Bán, who this time sought to secure himself by dividing the kingdom with Edmund, the eldest surviving son of Malcolm and Margaret. The younger 'Margaretsons'* had taken refuge at the English court, where they formed the relationships and the tastes which led them to introduce Norman innovations into Scotland in later years. William Rufus extended his patronage of them so far as to provide the army with which Edgar defeated Donald Bán and Edmund in 1097. Edmund was imprisoned for the rest of his life and Donald Bán was blinded. On his death his remains were taken to Iona, where he was the last king of Scots to be buried. It was an appropriate resting place for a king who represented the traditions of Dalriada.

The challenge to the 'Margaretsons' was taken up by the surviving members of the house of Moray. Lulach had left two children: a son, who seems to have left no descendants, and a daughter who married Áed (or 'Heth'), Earl of Moray.† His descendants, the 'MacHeths', received strong support in their own country of Moray, in Argyll, and in the Western Isles, where the re-emergent Gaels would have had little sympathy for the Anglo-Norman connections of the ruling house. In 1130 Áed's sons, Angus and Malcolm MacHeth raised a rebellion in Moray; but the men of Moray were no match for the mailed knights sent north by David I. The MacHeths were defeated at the battle of Stracathro, where Angus was killed. Malcolm continued in rebellion until he was captured in 1134, after which he remained

---

* This useful term was coined by Professor Gordon Donaldson. It is worth remarking the odd fact that a 'matronymic' should provide the most convenient name for a family which established primogeniture in the male line.
† This is the first use of the title 'earl' instead of 'mormaer'.

a prisoner for twenty-eight years.

However, Malcolm MacHeth was married to a sister of Somerled, lord of Argyll, the formidable descendant of the Airgialla who created for himself a Gaelic principality in Argyll and the Isles, and was acknowledged by Irish contemporaries as *rí Innse Gall* ('king of the Hebrides'). Malcolm MacHeth's sons appealed to Somerled, who made war on their behalf against King Malcolm IV. Somerled secured the release of Malcolm MacHeth and the grant to him of the earldom of Ross for his lifetime. Somerled made his peace with Malcolm IV, but he invaded western Scotland in 1164 – not apparently for any purpose connected with the MacHeth's – and met his death in battle at Renfrew. When Malcolm MacHeth died his earldom reverted to the crown. His daughter Gormflaith, wife of Harald Maddadson, Earl of Orkney, urged her husband to occupy it. He did so, but was defeated by William the Lion, who was strong enough to wrest Sutherland from him, leaving the earldom of Orkney in possession of Caithness alone on the Scottish mainland. In Caithness the kindred and dependants of Malcolm MacHeth may have found refuge; they are believed to have been the forebears of the Clan Mackay (*Mac Áed*).

The MacHeths were not the only claimants to the throne to contest the linear succession. Duncan II had a son whose Norman affinities are suggested by the form of his name, William FitzDuncan. He may have married a kinswoman of Malcolm MacHeth, for he fathered Donald MacWilliam who found support in Moray for his claim to the throne. (This is not as surprising as it sounds, for if the old system of succession had been reinstated MacHeth and MacWilliam claimants could have alternated, doubtless with a good deal of intermittent bloodshed). Donald MacWilliam spent years in revolt and was evidently regarded as a serious threat by William the Lion, who sent an army to Inverness in 1187 and dispatched search parties to apprehend him. It was Roland, Lord of Galloway, who slew him at Mamgarvie, on the borders of Moray.

This was probably the last serious threat to the 'Margaretson' succession, though it was not the last of the Celtic revolts. In 1215 Donald Bán MacWilliam and Kenneth MacHeth brought an army from Ireland to invade Moray. They were defeated by Farquhar MacTaggart (*mac an t'-sacairt*, 'son of the priest'), who is thought to have been the secular heir of the abbots of Applecross.[14] Farquhar, in ancient Celtic style, brought the severed heads of the defeated claimants to the new king Alexander II, who rewarded him in the

A goose and a
salmon, incised on
a Pictish symbol
stone from
Easterton of
Roseisle.

Pictish silver

The Hunterston brooch

The Brecbennock of St Columba, or 'Monymuste Reliquary'

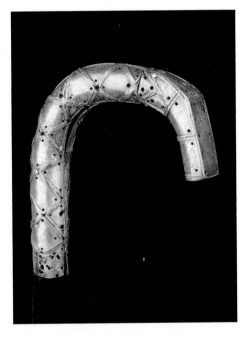

The head of the Crozier of St Fillan

The Inauguration of King Alexander III, showing the recitation of the King's genealogy by a Highland *seannachie*.

A page of the Book of Deer, a ninth-century Latin gospel with mid-twelfth-century Gaelic 'notitial' written in its blank spaces.

sixteenth-century clarsach or Highland harp, known as the 'Queen Mary Harp'.

Left: Effigy of Bricius MacKinnon, who may have fought at the Battle of Bannockburn. *Right*: Effigy of Cristinus MacGillescoil, Prior of Iona.

Monument of Anna MacLean, Prioress of Iona.

Left: The Cross of Colinus MacDuffie, Oronsay. *Right*: The reverse side of the Campbeltown Cross.

modern Norman style, with a knighthood, a cost-free method of giving gratification, which retains its power in the late twentieth century. However, in 1226 Farquhar MacTaggart was more substantially rewarded with the earldom of Ross. He was a significant figure, a Celtic magnate who might have been expected to support the old order, but chose to seek his fortune with the new.

The MacHeths and MacWilliams fought not only to restore the form of succession which allowed them access to the throne but to resist the Norman Conquest of Scotland from within, which took place under the 'Margaretsons' and the grandsons of David I, through the introduction of feudalism.

According to feudal theory only the king held his land 'allodially', i.e. in absolute possession. He was the proprietor of his kingdom and his vassals, or tenants-in-chief, held their lands from him in return for military service. They in turn had tenants of their own, whose tenures and obligations were similar in concept but smaller in scale. The characteristics of feudalism were: the oath by which lordship and vassalage were acknowledged and confirmed; the *feudum* or fief, the land granted by king or lord in return for the service performed; the knight, or mailed warrior trained to fight on horseback, who performed the service; and the castle, or fortified residence, which lord and vassal alike required to house his family, household officers, servants and military resources. The power which the hierarchical structure of feudalism, cemented by the oath of 'vassalic commendation', could give to a strong king was a lesson which the 'Margaretsons' learned from the sons of William the Conqueror.

Edgar and Alexander I aspired to imitate the Norman kings but David I possessed the means to do so. David married an Anglo-Norman heiress, Maud de Senlis, Countess of Huntingdon, and the great estates of the 'honour of Huntingdon' in the English Midlands provided him with a reservoir of feudal tenants who could be granted lands in Scotland, where their advancement would create a loyal and efficient military caste like that which had secured the Norman kings' hold upon England. The feudalization of Scotland under David I chiefly affected the Lowlands but about 1130 he granted Duffus in Moray to Freskin, a Fleming. By the middle of the next century Freskin's descendants had prospered greatly. They took the surname de Moravia (later Scotticized as 'Murray') from their northern possessions and acquired the earldom of Sutherland after William the Lion's defeat of Harald Maddadson of Orkney.

The advancement of Freskin serves as a reminder that the feudalization of Scotland was not carried out by the importation of Normans alone. Three families from which later kings of Scots were descended illustrate the diverse origins of the incoming families. The Bruces were Normans, from Brix, near Cherbourg; the Balliols came from Bailleul-en-Vimeu, in Picardy; the Stewarts from Dol, in Brittany. The Cumins, or Comyns, advanced by David I, were Normans of quite humble origin, who in the thirteenth century became one of the most powerful families in Scotland and especially in the Highlands. William Comyn (d. 1233) was the first member of an imported family to acquire an earldom: in 1212 he gained the earldom of Buchan through marriage to its heiress. His sons Walter and Alexander became earls of Menteith and Buchan respectively and around 1230 Walter became lord of Badenoch. The Comyns established their power both by acquiring feudal tenures and by intermarriage with the Celtic aristocracy. They demonstrated that feudal and kin-based power were not necessarily mutually exclusive.[15] Many other families which arrived in Scotland as feudal tenants, like the Comyns, evolved into clans: the Chisholms, Frasers, Grants, Grahams and Menzies are but a few examples.

The construction of new motte-and-bailey castles of the Norman pattern marked the establishment of feudal power in post-Norman Conquest England, and its exportation to lowland Scotland. Some motte-and-bailey castles were built in the Highlands, especially on its fringes, but more characteristic of the establishment of feudalism in the Highlands was the occupation and reconstruction of ancient strongholds by new overlords. Loch-an-Eilean, which had begun its history of human habitation as a crannog, became a stronghold of the Comyns. The castles of Dunollie, Dunstaffnage and Dunaverty were medieval castles which occupied and strengthened the sites of ancient forts. The local societies which had followed patrimonial warlords were often obliged to transfer their loyalty to feudal overlords. Sometimes they did so readily and sometimes refused. The interaction and conflict between patrimonial and feudal loyalties is a continuing theme in the history of the development of Highland clans.

David I did not intend merely to infiltrate his kingdom with a network of military tenures which would increase his control over it; he aspired to metamorphose it in accordance with ideals which he admired, in part perhaps acquired from his mother, in part absorbed through his own experience. St Margaret had brought a small community of Benedictine monks from Canterbury to Dunfermline; David I transformed the religious life of Scotland by a large-scale importation of European monasticism. He founded communities of Cistercians at Melrose, Dundrennan, Newbattle and Kinloss, and of Augustinian Canons at Holyrood, Jedburgh and Cambuskenneth, near Stirling. He brought Tironensians to Kelso and Cluniacs to the Isles of May. The first of the Stewarts founded another Cluniac community at Paisley, and the Premonstratensians were brought to Dryburgh by Hugh de Morville. In the reign of Alexander II the austere order of the Valliscaulians arrived, and was established at Pluscarden, near Elgin, at Beauly, near Inverness, and at Ardchatten, on Loch Etive, in Argyll; they, it seems, were the order which adapted most successfully to life in the Highlands. However, Somerled and his son Ranald founded the Cistercian abbey of Saddell in Kintyre[16] and this was followed by the foundation of a Benedictine priory and an Augustinian nunnery on Iona (*c.* 1208). In the middle of the following century John, Lord of the Isles, founded the Augustinian priory of Oronsay.

Not all the ecclesiastical innovations were monastic; the diocesan and parochial system was extended to cover the whole of Scotland. About 1190 a new diocese of Argyll was created out of scattered properties which hitherto had been subject to the diocese of Dunkeld. Parishes were organized in the Highlands as in the Lowlands, and churches were built to take the place of the shrines, chapels and hermitages dedicated to Celtic saints, though the parish churches of the twelfth and thirteenth centuries preserved some of these dedications: the church of St Adomnán at Insh in Badenoch is a surviving example.[17] However, parishes, like monastic foundations were more plentiful in the Lowlands: at the end of the thirteenth century Fife and Dumfriesshire had seventy parishes each, while Sutherland and Wester Ross had only eight parishes between them.

These examples represent the extremes, and do not imply that where there were few parishes the spiritual life of the people was necessarily neglected. Communities of Culdees survived the importation of European monasticism, at least for a time. During the twelfth century Culdee communities existed at Abernethy, Brechin, Dunkeld, Inchaffray, Iona, Loch Leven, Monifieth, Monymusk, Muthill and St Andrews; during the next century some of them continued to survive as colleges of secular clergy who continued to attend to the spiritual needs of areas which were not necessarily organized as parishes.

At the same time veneration of the Celtic saints continued, often centred not so much upon sacred sites as upon their relics. Whereas the Roman church preserved corporeal relics – such as incorrupt bodies, limbs, bones or phials of blood – characteristic relics of the Celtic saints were ecclesiastical insignia or personal possessions, often preserved by their *comh-arba* or 'coarbs', secular descendants or collateral descendants. For example the crozier of St Fillan was preserved by the family of MacNab or *Mac an aba* ('Son of the Abbot'), and the staff or *bachull* of St Moluag of Lismore still remains in the keeping of the Livingstone family. The surname of Dewar recalls the office of *Deòradh*, a keeper of holy relics. The *deòradh* who guarded the *brecbennoch* or reliquary of St Columba was required to carry it on campaigns with the royal army, whose success it was expected to ensure. After the victory of Bannockburn the Abbot of Arbroath, who had performed that function, resigned his office of *deòradh* to Malcolm of Monymusk. The *brecbennoch* is known as the Monymusk Reliquary to this day.[18]

The third great innovation of David I, the foundation of the Royal Burghs had little immediate effect upon the Highlands, except that insofar as the burghs were granted the monopoly of trade and of import and export their establishment must have discouraged the development of local manufactures. However the planting of communities of burgesses assisted in extending the authority of David I and his successors into the north of Scotland. An important series of early burghs – Inverness, Elgin, Kintore, Aberdeen, Perth, Stirling, Dumbarton – follows the Highland Line fairly closely; but all these burghs lie on the Lowland side of it, including Inverness, which later became known as the 'Capital of the Highlands'. On the whole, the Gaels did not take to town life and the communities of the burghs were formed of Lowlanders of Anglian stock and of English and Flemish immigrants.

Though the townsfolk were few in number they were great in influence. They spread the northern dialect of English, which had been spoken in Lothian, throughout the areas of Scotland in which burghs were established. It underwent acclimatization and became the Scots vernacular, a vigorous and expressive language in which some of the greatest Scottish poetry was written in the fifteenth and sixteenmth centuries. The subtle and beautiful Gaelic tongue retreated before it and by the end of the fourteenth century it was spoken only in the Isles, beyond the Highland Line and in separatist Galloway, where it declined more slowly than in the rest of the Lowlands. French was imported by incoming feudal families but it never struck deep roots in Scotland. The Bruces, Balliols, Comyns, Stewarts and others would have spoken it among themselves, but it did not long remain the language of the aristocracy, as it did in England. Gaelic and Scots, in their appropriate areas, became the languages of the dominant families, while Latin was the ecclesiastical and diplomatic language of Scotland, as of all other western Christian kingdoms.

When Scotland, as a result of the innovations of David I and his successors, ceased to be an exclusively kin-based Celtic society and became at least in part a feudal kingdom, it took its place as 'one of the recognized powers of middle rank within the family of west European states'.[19] As an accompaniment to this development the royal house itself became less Celtic: Malcolm IV and William the Lion, Alexander II and Alexander III were all the sons of Norman or French mothers. It might have appeared that the kings of Scots were turning away from their Celtic origins but this was not so: the most Europeanized scion of the royal house was inaugurated with ritual which deliberately recalled them.

In accordance with the ancient rite of Dalriada the eight-year-old Alexander III, on his accession in 1249, was neither crowned nor anointed. He was brought to Scone and enthroned out of doors on the sacred stone of inauguration which the Scots had brought from Irish Dalriada. Then a *seanchaidh* (historian or genealogist) recited in Gaelic his ancestry, 'Benach de Re Albanne Alexander, Mac Alexander, Mac Uleyham, Mac Henri, MacDavid – and reciting thus he read off even unto the end, the pedigree of the kings of Scots', extending beyond Fergus Mór mac Eirc, through a long list of legendary predecessors to the mythical and eponymous ancestress of the Scots, Scota, daughter of the Pharaoh from whom the Israelites had fled. This ancient ritual would have seemed very alien to the more recently established tenants-in-chief, but it would have reminded the Gaels of the fabulous antiquity of their royal line.

The 'Margaretsons' had not neglected to claim authority over the outlying areas of the kingdom, but the substance of their claims required to be enforced by their successors. William the Lion, by the end of his reign, had extended his control as far as the Pentland Firth; effective rule of the west and the recovery of the Western Isles awaited the attention of his son and grandson. Two political changes enabled them to turn their attention to it: the first was the improvement of Anglo-Scottish relations; the second was the weakening of Norwegian power.

Throughout his long reign William the Lion had had troubled relations with England, as a result of the expansionist ambitions of Henry II, the first of the Plantagenet kings. The marriage of Alexander II to Joan, sister of Henry III, in 1221 inaugurated a happier period, which allowed the king of Scots to turn his attention to the west. Meanwhile, civil war in Norway, between 1161 and 1208, had loosened the hold of the Norwegian kings over the Western Isles. During the early years of his reign Alexander II increased his authority over both Galloway and Argyll, and during the 1240s he took the initiative against Norway. He sent a series of embassies to King Haakon IV, by which he complained of the treaty forced upon Edgar by Magnus Barelegs, and offered to purchase the isles from Norway. On Haakon's refusal he moved from negotiation to force and gathered a fleet for the purpose of annexing the Western Isles. He sailed round the Mull of Kintyre into the Fifth of Lorn, but his sudden death on the Isle of Kerrera left his plan in abeyance. Its resumption had to await the maturity of Alexander III, the late born son of his second marriage, to his French queen, Marie de Coucy.

Alexander III began his personal rule in 1261 and immediately provoked a confrontation with Norway. In 1262 William, Earl of Ross, son of Farquhar MacTaggart, invaded and devastated the Isle of Skye. Haakon IV, by this time an old king, prepared to defend his possession of the Western Isles by having his son Magnus crowned as his successor before he embarked on the expedition which might – and indeed did – prove to be his last. In the autumn of 1263 he brought a great fleet to the Western Isles, but the weather turned against him and the Scots were ready for him. Equinoctial gales battered his fleet, and his landing force was mauled at the battle of Largs. Haakon withdrew to Orkney, where he fell ill and died in mid-December.

The transfer of the Isles was negotiated in 1266 between his successor, Magnus the Law-Mender, and Alexander III. By the Treaty of Perth the Western Isles became subject to Scotland for the sum of 4,000 marks and an 'annual' of 100 marks to be paid in perpetuity (a payment which lapsed in the next century). The Northern Isles were expressly reserved to the Norwegian crown, though the line of the Norse earls of Orkney had already died out (1231) and Orkney and Shetland fell increasingly under Scottish domination. However, the

Treaty of Perth opened a period of close relations between Scotland and Norway, cemented in 1281 by the marriage of Alexander's daughter Margaret to King Magnus's successor, Eric.

Though the Western Isles became officially part of Scotland the unification was more apparent than real; they retained a semi-independence under the descendants of Somerled until the end of the fifteenth century.

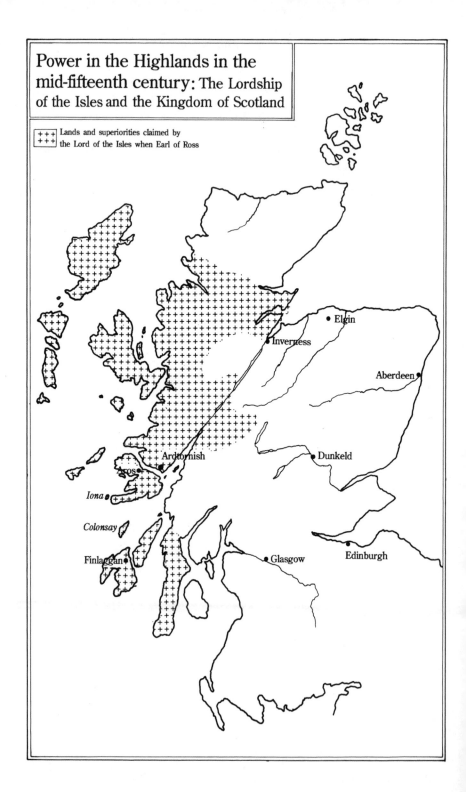

Power in the Highlands in the mid-fifteenth century: The Lordship of the Isles and the Kingdom of Scotland

+++
+++ Lands and superiorities claimed by the Lord of the Isles when Earl of Ross

Elgin

Inverness

Aberdeen

Dunkeld

Ardtornish

Ross

Iona

Colonsay

Finlaggan

Glasgow

Edinburgh

4

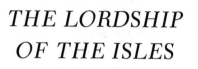

THE LORDSHIP
OF THE ISLES

There is no clan like the Clan Donald
The noble clan of firmest mind.
Who is there can number their gifts? . . .
First of all with the Clan Donald
There is knowledge which they learn;
Last of all there is among them
Polish, generosity and modesty.
'Tis in sorrow and in grief
Understanding and learning are got
By him who them would have . . .
Loud was the sound of their thunder,
This race so wise and faithful,
Though now they be reproached . . .[1]

The rise of the Lordship of the Isles was made possible by the misfortunes of the three kingdoms which aspired to control the Western Isles: the kingdoms of Man, Norway and Scotland.

The links between the Manx kingdom of the Isles and Norway were strong. Theoretically the Manx kings were subject to Norwegian overlordship but the weakening of Norwegian power in the Isles simultaneously permitted them greater independence and deprived them of Norwegian support when they most needed it. Olaf the Red, the last king of the entire Manx kingdom of the Isles, ruled from 1115 to 1153 and gave his daughter Ragnhild in marriage to Somerled, probably with the intention of converting an ambitious potential enemy into an ally.

Somerled, as previously mentioned, was probably a *Gall-Gaidheal* (i.e. a man of Norse-Gaelic extraction). His name was of Norse origin. Somarlidi (gaelicized as Somerled, Somhairle or Sorley) meant 'summer warrior' or 'Viking'. It was a noun which became a personal name.[2] Both his father and his grandfather had Gaelic names: Gilla-Brighte ('servant of St Bride') and Gilla-Adomnáin ('servant of St Adomnán') respectively. Somerled claimed descent from Godfrey mac Fergus, a chief of the Airgialla, who had fought for Kenneth mac Alpin and won great possessions in the Western Isles which were lost again under the Norse overlordship. Somerled's father attempted to recover this lost patrimony, and the desperate condition to which he was reduced in the course of his struggle is recalled by his nickname *Gilla-Brighte nan Uamh* ('Gilla-Brighte of the cave') – the cave in which he had been obliged to hide from his enemies. Somerled succeeded where his father had failed and built up a powerful principality, Gaelic in culture, based on Argyll, Arran and Bute. His alliance with the MacHeths has already been mentioned; by 1140 he was considered a valuable son-in-law by Olaf the Red.

Olaf's daughter Ragnhild bore Somerled three sons, Dugald, Ranald and Angus. When Olaf died he was succeeded by his son Godfrey, who proved to be a tyrannous ruler. Some of Godfrey's subjects approached Somerled and offered to make Dugald their king, if Somerled would assist in Godfrey's overthrow. Somerled agreed and about 1156 he defeated Godfrey in a sea battle, after which the kingdom of the Isles was divided. 'And this,' in the words of the Manx Chronicle, 'was the downfall of the kingdom of the Isles, from the time when the sons of Somerled took possession of it.'

When Somerled died in 1164 his vast and scattered possessions were divided among his sons. Dugald inherited his father's mainland territories of Lorne, Morvern and Ardnamurchan, together with the Isle of Mull and its adjacent group, and became the ancestor of the Clan Dougall. Ranald inherited Kintyre with Islay and its surrounding group of islands. On his death this inheritance was divided again, between his sons Donald and Ruaridh: Donald inherited Islay and was the ancestor of the later Lords of the Isles and of other branches of the Clan Donald (Glencoe, Glengarry, Clan Ranald and MacIains of Ardnamurchan) and Ruaridh inherited part of Kintyre and became the ancestor of the Clan Ruari. Angus, the third son of Somerled, inherited Bute but in two generations the only survivor of this branch of the family was Angus's granddaughter, who married a Stewart thus transferring Bute to the possession of the future royal house.

The Isle of Man and the Outer Hebrides remained in the possession of the descendants of Olaf the Red, the last of whom, Magnus, died in

1265. These islands, together with the rest of the Western Isles, were transferred to the Scottish crown by the Treaty of Perth the following year.

Alexander III rewarded the support of the Earl of Ross by granting him Skye and Lewis. These additions to his earldom and his hereditary lands of Applecross made him one of the greatest among the northern magnates. This enlarged earldom of Ross was to be of great importance in the future history of the Lordship of the Isles. By the end of Alexander's reign Alan MacRuari, great-grandson of Somerled, had acquired Garmoran or *Garbhcriochan* ('the rough bounds'), an area extending from Glenelg to Ardnamurchan. He was also lord of Uist, which the MacRuaris may have held nominally from the crown of Norway before the Treaty of Perth.

The chiefs of the *Clan Somhairle* (descendants of Somerled) might have preferred to remain as semi-independent rulers, kings in their own estimation, under the ineffectual sway of Norway but after the Treaty of Perth they accepted the overlordship of Alexander III and became subjects of the Scottish crown. In 1284 Alexander MacDougall of Argyll, Angus Mór MacDonald of Islay and Alan MacRuari of Garmoran attended as barons of Scotland a council which met at Scone to deliberate on the Scottish successions. Throughout Alexander III's reign his preoccupation had been the unity of his kingdom, and the progress he had made in achieving it in the eighteen years following the Treaty of Perth was well illustrated by the presence of the chiefs of the Clan Somhairle at Perth.

The council was summoned to avert an impending succession crisis. Alexander's sons had predeceased him, as also had his daughter Margaret, the wife of Eric II of Norway. His only surviving descendant was the child of this marriage, Margaret 'the Maid of Norway' whom the lords assembled at Scone were requested to recognize as heiress to the throne. This they did and on Alexander III's death in 1286 they kept faith with their agreement and acknowledged her as 'Lady and Queen' of Scotland.

The events which followed are well known. The death of the Maid of Norway in 1290 precipitated the very crisis which Alexander III had sought to avert. There were thirteen claimants to the throne, known as the 'Competitors' a term which no doubt accurately conveys their state of mind. Only two of them had claims which merited serious consideration: they were descendants of David, Earl of Huntingdon, brother of Malcolm IV and William the Lion. Earl David's eldest daughter, Margaret, married Alan, Lord of Galloway, and their daughter Derbforgaill (or Dervorguilla), Lady of Galloway, married John Balliol, a member of the Picard family which owed its advancement to David I. Their son, John Balliol the younger, was the leading competitor. Earl David's second daughter, Isabella, married the Norman Robert Bruce, Lord of Annandale, and their son Robert Bruce was the other competitor with a serious claim. Bruce contested Balliol's claim on two counts: first, that he was the grandson of Earl David, whereas Balliol was the great-grandson, and therefore at one further remove from royalty; and second, that Alexander II, while still childless, had designated Bruce his heir. Since these two men, and the remaining competitors were unable to agree among themselves, they submitted their claims to the arbitration of Edward I of England, who had been the brother-in-law of Alexander III.*

Edward I demanded as a preliminary that the competitors should acknowledge him as their overlord, which seemed a reasonable demand, if only to ensure their acceptance of his decision. Edward considered the claims with every appearance of impartiality and decided with scrupulous fairness in favour of John Balliol, who was inaugurated as king in November 1292. Edward then demanded that Balliol should accept him as overlord of Scotland. Balliol was trapped. He had already acknowledged Edward as his personal overlord (which he could scarcely have failed to do, since he held lands in England); but once he had become King of Scots he continued to need English support because the powerful faction of Bruce refused to acknowledge his kingship. It was not long before Balliol found his position as a vassal king intolerable. In 1295 he abjured his homage to Edward and formed an alliance with France, the beginning of the lasting bond between the two countries which came to be called the *auld alliance*.

Edward I, as his conquest of Wales revealed, was a ruthless imperialist and he must have planned the conquest of Scotland from the moment when the request for arbitration delivered the fate of the kingdom into his hands. His contemptuous treatment of Balliol goaded the latter to revolt, an action which legally justified the attempted conquest of Scotland as the crushing of a rebellious vassal. Though his plan came close to success, he obviously underrated the resistance which he would meet, for it outlasted his lifetime, and continued during the reigns of his son and grandson, Edward II and Edward III.

* Alexander's first wife had been Edward's sister, Margaret of England.

The Wars of Independence fell into four distinct episodes: the first was the rebellion of John Balliol, which ended in his abdication (1296) and the apparent triumph of Edward I; the second was the national rising led by Sir William Wallace and his supporter Sir Andrew Murray (or 'de Moravia'), which seemed to have been totally crushed when Wallace was captured and executed by the English in 1305; the third was the renewed struggle under Robert Bruce, grandson of Bruce the Competitor, which began with his inauguration as King Robert I (1306), culminated in his victory over Edward II at Bannockburn (1314) and concluded with Edward III's acknowledgement of Scottish independence in the Treaty of Northampton (1328); the fourth and final phase was the attempt of Edward Balliol, the son of John to regain his father's throne on the same terms, as the vassal of Edward III, an attempt which was frustrated by the supporters of Robert I's young son, David II.

Though the Wars of Independence ultimately secured Scotland's freedom and autonomy, they would have been much less protracted if the Scots had not been divided amongst themselves. The course of the struggle in the Highlands was decided by patterns of family alliance and enmity. The sisters of John Balliol were married to John Comyn, Lord of Badenoch and Alexander MacDougall of Argyll, alliances which assured Balliol of powerful support in the Highlands. The Bruces initially enjoyed the support of the MacDonalds of Islay and the MacRuaris of Garmoran, but Alexander, eldest son of Angus Mór MacDonald of Islay, married a daughter of Alexander MacDougall of Argyll, which brought him within the orbit of the opposing faction. These alignments were converted into a violent feud in 1306, when Robert Bruce, shortly before he claimed the throne, met John 'the Red' Comyn, Balliol's nephew, in the Greyfriars' church at Dumfries, possibly with a view to bargaining for his support. But a violent quarrel ensued, in which Bruce stabbed Comyn to death in front of the altar. The sacrilegious murder laid the obligation of a blood feud on all Comyn's relations and connections by marriage. When Bruce was inaugurated at Scone by a handful of supporters he became a fugitive king, pursued by the enmity of England, threatened by the combined power of the Comyns, the MacDougalls and Alexander of Islay, and faced with the certainty of excommunication by the Church.

Shortly after his inauguration Robert I suffered two defeats in rapid succession, at Methven and Dalrigh. He was obliged to flee the country, and in this desperate situation he was aided by the MacRuaris and by Angus Óg MacDonald, younger brother of Alexander of Islay, who remained his steadfast supporter. Angus Óg deserved the rewards which he ultimately received, for he supported Robert I when his fortunes were at their lowest, and probably assisted both his flight from Scotland and his return. In 1307 Robert I won his first victory at Loudoun Hill and in 1308 or the following year broke the power of the MacDougalls at the Pass of Brander. Angus Óg brought a contingent from the Isles to the battle of Bannockburn.

When his authority was fully established Robert I required Angus Óg to resign his lands in Kintyre, which were bestowed on Robert Stewart, the son of the King's daughter Margery and her husband Walter, High Steward of Scotland. But Angus Óg received a princely compensation by being granted Mull, Coll, Tiree, Morvern, Ardnamurchan, Duror, Glencoe, and part of Lochaber. He already possessed Islay, Jura, Gigha and Colonsay. He gave Ardnamurchan to his younger brother Iain Sprangach, who had supported him in fighting for Robert I. The MacRuaris were also rewarded: Roderick, the son of Alan MacRuari of Garmoran, received part of Lochaber, in addition to his mainland possession of Garmoran and the islands of Benbecula, Barra, Eigg, Rhum and the Uists.

King Robert's enemies suffered commensurately. The power of the Comyns was broken, and never revived. Many of the MacDougalls and the disinherited branch of the MacDonalds – those descended from Alexander of Islay – took service as soldiers of fortune in Ireland. They became members of the military caste known as 'galloglasses' (*gall-oglaich*, 'foreign young men'), a popular career for men of the Western Highland and Isles.

John of Islay, son of Angus Óg, was known as 'the good John of Islay' for reasons which are not apparent, apart from his generosity to the Church. He succeeded to his father's possessions in about 1330, at the outset of the fourth phase of the Wars of Independence, when Edward Balliol attempted to seize the throne of Scotland, while the child-king David II was sent to France for safety.

The adherence of John of Islay, the most powerful magnate of the west, was sought by the partisans of both Balliol and David II. In 1336 Balliol wooed his support with a grant of Kintyre, Knapdale and Skye; but Balliol failed to establish himself as king of Scots and David II returned from France in 1341. David rescinded the grants which

Balliol had made to John of Islay but confirmed him in his hereditary possessions. In 1346 David II was obliged to repay French hospitality by invading England on behalf of his allies; he was defeated and captured at the battle of Neville's Cross, near Durham, and remained Edward III's prisoner for eleven years. His long absence from Scotland allowed John of Islay renewed scope for self-aggrandizement.

In 1337 John had married Amie, daughter of Roderick MacRuari, who on the death of her brother Ranald in 1346 inherited all the MacRuari lands, which passed in effect to her husband. A few years later he divorced Amie though he kept her lands (for possession of which he secured recognition from the crown in 1372). In 1350 he married Margaret, daughter of Robert Stewart, Robert I's grandson, and acquired Kintyre and Knapdale as her dowry. In the dispensation for this marriage, granted by Pope Clement VI, John was described as *dominus Insularum Scotie* ('lord of the Isles of Scotland'), a title which was thenceforward acknowledged throughout Scotland. To the Irish and the Gaelic-speaking Scots he was *Rí Innse Gall* ('King of the Hebrides').

The marriage of John, Lord of the Isles, and Margaret Stewart linked the two most powerful kindreds of Scotland. In 1350 Robert Stewart was acting as regent of Scotland during David II's captivity and he was also heir presumptive. As the years passed and David II remained childless it seemed increasingly likely that Robert would become king. He eventually succeeded as Robert II in 1371 and confirmed the Lord of the Isles in all his possessions. John, before his death in 1387, gave Glencoe to his brother Iain Fraoch and persuaded Godfrey and Ranald, his sons by Amie MacRuari, to agree that Donald, his eldest son by Margaret Stewart, should succeed him as Lord of the Isles. It may have been acknowledged that the whole kindred would benefit, if the chief were the grandson of the king.

Thanks to his father's successful policy of self aggrandizement Donald, Lord of the Isles, inherited immense power and prestige, which he was able to enhance under circumstances very similar to those which had assisted his father. His uncle, Robert III, who described himself as 'the worst of kings and the most miserable of men' failed to keep order in either his kingdom or his family; shortly before his death in 1406 he decided to send his son Prince James to the French court to ensure his safety. The unfortunate prince was captured at sea by English pirates and sent to the court of England, where he remained a prisoner for eighteen years. After the death of his father he was acknowledged as James I of Scotland *in absentia,* and the regency was assumed by Robert III's brother, Robert, Duke of Albany, whose protracted failure to ransom the king suggested that he aspired to the throne.[3] A regency and a royal captivity reproduced the conditions in which John of Islay had been able to enhance the power of the Lordship of the Isles; the difference lay in the Lordship's relations with the regency. The ambitions of Donald, Lord of the Isles, and Robert, Duke of Albany, clashed over the earldom of Ross.

Donald married Mariota Leslie, sister of the Earl of Ross. In 1402 the earl died, leaving a daughter, Euphemia, who became a nun. In taking the veil she became dead to the world, and in the normal course of events, under feudal law her claim to her father's earldom would have reverted to her aunt Mariota; but Albany demanded and obtained her agreement that it should revert to her maternal uncle, the Earl of Buchan, who was his own son. Donald claimed the earldom in right of his wife and backed his claim with force. This was the background to the battle of Harlaw (1411), which entered popular history as a confrontation between the Highlands and the Lowlands, a clash of cultures as well as of arms.

A Gaelic *brosnachadh catha* ('incitement to battle') was composed to inspire the warriors who fought for the Lord of the Isles. Addressed as 'Children of Conn' – descendants of the legendary Irish king 'Conn of the Hundred Battles' – they were exhorted in a hypnotic chant which progressed through the alphabet in alliterative couplets, to display their warlike qualities. It would be impossible to translate the *brosnachadh* retaining its original alliterations, but it concluded:

> O Children of Conn of the Hundred Battles
> now is the time for you to win recognition,
> O raging whelps,
> O sturdy bears,
> O most sprightly lions,
> O battle-loving warriors,
> O brave heroic firebrands,
> the children of Conn of the Hundred Battles,
> O children of Conn remember
> Hardihood in time of battle.[4]

The *brosnachadh* would have been sung or chanted to the accompaniment of the *clarsach,* the highland harp, perhaps to a chosen band of warriors feasting in the hall of the Ardtornish Castle, where Donald mustered his army.

Donald took a circuitous route to meet the enemy. He first advanced up the Great Glen, to capture Inverness, and then marched on through the low-lying lands of the Laigh of Moray, well beyond the boundaries of Ross. Perhaps, since his army had to live off the land, he was determined it should not despoil the land he was claiming. He encountered the forces of the Duke of Albany, commanded by the latter's nephew, Alexander, earl of Mar, at Harlaw, near Aberdeen.

The Lowland view of the battle was preserved in several ballads. In the words of one of the balladists:

> As I cam' in by Dunideer
>   And down by Wetherha'
> There was fifty thousand Hielan' men
>   A' marching to Harlaw
> In a dree dree drady drumtie dree.[5]

The refrain is an ingenious attempt to suggest by onomatopoeia the sound of the Highlanders' pipes, and this detail dates the ballad at least a century later than the battle, for at the time of Harlaw the development of *Ceòl mór*, the 'great music' of the pipes was still in the future. However, the ballad may enshrine genuine memories of the battle, such as the terrifying appearance of Donald's army – even if it were ten thousand and not fifty thousand. The battle was bloody but indecisive, as the ballad relates:

> On Monanday at mornin'
>   The battle it began;
> On Saturday at gloamin'
>   Ye'd scarce tell wha had wan

It concludes with a chilling impression of the aftermath of battle:

> An' sic a weary burying,
>   The like ye never saw,
> As there was the Sunday after that
>   On the muirs doun by Harlaw.

Donald withdrew from the field of battle with heavy losses, but he did not withdraw his wife's claim to the earldom of Ross. It has been speculated that had the battle been a victory for the Lord of the Isles, he might have gone on to claim the throne of Scotland. There is no evidence that this was in his mind but he was a son of a daughter of Robert II and he must have been well aware that Robert II had succeeded to the throne as the son of the daughter of Robert the Bruce. Had he won the battle of Harlaw, his claim might have appeared stronger than that of the young Prince James, imprisoned in England.

Since Donald's advance was brought to a stop at Harlaw, the scope of his ambition remained untested. Within the Lordship his powers suffered no diminution. He was able to make generous provision for his brothers. He bestowed the lands of Dunyvaig in Islay on his younger brother John Mór, who married the heiress of the Glens of Antrim and was the ancestor of the earls of Antrim; to his younger brother, Alasdair Carrach, Donald gave Brae Lochaber and from this branch of the family descended the MacDonalds of Keppoch.

The power of the Lordship of the Isles reached its zenith under Donald, who died about 1420. Its decline began under the rule of his son Alexander, who was described as 'a man born to much trouble all his lifetime'. The origin of Alexander's troubles was that he had James I to deal with. In 1424 James secured his freedom and rapidly made it clear that he intended to set his kingdom in order. He was in a vindictive mood towards the family of the regent who had failed to ransom him. The old Duke of Albany was fortunate that he had died already for as soon as James's position was secure he executed Albany's son, Duke Murdoch, and the latter's father-in-law and sons. In 1428 he invited fifty Highland chiefs to a gathering at Inverness and had them seized and imprisoned. A few were executed, as a warning to the rest, while the remainder were distributed as prisoners among the royal castles. The Lord of the Isles was imprisoned for a time at Perth but he escaped and burned Inverness to avenge his wrongs. He was defeated in battle by the royal forces, recaptured and forced to make a humiliating act of submission to the King and stand before the altar in the abbey of Holyrood dressed as a penitent, before being imprisoned in Tantallon Castle on the east coast.

In 1431 his uncle Alasdair Carrach and his cousin Donald Balloch of Dunyvaig and the Glens (the son of John Mór) raised a rebellion on his behalf and defeated a royal army of local levies at the battle of Inverlochy. Their success evidently decided the King to change his tactics, as the Lord of the Isles was released and pardoned, possibly on condition of his keeping the peace, and in 1435 he was recognized as earl of Ross in right of his mother. After the assassination of James I in 1437, Alexander, Lord of the Isles, was appointed justiciar of Scotland north of the Forth. He died in 1449.

Though Alexander had experienced extremes of fortune, the words 'a man born to much trouble all his lifetime' might have been applied more aptly to his son. The accession of John, Lord of the Isles and Earl of Ross coincided with the coming of age of King James II, against whom he was unwise enough to ally himself with the ambitious house of Douglas. The earls of Douglas, like the Lord of the Isles, had increased their estates by advantageous marriages. The lands of the eighth Earl of Douglas included Galloway and stretched across the Borders. It is probable that James II feared the development of a Lowland principality as powerful as the Lordship of the Isles itself. The crisis came in 1452, when James II discovered the existence of a network of alliances between England, the Lordship of the Isles, the Earl of Douglas and the Earl of Crawford. He summoned Douglas to Stirling and demanded that he reaffirm his allegiance and repudiate his allies. When Douglas refused, in the ensuing quarrel the king stabbed him to death, a strange re-enactment of the fatal quarrel of Bruce and Comyn. The murdered Earl was succeeded by his brother, who continued his resistance to the crown; but the Douglas power was broken at the battle of Arkinholm in 1455, after which the Earl's estates were forfeited, and he fled to England. John, Lord of the Isles remained neutral in the last stages of the struggle, and was rewarded for his passive assistance with a grant of Urquhart Castle and Glenmoriston for life.

The death of James II in 1460 tempted him to renewed intrigue, by which he hoped to increase his independence of the crown during the minority of James III. No doubt the enhanced power of the Lordship during previous minorities encouraged him to make the best of a long opportunity (James III was only eight in 1460). In 1462 the Treaty of Westminster-Ardtornish was signed by Edward IV of England, the Lord of the Isles, Donald Balloch of Dunyvaig and the Glens, and the exiled Earl of Douglas, in which the Scottish signatories agreed to accept Edward IV as their overlord and, in the event of a successful conquest, to divide Scotland north of the Forth among themselves.

The existence of the treaty was revealed when the regency government, which had hitherto supported the Lancastrian party in the English Wars of the Roses, came to terms with the victorious

Yorkist, Edward IV. The Lord of Isles submitted to the young King of Scots at Inverness in 1464, but the details of the Treaty of Westminster-Ardtornish were not fully revealed until a treaty was concluded between Edward IV and James III in 1474. Thereupon, John, Lord of the Isles, was summoned to appear before parliament on a charge of treason. He was stripped of the earldom of Ross, which was annexed to the crown, and deprived of Kintyre and Knapdale. Henceforth the title 'Lord of the Isles' was no longer to be self-assumed, but conferred by the king, i.e. 'Lord of the Isles' became a Scottish title, and was no longer the style of an independent prince.

In reality the change involved more loss of face than loss of status since it left the greater part of the Lordship intact; but it was unacceptable to John's illegitimate son, Angus Óg, who had been designated his heir. Angus Óg rebelled against his father and defeated him in the sea battle of Bloody Bay, fought in the bay of Tobermory, Isle of Mull. He went on to attempt the recovery of the earldom of Ross by force of arms, but in 1490 he was assassinated by an Irish harper named Diarmaid O'Cairbre. A remarkable lament for him was preserved in *The Dean of Lismore's Book*. It takes the form of an address to the head of the executed assassin, exposed on a stake:

> Thou head of Diarmaid O'Cairbre, though
> great enough are thy spoils and thy pride,
> not too great I deem the amount of thy
> distress though thou hangest from a stake.
>
> I pity not thy shaggy mane, nor that it is
> tossed in the wind of the glens however
> rough; I pity thee not that a withy is
> in thy jaws, thou head of Diarmaid
> O'Cairbre . . .
>
> By thee was destroyed the King of Islay,
> a man who dealt wine and silver; whose
> locks were fresh and crisp, thou head of
> Diarmaid O'Cairbre . . .
>
> Dear to me was his noble palm, ungrudging of
> gold or silver; who joyed in feast and
> hunting, thou head of Diarmaid O'Cairbre . . .[6]

The support which Angus Óg had won is shown by the use of the style 'King of Islay'. His role was taken over by John's nephew, Alexander of Lochalsh, who invaded Ross in 1491. These attempts to reassert the independence of the Lordship of the Isles and recover its lost territories led directly to its ruin. John, who lost the support of most of his MacDonald kindred, though he retained that of his non-MacDonald vassals including the powerful MacKenzies of Kintail, was unable to restrain the activities of Angus Óg and Alexander of Lochalsh. It was probably the latter's invasion of Ross which led to the final forfeiture of the Lordship of the Isles in 1493. John, who had lost control of his patrimony when Angus Óg rebelled against him, was not held responsible; he lived on as the pensioner of James IV until 1503. He died in Paisley Abbey and his remains were buried on Iona.

Attempts to revive the Lordship of the Isles, by Donald Balloch's son, John Mór of Dunyvaig and the Glens and his son John Cathernach (who were executed on the Boroughmuir of Edinburgh in 1499) and by Angus Óg's son Donald Dubh (d. 1545), have been compared to the Jacobite attempts to restore the house of Stuart in later centuries. In both instances, irrespective of rightful claims, power had passed into other hands.

Though the Lord of the Isles might be called *Rí Innse Gall* ('King of the Hebrides') he had another, more apt title, *Buachaill nan Eilean* ('Herdsman of the Isles'), which suggests his role as a leader and protector rather than a ruler. While some clans looked to him for protection and leadership, others opposed what they considered to be the threat of MacDonald hegemony. Among those who opposed the power of the Lordship were the Frasers, the Munros, latterly the Mackenzies and above all the Campbells, whose power superseded but did not replace that of the fallen Lords of the Isles.

In its heyday the Lordship of the Isles had its own highly intricate organization, which provided a focus for Scottish Gaelic culture. A historian of the MacDonalds described the quasi-royal ceremonial with which the Lord of the Isles was inaugurated:

At this [ceremony] the Bishop of Argyll, the Bishop of the Isles, and seven priests were sometimes present; but a Bishop was always present, with the chieftains of all the principal families and a Ruler of the Isles. There was a square stone seven or eight feet long, and the tract of a man's foot cut thereon, upon which he stood, denoting that he should walk in the footsteps and uprightness of his predecessors, and that he was installed by right in his possessions. He was clothed in a white habit, to show his innocence and integrity of heart, that he would be a light to his people and maintain the true religion . . . Then he was to receive a white rod in his hand, intimating that he had power to rule, not with tyranny and partiality, but with discretion and sincerity. Then he received his fore-fathers' sword, or some other sword, signifying that his duty was to protect and defend them from the incursions of their enemies in peace or war, as were the obligations and customs of his pre-decessors. The ceremony being over, Mass was said, after the blessing of the bishop and seven priests the people poured out their prayer for the success and prosperity of their new created Lord. When they were dismissed the Lord of the Isles feasted them for a week thereafter; [and] gave liberally to the monks, poets, bards and musicians . . .[7]

The inauguration of the Gaelic Kings of Scots may have been similar, for this description recalls the footprint carved on the table-like block of stone on the summit of the rock of Dunadd. A detail which the two rites certainly shared was the recitation of the new ruler's genealogy, by a *seanchaidh* (historian or genealogist). The inauguration ceremony of the Lords of the Isles outlasted that of the kings of Scots, for King Robert I gained papal permission that his successors should be crowned and anointed in the same manner as other European monarchs.

The Lord of the Isles was advised by a council, the *Concilium Insularum* ('Council of the Isles'), by which he was theoretically elected. (Probably the agreement of the Council would have been required to sanction the succession of Donald, Lord of the Isles, in the place of one of his elder brothers by his father's first marriage.) In the fifteenth century the Council was composed of: four chiefs of the 'royal blood of clan Donald lineally descended' – MacDonald of Dunyvaig and the Glens, Clanranald, MacDonald of Keppoch and MacIain of Ardnamurchan; four chiefs of other kindreds which acknowledged the authority of the Lordship – MacLean of Duart, MacLean of Lochbuie, MacLeod of Dunvegan and Harris and MacLeod of Lewis; four lesser chiefs – MacKinnon, MacQuarrie, MacNeill of Gigha and MacNeill of Barra; and four substantial freeholders – MacKay of the Rhinns,

MacNichol in Portree, MacEachern of Killelan, MacKay of Ugadale, MacGillevray in Mull and MacMillan of Knapdale. (The fact that six men are named in the fourth category suggests that the four representatives were selected from a larger group.)[8] The Council also had ecclesiastical members: the Abbot of Iona and the Bishop of the Isles.

Traditionally the Council met at Finlaggan in Islay, where there was a stone table at which it gathered, perhaps also the site of the inauguration ceremony. The Council also met at Aros in Mull and on Eigg and Oronsay. No doubt it met at whichever place the Lord of the Isles chose to summon it and its membership would have varied according to the feasibility of attendance. The functions of the Council were not only elective and consultative but also judicial. It was the supreme court of appeal in the Lordship from the decisions of local judges. Each island had its own judge or *brithem*, who was chosen from one family; the Morrisons, for example, were the hereditary judges of Lewis. The *brithem* arbitrated in cases which were brought before him by the disputing parties and received an eleventh part of the compensation agreed. If the case went to appeal the member of the council who was *archijudex* ('chief justice') received the eleventh part instead.

Hereditary professions were characteristic of Gaelic society. One of the most famous examples is provided by the medical family of Beaton or MacBeth, who were described in a Gaelic poem as,

> The Clan MacBeth, accurate in their
> practice,
> Carvers of bones and arteries.[9]

The first member of the family to practise in Scotland was said to have arrived in the retinue of Aine O'Cathan or O'Kane, the Irish wife of Angus Óg of Islay, the father of John, first Lord of the Isles. Her following was called *Tochradh Nighean a' Chathanaich* ('the dowry of O'Kane's daughter') because it contained many men of talent who brought their skills to Scotland.[10] It was prestigious for a family to claim that an ancestor had been a member of it. The Beatons could probably make the claim with truth, for a Beaton was always physician to the Lords of the Isles from whom the family held lands in Islay. After the fall of the Lordship the Beatons still continued to practise medicine in the Isles until the eighteenth century. Another medical dynasty which originated in Ireland was that of O' Conchubhair or MacConacher, members of which were physicians to the Campbells and the MacDougalls of Dunollie. Some of the Gaelic manuscripts which belonged to these families are still in existence, for the most part Gaelic translations of fourteenth, fifteenth and sixteenth century works from the medical schools of Salerno, Padua and Montpelier.

A book evidently held in high esteem was the work of a Scot, the *Lilium Medicinae* by Bernard Gordon, Professor of Physic at the University of Montpelier. The *Lilium Medicinae* appeared in 1305 and was soon translated into Gaelic, in which there are several surviving copies. A copy handed down in the Beaton family was so highly valued that when the doctor had occasion to cross a sea-loch he sent the book round by land. In the sixteenth century a John MacBeath wrote the *Regimen Sanitatis* which was based on an earlier book of the same name, produced in Salerno and incorporating the traditions of Greek medicine. Gaelic medicine was characterized by continuing veneration for the great physicians of antiquity, Hippocrates and Galen; the earlier, Hippocrates, was honoured in Gaelic as *iuchair gach uile eolas* ('the key of all knowledge').[11]

Other hereditary professions were those of the *oes dana* ('men of art') the poets, musicians, historians, artists and craftsmen, who, like the jurists and physicians, enjoyed the status of nobles in society and received lands in reward for their services.

High honour was accorded to the MacMhuirich family of poets, who were descended from *Muredach Albannach* ('Muredach the Scot') who came from Ireland and settled in Scotland in the thirteenth century. Among his descendants were Lachlan Mor MacMhuirich, who composed the *brosnachadh catha* for the battle of Harlaw, and John MacMhuirich (who was also Dean of Knoydart) who composed the lament for Angus Óg, natural son of the last Lord of the Isles, after his murder in 1490. The MacMhuirichs held lands from the Lords of the Isles in south Kintyre, where their near neighbours were the O'Senog or MacIlshenaich family of harpers. The relationship between them would have been close, for the bardic poet's recitation was accompanied by the music of the harp.

The bardic poet might be both poet and harper, who composed the poem and sang it to his own accompaniment. A poem survives addressed by a Scottish bard Giolla Críóst Brúilingeach to an Irish chief Tomaltach MacDiarmada of Moylurg, Connacht, requesting the gift of a harp for his own use:

I have come to make a request of you
from Scotland, O golden-haired one,
over the stormy sea with its clustering wave-tops,
chill and huge, the home of grilse and salmon.
A harp in special, in return for my poem,
grant me at my request, O king,
O countenance like the ripe fruit of the apple-tree,
for this is something that you happen to have.[12]

A harp like this would be strung with strings of brass wire, which could be plucked by long, strong fingernails, or with plectra. It might be decorated with precious or semi-precious stones, according to the status and success of the bard.

Sometimes the bard sang the words of his own composition, accompanied by the harper. A third possibility was that the words were memorized by a *racaire* ('reciter') who sang them to the harper's accompaniment, while the poet listened, seated beside the chief to whom the poem was addressed. Bardic praise poems were extremely fulsome and were composed in the expectation of great rewards, for praise enhanced the prestige of a chief, even the Lord of the Isles. But if the rewards were deemed stingy, then the bard might turn upon the unworthy patron with scathing satire. The satire of a great bard was dreaded, for words possessed almost magical power and the contempt of such a man was expected to bring misfortune in its train. As Giolla Criost's poem to Tomaltach MacDiarmada illustrates, the bard would travel from one chief's court to another, collecting his rewards.

Membership of the Church was recruited from the families of the learned professions and the *oes dána*, but the clerical profession was itself kin-based, and could even be hereditary. All the religious houses within the Lordship of the Isles had been founded by members of the Clan Somhairle, and the founders' families continued to be generous patrons of their respective foundations. Other families were also closely connected with particular monasteries: the MacKinnons with Iona, the MacDuffies and MacMhuirichs with Oronsay, and the MacDougalls with Ardchatten. In a large and ramifying kindred like that of the ruling house it was natural that some members should turn to the religious life, or be found advantageous positions within it. Bethoc, daughter of Somerled, was the first prioress of Iona, and Angus, son of Donald, Lord of the Isles, was Bishop of the Isles from 1426 to 1438. From the automatic nepotism of a powerful kindred to the inheritance of clerical office was a short progression. Angus, son of Bishop Angus of the Isles, petitioned the papacy to be appointed Abbot of Iona, on the grounds that he was the son of 'a bishop of royal blood', and later he also became Bishop of the Isles (1472–80). A father and son were priors of Oronsay between 1362 and 1426, and there is an example of a father and son serving as parish priests.[13] The disregard for clerical celibacy which gave rise to these situations seems to have been an accepted condition among a kin-based clergy and not a symptom of demoralization. Perhaps precisely because the clerical profession was kin-based, the supply of both regular and secular clergy remained plentiful in the late fifteenth and early sixteenth centuries. The monasteries of the Lordship of the Isles, with the exception of the Abbey of Saddell, continued to flourish until the eve of the Reformation.

The generally devout temper of society is suggested by the great West Highland tradition of monumental sculpture, which is the most remarkable artistic survival of the Lordship of the Isles. Four schools of stone carving have been identified, based on Iona and Oronsay, in Kintyre and in the district of Loch Awe. Of these the Iona school was pre-eminent, and owed its excellence to the Ó Brolchán family, who had been sculptors in Ireland, centred at the monastery of Derry, throughout the twelfth century; by the middle of the fourteenth century they were established at Iona. They were joined by a second Irish family, the Ó Cuinns, who were also active at Oronsay, where in about 1500 Mael-Sechlainn Ó Cuinn carved and signed a great cross which bears the inscription *Hec est crux Colini fillii Cristini MeicDu-faci* ('This is the cross of Gille-Coluim son of Gille-Criósd MacDuffie'). To commission and dedicate a cross was considered meritorious and conducive to salvation. Scattered throughout the lands of the Lordship some sixty crosses survive, dedicated by both churchmen and laymen.

Far outnumbering the crosses are grave-slabs carved in relief, of which some six hundred examples are known. Some of them bear effigies, mostly of churchmen in canonical vestments or of warriors, though one of the most individual and appealing is of a woman, Anna MacLean, Prioress of Iona (*c.* 1509–1543), a stout nun with little lapdogs nestling in the folds of her habit. On the effigies of warriors the form of military costume most frequently represented is the *aketon*, a thickly padded knee-length surcoat. Worn over it is a *coif*, a head and shoulder covering of chain-mail, and a *bascinet* or smooth conical helmet, called in Gaelic the *clogaid*, or else an *aventail*, or chain-mail shoulder covering joined to the lower rim of the helmet. Each warrior is armed with a large cross-hilted sword, the *claidneamhmor* or claymore, and a long spear. Some carry shields with armorial bearings on them, which demonstrate that heraldry was used for identification in war in the Highlands as in the Lowlands.

The grave-slabs without effigies bear symbols appropriate to the people commemorated – swords, ships or craft-tools – and the remaining surfaces are carved with intricate designs of foliage or, more rarely, with interlace patterns. The swords presumably commemorate warriors and they are shown with such variation of detail that it seems probable that portrayals of individual weapons were intended. The ships may commemorate men who owed service on board a *berlinn* ('galley') or *long fhada* ('lymphad' – a larger type of vessel propelled by both oars and sail). The craft-tools would have commemorated craftsmen of high status, members of such families as the MacEacherns of Morvern and Islay or the MacNabs of Dalmally, who were swordsmiths and armourers.

Though the sculptors of the West Highland tradition owed much to Irish origins and inspiration, their art was not merely imported. Like the Pictish sculptors of earlier centuries, they absorbed external influences and produced a style which was vigorous, inventive and indigenous.

The forfeiture of the Lordship of the Isles did not bring the cultural life of the area to a sudden end. Monastic life ended with the Reformation in the mid-sixteenth century; but Gaelic society was too conservative to abandon Catholicism with the rapidity which was shown in lowland Scotland. Monumental sculpture ceased to be produced after the Reformation, probably because the schools had been based on religious houses or heavily dependent on ecclesiastical patronage. Gaelic medicine, poetry and music, however, continued to flourish, for other families besides the ruling house required their doctors, poets and musicians. The effect of the forfeiture of the Lordship was more obvious in political terms, for there was no other chief who was acknowledged as *Buachaill nan Eilean* ('Herdsman of the Isles'). In the period of inter-clan strife which followed the forfeiture of the Lordship a poet expressed the deep sense of loss experienced by the erstwhile subjects of the Lords of the Isles:

There is no joy without the Clan Donald.
This people so great in fame,
In courtesy, mind and firmness,
There is no right without them.
There is no joy without the Clan Donald.
The Son of His Virgin Mother
Who hath earned us freedom from pain,
Though He be faithful and true,
There is no joy without the Clan Donald.
 There is no joy.[14]

THE CLANS IN THE
AGE OF FORAYS

'. . . I and my frenndis hes als gret experience in the
danting of the Ilis . . . as ony utheris of the realme,
and specialie for the distructioun of thaim inobe-
dient to the kingis grace and in the rewarding of
thame that makis gud service to his hienes.'

I sit here alone by the level roadway
Trying to meet in with a fugitive
Coming from Ben Cruachan of the Mist,
One who will give me news of Clan Gregor
Or word of where they have gone.[1]

Clanship, the society which characterized the Highlands in the
sixteenth century, had been evolving over many centuries.

In Scottish Dalriada there had been several words for different types
of kin-groups: *tuath* for the whole people (e.g. the Scots themselves, or
the Airgialla from whom Somerled was descended); *cenel* for a
particular kindred within that people (e.g. the Cenel Loairn, as a
kindred of the Scots); *fine* (as in *derbfine*) for a particular kin-group
within a kindred; *clann* for children or offspring. *Tuath*, *cenel* and *fine*
retained their meanings, but gradually came to represent archaic
concepts of kinship. *Clann* acquired an extended meaning as
'descendants'.

Possibly the earliest use of the word 'clan' in this sense is the
reference to a 'Clan Canan' and a 'Clan Morgan' in the twelfth century
Gaelic notes written in the blank spaces of a ninth century Gospel, the
'Book of Deer', but nothing is known of these clans beyond their
names. Early clans are assumed to have resembled the Dalriadic

kindreds: to have been tribal groups occupying an area which maintained the whole community, and to have been ruled by chiefs who succeeded in accordance with the rules of tanistry.

The history of the descendants of Somerled illustrates the way in which many clans could develop from a single stock. The immediate descendants of Somerled were known as the Clan Somhairle and, when this name fell out of use, Clan Donald remained a general term for the descendants of Somerled's grandson Donald. The various branches of this clan remained vassals of the Lord of the Isles but after the fall of the Lordship they evolved into autonomous clans. These clans were: the MacAlisters of Loup; the MacIains of Ardnamurchan; the MacDonalds (or MacIains) of Glencoe; the MacDonalds of Clanranald (with cadet branches of Glengarry, of Knoydart and of Morar); the MacDonalds of Kintyre and Islay (also known as Clan Donald South, with a cadet branch of Largy); the MacDonalds of Loch Alsh; the MacDonalds of Sleat (also known as Clan Donald North).

Clanship was profoundly affected by the introduction of feudalism, which in some respects strengthened the position of a chief. If a clan chief acquired a feudal charter as a tenant-in-chief of the king he gained a certain title to his lands which gave him a great advantage over any of his neighbours who lacked a charter. He gained the right to hold a feudal court, which facilitated the dispensing of justice; he could establish primogeniture, which as the example of the Margaretson and Stewart monarchy proved, stabilized succession. Feudal law did not recognize male co-heirs, so that when succession took place in accordance with it a large inheritance did not have to be subdivided among sons, as had happened on the death of Somerled. Under feudal law the eldest son, or nearest heir-male, inherited the territory intact and then made provision for his younger brothers as he felt obliged or inclined, or not at all. If a chief succeeded as a minor, it was customary for a mature kinsman, who was known as the Captain of the clan, to rule on his behalf. In most instances the Captain honourably resigned his charge when the chief attained his majority.

For any clan the greatest hazard of inheritance under feudal law was the failure of the male line. Territory could be divided among co-heiresses, but even if an only daughter inherited, her marriage could transfer the chiefship to a different clan, as occurred when the heiress of Cawdor (or Calder) married a Campbell in 1510. This problem could be resolved more satisfactorily for an heiress's clan if it were already very powerful, in which case her husband might prefer to identify himself with it. This happened when the heiress of Gordon married a Seton. Her husband called himself 'Seton of Gordon', but their son, the first Earl of Huntly, took the surname of Gordon (*c.* 1457).

Terrible confusion could occur if a feudal charter were granted to a man who was not a clan chief. Then clansmen might find that they had both a natural chief and a feudal lord, both of whom demanded their loyalty, services and rents. Painful conflicts of loyalty as well as economic difficulties could result. For these reasons a landless chief would lay stress upon the demands of natural loyalty and a chief who had good relations with the crown would secure the advantage of a feudal charter (as did John, first Lord of the Isles, to the lands of the MacRuaris). The most successful chiefs were those who possessed both advantages. The chiefs of the Campbells and the MacKenzies, for example, are often described as having practised 'aggressive feudalism' by securing charters to the lands of their unlucky neighbours but they did not despise the claims of kinship, or even of mythical, notional or adoptive kinship, to bind their clans together.

The history of the MacDonalds illustrates that a claim to descent from a remote ancestor (in their instance Godfrey mac Fergus of the Airgialla) could be genuine. Such a claim was frequently extended through a traditional but non-verifiable genealogy to an even more remote progenitor, in the instance of the MacDonalds to Conn of the Hundred Battles, who was cited in the Harlaw *brosnachadh*, and beyond him again to the legendary High King of Ireland, Colla Uais. Most Gaelic clans possessed an eponym, or name-father. The name Clan Chattan, for instance, meant 'Children of Saint Catan', and their eponym was Gillechattan, 'the Servant of Saint Catan'; yet the Clan Chattan was a confederation of clans, amongst whom the Mackintoshes, MacPhersons and MacBeans claimed descent from Gillechattan, while the MacGillievrays did not. Their chief was Mackintosh of Mackintosh, whose name means 'Son of the Toiseach' (*toiseach* being a Gaelic title uncertainly equated with 'thane').

Some clans, as previously mentioned, were not of Gaelic or Gall-Gaidheal origin. A few, for example the Clan Gunn, claimed pure Norse ancestry. Many had evolved from the families, followings and non-related tenants of early feudal landholders. These could not claim a Gaelic eponym, historical or mythical. Their chiefs relied on the concept of the patriarchal authority of a chief as bestowing a notional fatherhood on them. As the authority of the father was acknowledged as being the most basic type of authority, exemplified by the biblical patriarch, so it was natural for the tribal leader, the chief or the king, to adopt the style of 'Father of his People'. By claiming to be the father of his followers a clan chief was complimenting them by acknowledging them as his kin and at the same time he was placing them under a greater obligation to him.

It was genuine kinship, however, which conferred power within a clan. A chief would provide land for the cadets of the family. If they did not become chieftains of septs they remained the *daoine uasile* (the gentry of the clan), its military leaders in time of war, and the chief's advisers in time of peace. With the passage of time their status changed to their disadvantage. During the seventeenth century the clan chiefs became reluctant to allow their kinsmen 'kindly' (i.e. hereditary) tenure of their lands and began to insist upon granting a 'tack' (written lease) or a 'wadset' (a mortgage under revision after a set term of years). By the eighteenth century the *daoine uasile* had become 'tacksmen'; they were still influential, but they were vulnerable to change.

Change was the essence of clanship. A clan was a social organism which was continuously evolving. Where kinship did not exist, or could not be imagined or invented, it could be created. Gaelic society regarded fosterage as creating kinship. Fosterage could be used to strengthen an existing bond of kinship, as when a Campbell of Lochow was fostered by a Campbell of Glenorchy; or it could be used to create kinship, as when a Campbell of Glenorchy fostered his son with a 'native servant'. Kinship could be created even by recruitment, for a clan was always ready to welcome voluntary clansmen to increase its military strength. Often the recruits were 'broken' (i.e. landless) men, the followers of a chief who had lost his lands and with them the means to support his clansmen. In the seventeenth century many broken men were members of the unfortunate Clan Gregor, who were forbidden even to retain the surname of MacGregor. In the course of this century as surnames replaced patronymics, new clansmen would frequently take the surname of their adoptive chief, with the result that their descendants soon came to believe that they also shared their chief's ancestry. The Highland historian Dr I.F. Grant records a tradition that one of the Frasers of Lovat promised a boll of meal to any of his tenants who would take his name, with the result that 'meal Frasers' became a byword. The Frasers were a clan of feudal origin but they became sufficiently gaelicized for their chief to be known as MacShimidh ('Son of Simon') as though he had been the descendant of a Gaelic eponym.

The popular concept of a clan as a group of men all possessing the same surname and all descended from a common ancestor is completely erroneous; yet it was the chiefs themselves who had the greatest interest in propagating it, for so long as the maximum number of fighting men at their command was the measure of their power.

The century and a half which followed the fall of the Lordship of the Isles was called in Gaelic *Linn nan Creach* ('the Age of Forays'). It was a period of inter-clan strife in the power-vacuum which resulted from the fall of the Lordship and it was characterized by a hardening of the Lowland Scots' view that the Highlanders were inherently different: they might be fellow Scots, but they were dangerous neighbours, warlike, savage, potentially hostile.

This view had been long developing, influenced by such violent events as the 'Battle of the Clans', an organized combat between thirty champions from two clans, not certainly identified, but possibly the Clan Chattan and Clan Kay, which took place on the North Inch of Perth in 1396, witnessed by court and populace, like a gladiatorial show; or the burning of Elgin Cathedral in 1390 by Alexander Stewart, alias 'the Wolf of Badenoch', a wayward younger son of Robert II, who was feuding with the Bishop of Moray. His private army was described as a force of 'wyld wykked hielandmen'.

By their actions the Highlanders might seem wild and wicked but they seemed all the more so because they spoke a different language. As the use of Gaelic retreated beyond the Highland Line the speakers of Lowland Scots began to call the Gaelic language 'Erse' or 'Irish' and to ridicule it as an uncouth tongue. By the end of the fifteenth century the idea that the Highlanders were half-foreign savages was evidently well established. This was the court attitude accepted and echoed by Pedro de Ayala, a Spanish ambassador who visited Scotland in 1498, and reported that King James IV, in addition to speaking Latin, French, German, Flemish, Italian and Spanish, also spoke 'the language of the savages who live in some parts of Scotland and the Islands'. James IV had a natural facility for languages. He probably picked up spoken Gaelic without difficulty, but it is unlikely that he learnt to write it. However, it was symptomatic of the growing dichotomy between Highlands and Lowlands that he was the last King of Scots who had any Gaelic at all.

John Major, writing in the middle of the reign of James V, included in his *History of Greater Britain* (1521) a famous passage contrasting the characters and lifestyles of the Highlanders and Lowlanders, and containing as much Lowland prejudice as information:

> Some [Scots] are born in the forests and mountains of the north, and these we call men of the Highland, but the others men of the Lowland. By foreigners the former are called Wild Scots, the latter householding Scots. The Irish tongue is in use among the former, the English tongue among the latter. One half of Scotland speaks Irish, and all these as well as the Islanders we reckon to belong to the Wild Scots. In dress, in the manner of their outward life, and in good morals, for example, these come far behind the householding Scots – yet they are not less, but rather much more prompt to fight; and this ... because born as they are in the mountains, and dwellers in forests, their very nature is more combative ... One part of the Wild Scots have a wealth of cattle, sheep and horses, and these, with a thought for the possible loss of their possessions, yield more willing obedience to the courts of law and the king. The other part of these people delight in the chase and a life of indolence; their chiefs eagerly follow bad men if only they may not have the need of labour; taking no pains to earn their own livelihood, they live upon others, and follow their own worthless savage chief in all evil courses sooner than they will pursue honest industry. They are full of mutual dissensions and war rather than peace is their normal condition ...[2]

During the sixteenth century the evolution of Highland clanship and the warlike character of the clans enhanced the difference between Highlanders and Lowlanders. A strong sense of kinship was common to all Scots but in the Lowlands, where surnames developed earlier, attachment to the 'name' was declining at the same time as in the Highlands attachment to the clan was growing. In the fifteenth and sixteenth centuries the Lowlanders' sense of solidarity with other members of such great 'names' as, for example, Douglas or Hamilton was still undeniably strong. But as Lowland society grew more settled the need for the chiefs of these kin-groups to call upon their kinsmen for military support declined, and the readiness of individuals of the name, especially of men who had taken to professions or commerce, to stand or fall with their chief declined with it. The presence of thirty-eight Hamiltons in the army of Mary Queen of Scots at the Battle of Langside in 1568 was a late example of the action of a Lowland 'name' *en bloc*, though the solidarity of the Border 'names' such as Elliott, Armstrong and Kerr, and of their English counterparts, survived until the Union of Crowns of 1603, simply because the Borders remained a restless 'debatable land' between Scotland and England.

While the Border problem died away spontaneously in the early seventeenth century, the rift between Highlands and Lowlands was widened by religious differences. After the Reformation of 1560 the Reformed Church was slow to establish itself in the Highlands, with the exception of Argyll, where it was fostered by the Campbells. Many of the western clans remained nominally Catholic but as the supply of Catholic clergy declined the regular practice of Catholicism became impossible. In remote areas where there were neither priests nor ministers, pagan rituals and superstitions which had never been forgotten revived. To the predominantly Calvinist Lowlanders the papistical or godless condition of the Highlanders made them seem more alien and reprehensible than ever.

The Highlanders reciprocated the Lowlanders' contempt. In their eyes the Lowlanders were soft and effete, but inexplicably successful. Moreover, in the words of a modern Scottish historian, Dr David Stevenson:

> Many Highlanders felt a deep resentment at the way in which their language and culture had become limited geographically to the Highlands. Many Lowlanders who now spoke Scots were indistinguishable in blood from Highlanders who spoke Gaelic, but . . . Highlanders came to look on Lowlanders as men of a different race who had stolen the lands of the Gaels, driving them into the remoter, poorer parts of the kingdom.'[3]

The poison of racism, albeit a misapprehended racism, increased the enmity between Highlanders and Lowlanders. By the end of the sixteenth century the rift between Highlands and Lowlands was at its widest.

Yet despite this enmity, the Highlanders regarded themselves as subjects of the Scottish crown. They would never have denied their respect for the King and for the monarchy; but respect did not imply obedience to the King's laws. They simultaneously acknowledged the monarchy and ignored it. They were not threatening political separatism, as they might have done under the Lords of the Isles, but cultural separatism they already possessed, and by retreating into it and fighting among themselves they became ungovernable. To hold the kingdom together and to bring the Highlands under the law was a challenge which the Crown could not ignore.

It has become a historical cliché to blame the Stewart kings for delegating their power to certain great chiefs in their attempt to discipline the Highlands, but it is difficult to see what other course they could have taken. Without bureaucracy, without a centralized system of communications, and without the resources to establish either, they were reliant on the networks of power which existed in the localities.

Three clans which prospered beyond the rest through co-operation with the crown were the Campbells, the MacKenzies and the Gordons in their respective localities and at the expense of their neighbours. The earlier history of these clans demonstrates the diversity of clan origins.

The Clan Campbell, like many others, had a mythical origin and a very much later historical figure responsible for establishing its fortunes. The Campbells were also not alone in having contradictory accounts of their beginnings. They were sometimes known as the Clan Diarmaid, since by one account their chiefs were descended from the Fenian hero Diarmaid, companion in arms to Fionn and seducer of Fionn's wife Grainne. An entirely different genealogy gave the Campbells a British ancestry, with descent from King Arthur. The surname by one account derived from the marriage of a member of the family to a Norman heiress surnamed de Beauchamp, latinized as 'de Campo Bello', hence Campbell; but a more convincing explanation of the name was that it derived from the Gaelic *cam beul* ('twisted mouth'), which must have been a personal epithet converted into a surname. Indeed the earlier spelling of the name was 'Cambel', the 'p' being added in deference to the Norman legend. Recent research by Dr W.D.H. Sellar has suggested that the British genealogy was the true one, since the earliest members of the family were traced in the Lennox district of the old British kingdom of Strathclyde, though King Arthur was a fictitious addition.[4]

By the thirteenth century the family was established in Argyll in the person of a substantial tenant-in-chief of the crown called Cailean Mór ('Great Colin'), from whom the later chiefs took the title MacCailean Mór or MacCallummore ('son of Great Colin'). John Major in his *History of Greater Britain* made the often quoted statement 'in Argyll the people swear by the hand of Callum More just as in old times the Egyptians used to swear by the health of Pharaoh'.

The first 'Son of Great Colin' was Sir Neil Campbell, who supported King Robert I in the fugitive phase which followed the king's hasty coronation, when King Robert's fortunes were at their lowest ebb. The loyalty of Sir Neil Campbell and the continuing support of his son Sir Colin were rewarded after the king's triumph when he granted to Sir Colin the lands of Lochow and Ariskeodnish (now Kilmartin) as 'the one free barony of Lochow'. The Campbell lands were steadily extended and in the fifteenth century Lochow and Kilmun in Cowal were created burghs of barony by royal charter and a collegiate church was founded at Kilmun. In the earlier part of the century the lordship of Glenorchy was added to the Campbell possessions.

The fourth baron, Sir Duncan Campbell, was created Lord Campbell of Lochow in the reign of Robert III. He was twice married, first to Margery Stewart, daughter of the Duke of Albany, Governor of Scotland, and second to Margaret Stewart, daughter of Sir John Stewart of Ardgowan, a natural son of Robert III. By his first wife he had a son, Archibald Roy, who died young, leaving a late-born or posthumous son, Colin, who succeeded to the lordship of Lochow. To the eldest son of his second marriage Sir Duncan granted the lordship of Glenorchy, and younger sons of the marriage founded the Campbells of Auchinbreck, Kilberry, Kildalloig, Ellangreg and Otter. The fatherless Colin Campbell was brought up by his uncle Sir Colin Campbell of Glenorchy, who was said to have treated him with 'kyndness and fidelity' which were 'exemplarily remarkable'. Certainly he was more than conscientious, for he built the town and castle of Inveraray for his nephew, who in 1457 was created Earl of Argyll. Inveraray became the favoured residence of Argyll and his successors, for its position on Loch Fyne provided easy communications with both Highlands and Lowlands. This was advantageous for the Campbell chiefs in their later role as agents of the authority of the crown.

The MacKenzies, who became the predominant clan in the north-west, were almost certainly of purely Gaelic origin, descended from the same stock as the extinct line of the Celtic earls of Ross, with whom they shared a mythical progenitor, 'Colin of the Aird'. Their eponym was Kenneth, Colin's descendant, from whom they took their Gaelic name of Clan Chionnich. But, like the Campbells, the MacKenzies had an alternative account of their origins. When Norman forebears and feudal charters were perceived as advantageous, the MacKenzies discovered that their ancestor was Colin 'Hybernus', supposedly a scion of the Norman-Irish house of FitzGerald, who was said to have received a charter to the lands of Kintail in Wester Ross from Alexander III, an opportunist fiction. In closer touch with reality was Murdoch MacKenzie, said to have been fourth in descent from Kenneth, who held some of his lands from Donald, Lord of the Isles, but refused to follow him on the Harlaw campaign. Murdoch's son Alexander in 1463 received charters from John, Lord of the Isles and Earl of Ross, for the lands of Killin, Garve and Kinlochluichart. After the first forfeiture of the Lordship in 1476 he received the following year a crown charter for Strathconan, Strathgarve and Strathbraan. In 1509 the chief of the MacKenzies gained a feudal jurisdiction when his estates were created the barony of Eileandonan, named after his ancestral stronghold. His descendants continued to prosper and to increase their lands at the expense of the MacDonalds of Glengarry and the MacLeods of Lewis. By charter, lease and marriage the MacKenzies extended their possessions from sea to sea, from the north-west coast to the Cromarty Firth and into the Black Isle. By 1610 they had secured possession of Lewis from the MacLeods. The MacKenzie chiefs were ambitious to expand their influence but did not attempt to dispossess smaller clans if these were prepared to acknowledge their superiority. The MacKenzie acquisition of Lewis did not displace the Morrisons and the MacAulays, who had previously held their lands from the MacLeods. Before the end of the fifteenth century the MacKenzie chiefs removed from their ancestral lands of Kintail to Kinellan in lower Strathconan and early in the seventeenth century they built a new seat, Brahan Castle, near Dingwall. The Clan MacRae, constant supporters of the MacKenzies, provided custodians for the castle of Eilean Donan, which remained of strategic importance, guarding the seas between the MacKenzies' island and mainland possessions. In 1609 Kenneth MacKenzie of Kintail was created Lord MacKenzie of Kintail; in 1623 his son Colin was created Earl of Seaforth, taking his title from estates in Lewis.

The expansion of the Campbells and the MacKenzies in the west and north-west was mirrored on the eastern fringe of the Highlands by the rise of the Clan Gordon. This was a clan of feudal origin, descended from a family which probably originated in France, and came to Scotland from England in the reign of David I. The earliest records of the Gordons in Scotland show them holding lands in Berwickshire, where they were sufficiently prosperous to be benefactors of Kelso

Abbey. In the fourteenth century Sir Adam Gordon of Gordon, Berwickshire, supported Edward I in the early stages of the Wars of Independence but transferred his support to Robert I at about the time of the Battle of Bannockburn (1314). King Robert rewarded him with the grant of Strathbogie in northern Aberdeenshire, forfeited by David de Strathbogie, Earl of Atholl, who had supported John Balliol. Sir Adam's great-grandson married a Fraser heiress, and acquired her lands of Aboyne, Glentanar and Glenmuick on Deeside. Then the Gordon lands in turn devolved upon an heiress, Elizabeth. In 1408 she married Alexander Seton who, as previously mentioned, identified himself with his wife's family by calling himself Seton of Gordon. Their son Alexander took the surname of Gordon in 1457. He had been created Earl of Huntly in about 1445; he was created Lord of Badenoch in 1451 and by 1458 he had acquired the lands of Enzie in Banffshire.

Aberdeenshire and Banffshire remained the bases of Gordon power but Gordon influence extended itself further north when a younger brother of the third Earl of Huntly married the heiress of the earldom of Sutherland. In about 1516 he became Earl of Sutherland in right of his wife and the succession of Gordon Earls of Sutherland continued for two centuries, until the seventh Earl of the line changed his name to Sutherland. Normally clansmen took the name of their chief; in this instance the chief took the surname of the clan, a further instance of the diversity and flexibility of clanship.

The power of the Gordons in the north-east was demonstrated by the establishment of some hundred and fifty cadet branches, and it was enhanced by the appointment of several Earls of Huntly as King's Lieutenants in the North.

The Earl of Huntly as 'Cock o' the North' was the counterpart of MacCailean Mór in the west, and frequently his rival. Huntly and Argyll commanded opposing armies at the Battle of Glenlivet in 1594; the quarrel was between King James VI and Huntly, but the king was able to harness the enmity of the two earls for his own purposes.

The clan chiefs who supported the crown in the sixteenth century were Janus-like figures who watched their own interests on either side of the Highland Line. MacKenzie, the most genuinely Gaelic of the three, backed the crown against the Lordship of the Isles and gained his rewards without surrendering his Gaelic identity; Huntly, most of whose lands lay in the northeastern Lowlands, assumed the identity of a Highland chief among the minority of his tenants who were

Highlanders; the remote forebears of MacCailean Mór may have been Britons of Strathclyde, but he was perceived as being one of the greatest of the Gaelic chiefs. At the beginning of the sixteenth century a wandering bard could still address to the Earl of Argyll a praise poem beginning

> I shall journey with my prepared song
> To the King of the Gael,
> The man who keeps his house crowded
> Happy and plentiful.[5]

But the title proved to be inappropriate, and the expectation unfulfilled. Later hatred of the chiefs of the Clan Campbell by the Gaels was not only hatred of the persecutors of the MacDonalds, but of chiefs who might have deserved the title of *Buachaille nan Eilean* ('Herdsman of the Isles'), and who might have been leaders of Gaeldom, but who were perceived as its oppressors.

The forfeiture of the Lordship of the Isles in 1493 was obviously intended by James IV as a preliminary to the extension of the authority of the crown. James showed his intention by making frequent visits to the Highlands and Isles during the 1490s: in 1493, 1494, 1495 and then three visits in March, May and August of 1498. He established royal garrisons in the castles of Tarbert, Mingarry and Dunaverty, and probably intended to make the Clyde a base of royal naval power, as it had been in the reign of Robert I. He confirmed the charters of a number of former vassals of the Lord of the Isles and conferred knighthoods on several members of the Clan Donald. Much of the goodwill which he had won, however, was dissipated by his 'revocation' of 16 March 1498 – the customary revocation of the grants made during his minority which a King of Scots made on the eve of his twenty-fifth birthday, when he was regarded as having reached his 'perfect age', or complete maturity. This enabled a king to extricate himself from the grants which regents or guardians might have forced him to make when he was too young to refuse but it always caused feelings of insecurity in those who had received the grants and resentment in those who lost them and were not reinstated. The confirmation of charters made to the island vassals in the early months of 1498 were excluded from the revocation, but the sense of insecurity remained. James IV also lost more credibility in the Isles as a result of the executions of John Mór of Dunyvaig and the Glens and his son in 1499.

After 1500 foreign affairs increasingly claimed his attention. In 1500 the third Earl of Argyll was appointed his Lieutenant in the Isles and in 1501 the third Earl of Huntly received a similar commission for the North. These two noblemen survived until 1529 and 1524 respectively, holding their commissions throughout the rest of the reign of James IV and the minority of James V – Huntly for most of the latter and Argyll for all of it. James V emerged from tutelage in 1528.

James V soon gained the reputation of being a harsh, even a tyrannical, ruler with a personal determination to see law and order imposed. George Buchanan, who wrote his *History of Scotland* for the purpose of instructing James V's grandson James VI in the duties of kingship, described how James V would 'sit on horseback night and day, in the coldest winter, so that he might catch the thieves in their harbours at unawares; and his activity struck such a terror into them, that they abstained from their evil purposes, as if he had been always present among them'. James V was dissatisfied with the standard of law and order which had been maintained in the Highlands and Islands during his minority. One of his first acts on attaining his majority was to issue 'Letters of Fire and Sword' to his half-brother James, Earl of Moray, and several other chiefs, including MacKenzie, authorizing them to destroy the Clan Chattan with the exception of its women, priests and children, who were to be deported and set ashore on the coasts of Shetland and Norway. This is but one example of the 'Commissions of Fire and Sword' which were from time to time issued against Highland clans, empowering certain chiefs to extirpate the manpower of an enemy clan.[6] The commission against the Clan Chattan was not carried out effectively but it demonstrates the savage attitude of government against some of the Highland clans and explains the continuing enmity between the Earls of Moray and the Clan Chattan.

However, James V was not inflexibly inimical in his attitude towards the Highlanders. Following the death of the third Earl of Argyll in 1529, he was prepared to listen to the plea of Alexander MacDonald of Islay that Campbell policy had been to foment disorder and then to quell it, in order to reap the rewards of having been a champion of law and order. In 1531 the fourth Earl of Argyll was summoned to appear before the Privy Council to answer this accusation. He failed to do so, although he pleaded his experience in the 'danting of the Ilis'. James chose to believe Alexander MacDonald of Islay, who received the 'Commission of Lieutenandry', while Argyll was for a short time imprisoned, and thereafter remained out of favour for several years.

The rebellion of Donald Gorm of Sleat in 1539 determined James V to undertake his voyage round the north of Scotland in 1540, during which he visited Orkney and rounded Cape Wrath to sail through the Western Isles, visiting Lewis and Harris, and North and South Uist, and then Skye, Coll, Tiree and Mull, Arran and Bute, concluding his voyage at Dumbarton, seeing outlying parts of the kingdom which no previous king of his dynasty had visited. At each landing place the chiefs who came to greet the King were carried away captive, or hostages were taken from among their relatives. This rough and ready method of ensuring the temporary obedience of the chiefs was no way of investing in their future goodwill or trust. The Parliament which met later in 1540 confirmed the King's triumphal progress by re-enacting the forfeiture of the Lordship of the Isles.

James VI, crowned at the age of thirteen months in 1567, inherited a kingdom doubly in disarray as a result of the convulsions of the Reformation and the downfall of his mother, Mary Queen of Scots. The triumphant reformers determined that James VI should be educated to be the pattern of Protestant princes, pious, learned and ready to defend the reformed faith in arms or by disputation: 'in utrumque paratus', according to the motto on a coin issued while he was still a child, which showed him in armour and carrying a sword and an olive branch. Though James VI was on the whole a pacific and humane ruler, he wielded the sword rather than the olive branch in his dealings with the Highlands.

From the viewpoint of his Gaelic subjects the education of James VI was an opportunity tragically lost. The King's tutor, George Buchanan, was a distinguished classical scholar and a political philosopher of the Reformation. He was also a native Gaelic speaker but this aspect of his learning he regarded as irrelevant to the King's education. Buchanan admired the Gaels for their hardiness and austere lifestyle; he saw them as noble savages, though he did not coin the term. Unfortunately his love of classical languages led him to despise Gaelic and he passed on his contempt to James VI. The young King absorbed some of Buchanan's lessons and repudiated others. He declined to believe that the Gaels possessed any virtues. He admitted that Highlanders who had been exposed to Lowland influence might have gained some tincture of civility but most of them, and Islanders in particular, he considered 'utterly barbarous'. James had some justification for his prejudice. He had no impression of the achievements of Gaelic culture, its learning, poetry and music, but he was continually outraged by the atrocities committed by the Gaels, which flouted his ambition to make Scotland a peaceful and well ordered kingdom.

In 1578, during his minority, the so-called 'Battle of the Spoiling of the Dyke' was an episode of revolting savagery. At Trumpan, Isle of Skye, a marauding force of MacDonalds of Uist locked the door of the church on a congregation of MacLeods and set fire to the thatched roof. Everyone within the building died in the conflagration, except for one girl who struggled out, fatally burnt, to raise the alarm. The chief of the MacLeods led a force out of Dunvegan Castle, intercepted the departing MacDonalds in Ardmore Bay, and massacred them in revenge. The MacDonald corpses were laid out alongside a turf dyke and buried by overturning the dyke on top of them, a conclusion from which the episode took its name. This atrocity was recapitulated when the Glengarry Macdonalds burned the congregation in the church of Kilchrist, Easter Ross, in 1603. Meanwhile, quite large clan battles continued: in 1598 at the Battle of Gruinart in Islay, between the MacLeans of Duart and the MacDonalds of Dunyvaig, 280 MacLeans were killed; and at the Battle of Glen Fruin in 1603 the MacGregors slaughtered 180 Colquhouns, and suffered only two losses.

The MacGregor chiefs had been reduced to the status of leaders of 'broken men' by the aggressive feudalism of the Clan Campbell over several generations. Their victory at Glen Fruin was a fleeting success, which speedily brought the Clan Gregor to disaster. A battle, or massacre, only twelve miles from Dumbarton, on the fringe of the Lowlands, did not need to be tolerated by the government when the power of the Campbells could be mobilized to crush the offenders. The chief, Alasdair MacGregor, was captured and hanged, and all MacGregors who had fought at Glen Fruin were outlawed. After 1610 the campaign against the MacGregors was intensified: the very name of MacGregor was proscribed and a Commission of Fire and Sword was issued to a number of chiefs and lairds who had MacGregor tenants authorizing them to 'ruit out and extirpate all that race'.[7] A price of £1,000 was set on the heads of leading members of the clan, and of 1,000 merks on the heads of lesser men; any clansman could earn his own pardon by bringing before the Privy Council the head of another – an echo of the customs of the pagan Celts.

The 'wicked and unhappy race of the Clan Gregour', as the Register of the Privy Council described it, seemed destined for extinction. Its later revival was due to the 'resetting', or sheltering by other clans of individual MacGregors, who temporarily adopted the surnames of their benefactors. The notorious Rob Roy MacGregor ironically disguised himself with the name of Campbell. In 1611 the Earl of Argyll was given full powers against the Clan Gregor, with authority to fine the 'resetters' – 77½ per cent of the fines to be received by Argyll and the remainder by the Crown. Although the huge sum of £115,000 in fines was imposed, much less than half of it was ever collected, the Crown's share being a meagre £10,000.[8]

Circumstances which could permit a small clan to be persecuted and even destroyed by a stronger rival produced an obvious remedy in alliances between the weak and the strong, which were formalized in 'Bonds of Manrent and Maintenance'. The weaker chief signed a 'Bond of Manrent', promising his support to the stronger; the stronger signed a 'Bond of Maintenance', taking the weaker under his aegis. For example, in 1592 Colquhoun of Luss, fearing the power of Argyll, signed a 'Bond of Manrent' with the Earl of Huntly. Such bonds were limited in effect (this bond did not serve to protect the Colquhouns against the MacGregors) but they were of some help in creating local stability. They indicated that efforts were being made to reduce violence. Even Highland feuds, though notoriously long-lived, were not always endless and bloody vendettas. They could be brought to an end by negotiation, which often resulted in payments of reparation for injuries, or in the provision of husbands for widows or for orphaned daughters of men slain in feuds, or in the signing of bonds for the keeping of future peace. The 'Age of Forays' was also an age of local diplomacy.

In 1587 James VI endeavoured to extend the principle of the bond by an act of parliament imposing a 'General Bond' which made clan chiefs responsible for the good behaviour of their clansmen. A chief who held a feudal jurisdiction could try offenders himself; but a chief of 'broken men' whose clansmen were another man's tenants could only surrender them for trial, which further weakened his position. In 1597 another act ordered all landholders in the Highlands and Isles to 'compear' before the exchequer and show their title deeds; it followed that those who did not possess a legal title to their lands might be dispossessed and more amenable landholders established in their place.

James VI imagined that 'plantation' or colonization by Lowlanders was the key to making the Highlands and Isles more governable, and also more profitable to the Crown. Following the act of 1597 the Isle of Lewis was declared forfeit and a group of 'Gentlemen Adventurers' of Fife undertook to 'plant thameselffis tharin be force', but ten years later they retired defeated, after two unsuccessful attempts at colonization, and their rights were taken over by MacKenzie of Kintail.

A more successful plantation of Lowlanders was undertaken by the Campbells in Kintyre. In 1607 the seventh Earl of Argyll was granted a charter to the crown lands in Kintyre and the South Isles, for which he was also created Royal Lieutenant and Justiciar, initially for six months. He was commissioned to expel the MacDonalds and MacLeans and colonize the area with Lowlanders. In 1609 he founded the burgh of Lochhead (now Campbeltown); he crushed two risings by MacDonalds in 1614 and 1615, and in 1617 his charter to Kintyre was confirmed.

Argyll's success had much to do with timing: it followed the Union of Crowns of 1603, which had given James VI control of Ireland. Professor Gordon Donaldson has pointed out that 'Highlanders and Western Islanders had been exceptionally active in Ireland all throughout Elizabeth's reign, not only as mercenary troops but as something of an occupying force in certain coastal areas of Ulster'.[9] The Lowland plantation of Kintyre and the much larger scale plantation of Ulster in the years following the Union of Crowns were designed to prevent concerted action between the Gaels of Ireland and Western Scotland; but what appeared to be a far-sighted peace keeping measure at the time, ultimately proved to have been a sowing of dragons' teeth.

Andrew Knox, Bishop of the Isles, whose advice had considerable influence with James VI, viewed the advancing power of the Campbells with misgiving; he did not think it 'either good or profitable to his majesty or this country to make that name [Campbell] greater in the Isles than they are already, or yet to root out one pestiferous clan and plant in one little better'.[10] Bishop Knox, supported by Lord Ochiltree and other members of a Privy Council commission on the Isles, which did not include Argyll, stressed the advantage of a wider application of the principle of the 'General Bond', but not only making the chiefs responsible for the good behaviour of their clansmen, but responsible for the application of specific policies.

In 1608 Lord Ochiltree, acting as King's Lieutenant, and accompanied by Bishop Knox, led an expedition to the Isles, where he summoned a meeting of all the Island chiefs on the Isle of Mull. After listening to a sermon by the Bishop, the chiefs were carried away captive to spend the winter months in Lowland prisons. They were freed on provision of sureties that they would come to Edinburgh when summoned and that in the meantime they would give active support to the Bishop, as the King's agent. In 1609 the chiefs came to Iona to meet the Bishop and to sign the Statutes of Iona, which were then presented to them. These chiefs approximated very closely to those who in the days of the Lordship had constituted the *Consilium Insularum* (the 'Council of the Isles'); they were MacDonald of Dunyvaig, MacLean of Duart, MacLean of Lochbuie, MacDonald of Sleat and MacKinnon of Strathardle, MacLeod of Harris, MacLean of Coll, MacDonald of Eilean Tioram, Captain of Clan Ranald, and MacQuarrie of Ulva.[11]

The chiefs were obliged to sign a 'General Bond', swearing obedience to the King and to the laws of the land and the established church (at this point Episcopalian). The statutes which they swore to obey and to promulgate were: to aid the spread of the established church; to provide inns for travellers, so as to relieve the country people of the obligation of providing hospitality (this was also intended to prevent 'sorning', or exacting hospitality by force or threats); to accept the limitation of a specific number of followers for any chief; to aid the suppression of vagabonds, beggars and bards (bards because they kept alive the memory of old feuds and warlike deeds, and might inspire new ones); to submit to the control of both the import and production of 'strong wynis and acquavitie [whisky]'; to accept the prohibition of firearms; to arrest and try malefactors; to send their eldest sons, or daughters if they had no sons, to school in the Lowlands, until they could speak, read and write English; to be responsible for the obedience to the statutes of their kinsmen, friends and dependants. In 1616 the bond and the statutes were re-enacted, with the additional provision that no one should be eligible to inherit property in the Isles unless he could speak, read and write English.

The Statutes of Iona were not immediately or completely enforceble. They expressed the government's intentions rather than its immediate prospects of effective action. Indeed, Lord Ochiltree's expedition of 1608 did not appear very different from the disciplinary visits of James IV or James V. What was different was that the government of James VI, after the Union of Crowns of 1603, had the power to exert continuous pressure on the chiefs, and the purpose of this pressure was more than disciplinary. The intention was to metamorphose the chiefs from autonomous local rulers into agents of government. For this purpose it was sense that they should be fluent in English, the language of government. But the statutes also mirrored James's anti-Gaelic prejudice, which was shared by Bishop Knox, and they have been seen as the advance measures of growing official discouragement of the Gaelic language for general use. The statute condemning bards has been greatly deplored but it coincided with a decline in the long-lived tradition of formal bardic verse, which was being replaced by a more informal style of Gaelic vernacular poetry. The Statutes of Iona did not inflict a mortal wound on Gaelic culture, which, though it was changing, could still produce new and vigorous developments.

The composition of bardic verse had relied upon the transmission of an ancient tradition, supported by patronage. After the fall of the Lordship of the Isles the social structure which had supported the bardic tradition was weakened and gradually fragmented, and poetic style itself mirrored the change. The sixteenth and seventeenth centuries saw the rise of a new style of Gaelic poetry, known as 'semi-bardic', which has been described as 'a vernacularized but strongly literary version of bardic verse . . . familiar with some at least of the bardic thought-patterns . . . yet comprehensible to those who did not have bardic schooling'.[12] Its authors were for the most part educated amateurs, drawn from the social strata which in the previous age would have composed the bards' patrons and audience: local chiefs, *daoine uasile* (clan gentry), clergy and women of chiefs' families.

A group of such poems was inspired by the misfortunes of the MacGregors, and a powerful example is attributed to the widow of Gregor MacGregor of Glenstrae, who was executed in 1570:

> They placed his head on a block of oak,
> and spilt his blood on the ground;
> had I but had a cup then
> I'd have drunk my fill of it.

This form of communion with the dead belonged to the pagan Celtic tradition, for the ancient hero-tales and ballads recounted that Deirdre had drunk the blood of her murdered lover Naoise. A new husband was evidently found for the MacGregor widow; but he failed to comfort her, for she continued her lament:

> Far better to be with Gregor
> roaming heather and wood,
> than tied to the wrinkled Baron of Dull
> in a house of lime and stone.
>
> Far better to be with Gregor
> driving the cows to the glen
> than tied to the wrinkled Baron of Dull
> and drinking wine and ale.
>
> Far better to be with Gregor
> under tattered sealskin cloak
> than tied to the wrinkled Baron of Dull
> wearing satin and silk.[13]

Semi-bardic verse also includes religious poetry, sometimes written by clerics, on such traditional Christian themes as the conflict between flesh and spirit, or the necessity for repentance. For example, John Stewart of Appin, an aristocrat and cleric, used the fleeting beauties of nature to illustrate the transience of earthly pleasure:

> Like dew on a calm day,
> or snow that lies fines and white,
> the growth of leaves on the tree:
> men stay here but a space
>
> The most fragrant rose, or lily,
> the plum, or the red cherry,
> their bloom doesn't last long:
> So too with the people's mirth.[14]

With the metamorphosis of bardic verse into poetry of a more subjective and reflective kind, the status of the harper also changed. As a wandering entertainer the Highland harper did not disappear until the mid-eighteenth century but by that time harp music had lost its military role. A medieval band of warriors could be incited to deeds of prowess by the singing of a *brosnachadh* with its harp accompaniment but the larger clan armies of the sixteenth and seventeenth centuries and the later Highland regiments required a different kind of inspirational music.

The classical instrumental music of the Scottish bagpipes 'seems to emerge suddenly as the fully developed art of the *piobaireachd*' at the end of the sixteenth century or the beginning of the seventeenth. The bagpipe is a very early form of musical instrument known all over Europe and in parts of Asia since remote antiquity. The small medieval bagpipe, sometimes called the 'chorus' was used in courtly and rustic festivities to accompany dancing. The melody was played on the chanter and a single drone provided a continuous harmonic. The Highland bagpipes in addition have a tenor and a bass drone which give them the powerful and sonorous sound particularly suited to war music. It is often said that the music of bagpipes is either loved or loathed, that it cannot be heard with indifference. To those who love it, however, it is the most moving and inspiring of sounds.

Ceol mor ('great music', as opposed to *ceol beag* 'light music') is described by Dr I.F. Grant and Hugh Cheape as 'severe, intellectual music'. They wrote a brief explanation of its basic rules:

> Although individual tunes of *ceol mor* are very different from one another and definitely of different degrees of merit, they conform to certain rules of composition and follow a definite plan. The tune begins with the 'ground' or *urlar* . . . The theme can usually be discerned within the *urlar*, which will include different variations of it . . . The *urlar* itself is followed by a succession of conventional variations, achieving a slightly quicker tempo in successive movements and involving increasingly elaborate grace-noting. The tune reaches its culmination in the *crunluath* and the additional, often optional *crunluath a mach*, by which the piper's skill can be judged.[15]

From the late sixteenth century the greatest masters of *piobaireachd* were acknowledged to be the MacCrimmons, hereditary pipers to MacLeod of MacLeod (later of Dunvegan). Famous both as pipers and composers were Donald Mor MacCrimmon (born *c.* 1570) and Patrick Mor MacCrimmon (born *c.* 1595). They lived at Boreraig in Vaternish, Skye, where many aspiring pipers went to learn from them. It long remained a piper's proudest boast to have been taught by the MacCrimmons or to have inherited their traditions. Some three

113

hundred compositions by various composers both known and unknown survive from the classical age of *piobaireachd* (*c.* 1600–1760); gatherings and marches summoned the clans and accompanied them to war; battle tunes and laments celebrated victories or mourned defeat and death. *Piobaireachd* was the accompaniment to the wars of Montrose and the Jacobites, and of every other Highland campaign within the period.

Over the same century and a half the evolution of Highland dress was as characteristic and unique as that of Highland music. Throughout the middle ages the distinguishing dress of the Highlander, especially of the warrior, had been his voluminous *leine chroich* ('saffron or yellow shirt'), and his mantle woven in stripes or possibly in checks (since such adjectives as 'multicoloured' or 'particoloured' could have meant either). The bare legs which shirt and mantle revealed had given King Magnus Barelegs his nickname and caused the Highlanders whom the English encountered in Ireland to be nicknamed 'Redshanks'. In bitter winter weather they protected their feet by making *cuarans*, or improvised buskins of raw red deerskin, cut to fit as neatly as possible, laced with thongs and worn fur side out. These did not last long, but they could be renewed as opportunity offered.

From the sixteenth century onward descriptions of Highland dress proliferated, making it possible to trace its development. George Buchanan in his *History of Scotland* (1581) said that Highlanders 'delight in varigated garments, especially stripes, and their favourite colours are purple and blue', not the easiest colours to obtain from Highland plants and therefore probably especially prized. He also mentioned brown-toned plaids, worn for purposes of camouflage, and probably woven of undyed wool.

In the mid-seventeenth century a very detailed description by James Gordon of Rothiemay in *A History of Scots Affairs from 1637 to 1641* showed how Highland dress had evolved in the meantime:

> . . . next the skin they wear a short linen shirt, which the great men among them sometimes dye of saffron colour. They use it short, that it may not encumber them when running or travelling . . . In the sharp winter weather the highlandmen wear close 'trowzes' which cover the legs, thighs and feet . . . Above their shirt they have a single coat, reaching no farther than the navel. Their uppermost garment is a loose cloak of several ells, striped and party coloured, which they

gird breadthwise with a leathern belt so as it scarce covers the knees
... Far the greatest part of the plaid covers the uppermost part of the
body. Sometimes it is all folded round the body above the region of
the belt, for disengaging and leaving the hands free; and sometimes
'tis wrapped round all that is above the flank . . .[16]

This is a clear description of the jacket, trews and belted plaid, a
form of costume which continued to be worn until the second half of
the eighteenth century. The trews were close-fitting hose, or tights,
often bias-cut to give both fit and elasticity; when cut in this way the
checks of the tartan appeared in a lozenge pattern. Trews were worn
by chiefs and gentry; the ordinary clansmen continued to be
bare-legged.

Martin Martin, who wrote a *Description of the Western Isles* (1703)
mentioned the disappearance of the *leine chroich*; he said the
Islanders had 'laid it aside' about a century before. The shirt described
by Gordon of Rothiemay was a shirt of normal proportions, though an
affection for yellow dye remained. Martin Martin described the plaid
as being made of the finest wool and its dyes as being the subject of
great attention. 'It consists of divers colours, and there is a great deal of
ingenuity require in sorting the colours, so as to be agreeable to the
nicest fancy'. The women who were to weave it 'are at great pains, first
to give an exact pattern of the plaid upon a peice of wood, having the
number of every thread of the stripe on it'. This enabled patterns to be
reproduced as many times as required and sufficiently closely for
travellers 'at the first view of a man's plaid to guess the place of his
residence'. Martin Martin's description seems to indicate the development of district tartans at this date, but not of clan tartans. Indeed,
portraits of eighteenth century chiefs in tartan clothes often show them
wearing jackets, trews and plaids of two or even three different
patterns. Clan 'setts' were a later development and throughout the
century 'fancy' seems to have been the main influence on design,
subject no doubt to the availability of dyes.

Descriptions of women's costumes are usually less precise, but
Martin Martin describes the 'ancient' female costume of the Isles,
which was probably what had been commonly worn during the
sixteenth century. The woman's plaid or *earasaid* was a long mantle
which reached from neck to heel, woven of white wool, with a few
stripes of black, blue or red. It was secured at the breast with a round
brooch of silver or brass, perhaps set with semi-precious stones,

according to the status or prosperity of the wearer. A leather belt round the waist also might be ornamented with silver or set with stones. According to an eighteenth century poet:

> The *earasaid* is most becoming
> On many a surpassingly beautiful maiden
> Between Balavanich
> And the Sound of Barra . . .

A young girl wore her hair long and loose as a symbol of virginity, with a red *stiom* or head-band tied round it. After marriage a woman wore a white linen *breid tri chearnach* – a three cornered kerch or whimple, sometimes described as 'peaked', which suggests that it could be starched. The three corners or peaks symbolized the Three Persons of the Holy Trinity, her divine protectors.

During the seventeenth and eighteenth centuries women's costume, at least among the upper classes, began to show the influence of European fashions. The diary of a seventeenth century traveller, Hieronymus Tielssch, shows a Highland lady wearing a ruff and a skirt with a farthingale, covered by a tartan cloak. In the mid-eighteenth century Flora MacDonald was portrayed in a red tartan dress of fashionable cut, with elegant beribboned bodice and slashed sleeves. In the eighteenth century Highland women who did not attempt to follow rapid changes of fashion abandoned the *earasaid* in favour of a tartan plaid long enough to cover the head and reach the ground, and habitually woven in brighter colours and in larger checks than a man's plaid. A traveller in Scotland in 1723 thought that the women's plaids compared very favourably with the prevailing black mantles of continental women, and likened the pews of women in a Scottish church to a 'Parterre de Fleurs'.

When Highlanders, in the seventeenth and eighteenth centuries, became familiar figures on the international scene, it was by the wearing of tartan that they were identified.

THEATRE OF WAR

I climbed early on Sunday morning
to the brae above Inverlochy Castle;
I saw the army taking up position,
and victory lay with Clan Donald . . .

Many a well-saddled, armoured man
as good as the Campbells have alive,
could not escape with his boots dry,
but learned to swim at Nevis' foot . . .

You remember the place called the Tawny Field?
It got a fine dose of manure;
not the dung of sheep or goats,
but Campbell blood well congealed.

To Hell with you if I care for your plight,
as I listen to your children's distress,
lamenting the band that went to battle,
the howling of the women of Argyll . . .[1]

My great grief, the white bodies
that lie on the hills over there,
without coffin or shroud,
or burial even in holes!
Those that still live have scattered,
and are now herded close on the ships.
The Whigs got their own way,
and 'Rebels' is what we are called.[2]

At the beginning of the seventeenth century the idea that Highlanders
were 'Wild Scots' and 'savages' was long established in Lowland

Scotland and in England, and had been exported in Latin literary works intended for international consumption, such as those of John Major and George Buchanan, and in diplomatic dispatches like those of Pedro de Ayala. But simultaneously the idea was developing that Highlanders were not merely savage but interestingly picturesque. For example, in 1530 King James V took the Papal ambassador with him to an entertainment provided by the third Earl of Atholl on the fringe of the Highlands. To receive the court Atholl had built a rustic palace of green timber and leafy branches, its floors laid with green turfs and carpeted with rushes, meadowsweet and flowers, its windows set with glass and its inner walls hung with tapestries. Lodged in sophisticated rusticity, the court hunted by day and feasted by night. The ambassador was astonished that such entertainment could be provided in a country which other nations regarded as 'the arse of the world' (not an outstanding example of diplomatic tact). When the King and his guests departed and before they had ridden more than a short distance, the green palace, dried out by the summer heat, was set on fire together with all its luxurious contents. According to the chronicler who reported the episode:

> Then the ambassador said to the King, 'I marvel that you should permit yon fair palace to be burnt, that your Grace has been so well lodged in'. Then the King answered the ambassador and said, 'It is the use of our highland men, though they be never so well lodged, to burn their lodging when they depart'.[3]

It pleased the King to imply that a prodigal gesture involving the sacrifice of costly imported luxuries meant little to a Highland nobleman when honouring his native custom. Perhaps this was the first occasion on which Highlanders were cast in the role of picturesque savages. It was by no means the last. James V's daughter, Mary Queen of Scots, sometimes wore Scottish 'national dress' as a form of fancy dress at the court of France. This would have been some form of Highland dress, since the court dress of Scotland was identical in style with that of France, if usually less sumptuous in materials. Mary's biographer Lady Antonia Fraser suggests that Mary's Scottish costume was similar to the cloak of skins or furs shown in a contemporary French engraving entitled 'La Sauvage d'Escosse'[4] – a costume which was undeniably both savage and picturesque.

Travellers in the Highlands, of whom there were few before the sixteenth century and increasing numbers thenceforward, never failed to comment on Highland dress, sometimes admiring it as picturesque, sometimes despising it as uncouth. But they were unanimous in their condemnation of the Highland landscape; it was savage in itself and fit only to be the abode of savages. Taste was probably influenced by experience. Medieval, renaissance and early modern travellers had good reason not to admire mountainous landscapes, if they saw them only in terms of the dangers which they threatened and the discomforts which they promised. English or European travellers who were accustomed to roads which were at least discernible, and to inns which were provisioned to receive them, were daunted by trackless wastes and the random chances of local hospitality. Edward Burt, an English officer on the staff of General Wade, who wrote *Letters from a Gentleman in the North of Scotland* in the 1720s, saw the Highland landscape simply as 'most horrible'. As late as 1773 Dr Johnson, traversing the Highlands on his *Journey to the Western Isles*, reflected that 'an eye accustomed to flowery pastures and waving harvests is astonished and repelled by this wide extent of hopeless sterility. The appearance is that of matter incapable of form or usefulness . . . left in its original elemental state'.[5] But by the end of the eighteenth century a complete revolution in attitudes had taken place: the Highlander had become a heroic figure and his elemental landscape an appropriate habitat for heroes. The train of events which made possible these new perceptions began when the Highlands ceased to be a *terra incognita* and became a theatre of war which attracted international attention.

A century of conflict, extending from the mid-seventeenth century to the mid-eighteenth century, impressively demonstrated the military quality of the Highlanders. At the end of that period the royalist cause for which chiefs and clansmen had fought, sometimes willingly and sometimes reluctantly, was decisively defeated, but with paradoxical results. The royalists and Jacobites, transiently victorious and ultimately defeated, became invested with the aura of legend, and their personalities, motives and actions suffered the distortions of the mythopoeic process; meanwhile, the victorious British government, recruiting in the Highlands, created in the Highland regiments a military society which preserved the most genuine forms of Highland dress and music, while in the Highlands themselves Gaelic culture and language was subjected to ruthless repression.

*   *   *   *

The origins of this conflict dated from the Union of Crowns of 1603. The departure from Scotland of King James VI of Scotland and I of England, and the establishment of his court at Whitehall, led to the increasing anglicization of the royal house of Scotland. After the regnal union which James aptly called 'the Augmentation', the Stuarts could not have maintained an exclusively Scottish identity if they were to possess credibility as rulers of Great Britain. James VI and I wanted his kingdoms to be amalgamated in a fully incorporating union under his rule. Ireland, as a conquered territory, did not have to be consulted. James endeavoured to persuade the English Parliament of the desirability of an incorporating union in a famous speech, which fell upon deaf ears:

> What God hath conjoined, then let no man separate. I am the husband, and the whole isle is my lawful wife; I am the head and it is my body . . . I hope, therefore, that no man will be so unreasonable as to think that I, that am a Christian King under the Gospel, should be a polygamist and husband to two wives; that I, being the head, should have a divided and monstrous body . . .[6]

That this plea was rejected, and the body politic became increasingly 'divided and monstrous' was no fault of the far-seeing James. The year 1603 provided the best opportunity for an incorporating union, which James could have ensured did not take place to Scotland's disadvantage. But, since the union remained a purely personal one, under the King, the next best policy appeared to be one of creating as much uniformity as possible between the two kingdoms, with a view to facilitating full unification in the future. This was the policy which provided additional justification for James's anti-Gaelic prejudice: the Anglicization of the Gael was a step towards the unification of Britain.

To a seventeenth-century ruler religious uniformity was a desirable, if increasingly elusive, ideal. In pursuit of this ideal James VI and I was successful in imposing episcopacy on the reformed Church of Scotland, which was Calvinist in origin and Presbyterian by preference. Between 1603 and his death in 1625 James paid only one return visit to Scotland, in 1617, and on that occasion he discovered the limits he could not transgress in imposing the usages of the Church of England upon that of Scotland. James acknowledged that Scotland would not accept the high Anglican forms of worship and ritual which he had come to appreciate. His son, Charles I, in rejecting that lesson, began to tread the path which led to the signing of the National Covenant, and the outbreak of civil war.

The grievances which multiplied against the government of Charles I in England lie beyond the scope of this book. In Scotland Charles committed a series of errors which resulted from his exclusively English upbringing, for at the English court the Scots with whom he came into contact were as deracinated as himself. His accession was followed by a particularly sweeping Act of Revocation which annulled not only the grants made during his minority, in accordance with Scottish tradition but also all grants made since 1540 of properties which the Crown could claim. This included ecclesiastical properties which had fallen into lay hands both before and after the Reformation. It understandably alienated those members of the Scottish nobility who had acquired former ecclesiastical properties, the more so as Charles I's intention was to use at least some of these properties to provide more generously for the Scottish clergy. Moreover, while James VI and I had employed the Scottish bishops bureaucratically as agents of royal power, Charles I accorded bishops a veneration which appeared in Scottish eyes suspiciously popish. The elevation of the High Kirk of St Giles to the status of the cathedral of a new bishopric of Edinburgh, and the attempted imposition on the Church of Scotland of a revised Prayer Book, were dangerous causes of disaffection in Scotland. The fact that the new liturgy was the work of Scottish bishops and not of Archibishop Laud, who was widely blamed for it, and that it contained plenty of concessions to established Scottish usage, were not sufficient to prevent rioting when it was first used in St Giles on 23 July 1637. Resistance to the religious policy of Charles I led to the signing of the National Covenant on 28 February 1638.

The National Covenant was not in itself a dramatically innovative document. It was based on the 'Negative Confession' of 1581, which condemned popish practices. The National Covenant did not even repudiate episcopal government for the Church of Scotland, which was not abolished until nine months later, when the General Assembly of the Church which met at Glasgow resolved its abolition in November 1638, in defiance of the King's Commissioner, the Marquess of Hamilton. Military action followed, in which the ill-prepared and reluctant forces of King Charles were outfaced in the first so-called 'Bishops' War', which saw no actual fighting. The King was easily defeated in the second Bishops' War by the army of the Covenant commanded by Alexander Leslie, a veteran of the war in

Europe, in which he had served with distinction under Gustavus Adolphus. Charles visited Edinburgh in 1641 and attempted to woo his opponents with honours: the eighth Earl of Argyll, the Covenant's most powerful supporter, was created Marquess, and Alexander Leslie was created Earl of Leven, but this transparent appeasement did not change their allegiance.

Conflict between the King and the Covenanters rapidly escalated into the War of the Three Kingdoms. Catholic Ireland, having witnessed the weakness of the English King, broke out in revolt in 1641, and the Covenanters demanded the summoning of the English Parliament, which led to the outbreak of the Civil War in England in 1642. Thereafter, the Covenanters, growing increasingly fanatical, intervened in the English Civil War in support of Parliament and in 1643 signed with the Parliamentarians the Solemn League and Covenant, which proposed the establishment of a British Church with a Presbyterian polity. The Covenanters also sent an army to Ireland to protect the Scottish colonists of the Ulster Plantation against the insurgent Irish Catholics, who made a truce with the King in order to concentrate their forces against the more formidable adversary. This truce was later converted into an alliance against the Covenanters.

The Highlands became a new theatre of war in an increasingly ramifying conflict when James Graham, fifth Earl of Montrose, who had signed the Covenant and never repudiated it, opposed the extremist Covenanters' decision to support the Parliamentarian cause and offered his services to the King. In 1644 he was appointed the King's Lieutenant-General in Scotland and created Marquess. Montrose's original purpose was to invade Scotland from the south but failing to win sufficient support for the King in the Lowlands, he made his way to the Highlands almost alone, in the hope of raising royalist support among the Highland opponents of the Covenant, of whom there were many, both for religious reasons and for the sake of the more basic and territorial enmity, because the Covenant was supported by the Campbells, under the leadership of the Marquess of Argyll. So began a phase of conflict in the Highlands which was to continue, on and off, for a century, until the final defeat of the Jacobites on the field of Culloden in 1746. Only then, with Ireland reconquered and Scotland united with England, was the English government's Pax Britannica secured.

In Atholl Montrose joined up with a force which had invaded from Ireland with the intention of forcing the Covenanters to withdraw their invading army from that country. The Irish force was commanded by Alasdair MacDonald, usually known by his Gaelic patronymic, Alasdair MacColla. Alasdair was a kinsman of Randall MacDonnell, Earl of Antrim, chief of the Irish branch of the MacDonalds, and son of Coll Ciotach ('Left-handed') MacDonald of Colonsay, who had been deprived of his patrimony by the Campbells. Alasdair was inspired more by hatred of the Campbells than by loyalty to the King, but for the time being the two causes were one. Alasdair MacColla placed his forces under Montrose's command and thereby gained wider support than he would have won as a Catholic and an invader. Montrose, as a Presbyterian and as the King's Lieutenant-General, recruited Highlanders who would not have backed Alasdair alone. Together they won an astonishing series of victories: at Tippermuir, near Perth, on 25 September 1644; at Aberdeen on 13 September; at Inverlochy on 2 February 1645; at Auldearn on 9 May; at Alford on 2 July; and at Kilsyth on 15 August. Dramatically, albeit briefly, the royalist cause was victorious in Scotland.

Not only had Montrose and Alasdair defeated the Covenanters, they had temporarily destroyed the military power of the Campbells and three times caused Argyll to flee ignominiously from the battlefield. The massacre, which followed the Battle of Inverlochy and which was celebrated by the Gaelic poet Iain Lom MacDonald with bloodthirsty glee, was the nadir of Campbell fortunes. Montrose's triumph in Scotland had prevented the Covenanters from playing the decisive role in England which they had envisaged. While they assisted in the defeat of Charles I at Marston Moor in 1644 and at Naseby in 1645, it was the English Parliamentarian army under Oliver Cromwell which gained the kudos for defeating him. The defeat of the King in England freed the Scottish general David Leslie to bring his army back to Scotland, where he defeated Montrose at Philiphaugh, near Selkirk, on 13 September 1645. Alasdair MacColla, meanwhile, had separated from Montrose. He was finally driven out of Scotland by David Leslie in 1647, and murdered in Ireland after his capture at the Battle of Knocknanuss.

The defeat of the King by an English Parliament which showed little gratitude to the Covenanters and no disposition to implement the terms of the Solemn League and Covenant split the supporters of the Covenant in Scotland. The moderate adherents of the Covenant in 1647 signed the Engagement with Charles I, by which they promised to help him regain power in England on condition of his accepting the introduction of Presbyterianism for a trial period of three years. The army of the Engagement was defeated at Preston on 25 August 1648. It was in retaliation for the renewal of civil war in England that Charles I was tried by Parliament and executed on 30 January 1649.

Charles I had been King of Scots and King of Ireland, and his execution by his English subjects without consultation of either of his other kingdoms caused a blaze of resentment in both of them. Briefly the young Charles II faced the problem of choosing whether to seek his restoration at the hands of Irish Catholics or Scottish Covenanters. Cromwell solved this problem for him by a brilliant and ruthless campaign of conquest in Ireland, leaving Charles II reliant on the Covenanters, whose extremist wing suffered a heavy but not a final defeat by Cromwell at Dunbar on 3 September 1650. In the meantime Charles II had encouraged an independent invasion by Montrose, who had fled the country after Philiphaugh. Montrose failed to win support for Charles II's cause on the Continent, but none the less landed in Orkney in March 1650 and crossed to the Scottish mainland where he hoped once more to recruit an army in the Highlands. He was defeated at Carbisdale on 27 April, captured and hanged in Edinburgh by the Covenanting government on 21 May, protesting to the last his loyalty to both King and Covenant. Charles II, accepting the role of a 'Covenanted King', received the Crown of Scotland from the hands of the Marquess of Argyll on 1 January 1651. The Covenanters, though now reinforced by former Royalists, were defeated at Inverkeithing in July and Charles II's invasion of England was defeated at Worcester on 3 September, leaving the King a fugitive.

The monarchy was abolished and the Commonwealth established under an unloved but efficient military government. For a few years the Highlands benefited from better order than they had previously known. Cromwell's commander-in-chief in Scotland, General George Monck, built military forts to assist in controlling the Highlands, the principal ones at Inverlochy (where the fort was later renamed Fort William) and Inverness, at either end of the Great Glen. According to Dr I.F. Grant and Hugh Cheape, Gaelic speakers still call Fort William *An Gearasdan* ('the Garrison') perpetuating the memory of its original purpose. Abolition of the greater heritable jurisdictions and measures designed to limit the right to carry weapons prefigured later attempts to pacify and disarm the Highlands, and to assimilate them to the increasingly well-ordered society of Lowland Scotland and England itself.

From the Commonwealth period onward all the military actions initiated in the Highlands were rebellions against central government directed from England. They were, with one exception (the rebellion of the ninth Earl of Argyll) legitimist or nationalist in inspiration, though with continual changes of underlying motivation. In 1653/4 the ninth Earl of Glencairn led a Royalist rebellion against Cromwell, which was easily defeated. The Restoration of Charles II, which was welcomed in the Highlands, was followed by a restoration of the *status quo ante*, in so far as such a thing is ever possible: Scotland regained its Parliament, the Church became officially Episcopalian once more, and the heritable jurisdictions were restored. In the Highlands change toward a more peaceful society was halted and the martial character of clanship was reasserted. The greatest manifestations of the warlike spirit of the Highlands were yet to be seen. In 1685 the ninth Earl of Argyll, son of the Marquess whose devious life had been ended by execution after the Restoration, rebelled against the accession of Charles II's Catholic brother James VII and II, in co-ordination with the rebellion of Charles II's illegitimate son, the Duke of Monmouth. Both rebellions were defeated and both leaders executed. Even in the south-west of Scotland, where dissident Covenanters had defied the renewed Episcopalianism of Charles II's regime, Argyll had not found the support he had expected, for he was not himself a Covenanter. The execution of a second chief within a generation would have brought a less resilient and successful clan than the Campbells to ruin, but the Campbells emerged from the crisis more powerful than ever. The ninth Earl's son offered to fight against his father, and then went on to support the 'Glorious Revolution' against James VII and II. He joined William of Orange in Holland and accompanied him to England. Argyll was rewarded for his support of the victorious cause with a dukedom in 1701.

With the Revolution the supporters of James VII and II became known as 'Jacobites', the term derived from 'Jacobus' the Latin form of James. It applied successively to the supporters of James VII and II himself and then to those of his son, the *de jure* James 'VIII and III', acknowledged as King by his continental allies, Louis XIV and the Papacy. The Revolution may have been 'Glorious' in England for its lack of bloodshed but a great deal of blood was spilt in both Scotland and Ireland before the transfer of power from James VII to William and Mary was complete.

In John Graham of Claverhouse, Viscount Dundee, a kinsman of

Montrose, James VII had a dedicated adherent and a brilliant general, who raised a Highland army for him and won a spectacular victory over William's forces under General Hugh MacKay at the Pass of Killiecrankie, on 27 July 1689. Dundee was mortally wounded at the conclusion of the battle and William's answer to the advice that he should send reinforcements to Scotland has often been quoted: 'Armies are needless; the war is over with Dundee's life.' This was not entirely true at the time, but it appeared to have been so in retrospect. James VII's attempt to regain his kingdoms by way of an invasion of Ireland was defeated after hard fighting, in which William's victory was consolidated by the battles of the Boyne (1690) and Aughrim (1691).

The Scottish Parliament followed England in accepting the Revolution and the sovereignty of William and Mary. In the Highlands the Jacobite chiefs delayed taking the oath of allegiance to the new government until they had received the permission of the exiled James VII to do so. MacDonald of Glencoe failed to present himself before the Sheriff of Argyll at Inveraray to take the oath until after the last permitted date, 1 January 1692, and thus unfortunately provided the government with the opportunity to make an example of him, with the intention of terrorizing the Highlands into general acquiescence. The ensuing 'Massacre of Glencoe', which was intended to extirpate the small clan, failed in this purpose, but none the less caused widespread outrage. As an act of bad faith on the part of the government and as a flagrant abuse of the sacred law of Highland hospitality, the massacre had the reverse effect of its intention. It intensified Jacobite loyalties and centred Jacobite hopes on the restoration of the Stuarts.

A modern historian of the Jacobite movement, Dr Frank McLynn, has commented that as the objective conditions favouring a Stuart restoration worsened the Jacobite risings came closer to success.[7] The paradox is difficult to account for, other than by the simple explanation of better leadership. The first Jacobite attempt at invasion of Scotland in 1708 ought, according to McLynn, to have been a walk-over. Its timing was excellent for the Union of Parliaments of 1707 was widely and profoundly detested in Scotland and Jacobitism became the natural focus of anti-Union sentiment, a nationalist as well as a legitimist cause. The failure of a French expeditionary force to land James VIII in Scotland was for him a lost opportunity which was never repeated on such advantageous terms. The Rising of 1715 followed the Hanoverian succession, which a better co-ordinated opposition might have prevented altogether. Its leader, the eleventh Earl of Mar, had gained for himself the uninspiring nickname of 'Bobbing John', for his propensity for changing sides. He had supported the Union of Parliaments and despite his association with the Tory government of Queen Anne he had been prepared to welcome the Hanoverian succession, but had changed sides understandably when George I deprived him of his Secretaryship of State and of his hereditary governorship of Stirling Castle. When Mar raised the Jacobite standard at Braemar on 6 September 1715 the strength of Jacobite sentiment was demonstrated by a rapid muster of some 5,000 men. The Government forces in Scotland under the 2nd Duke of Argyll numbered only 1,500, so that with energetic leadership the Jacobites had another chance of easy victory. Mar behaved indecisively from the beginning, but even so, his army increased to 10,000. Argyll meanwhile had doubled his numbers. Mar divided his army, sending 2,000 men under William Mackintosh of Borlum to support Jacobite risings in south-west Scotland and north-west England. These combined forces advanced into England, but were surrounded and forced to surrender at Preston on 14 November. The previous day Mar and Argyll fought an indecisive battle at Sheriffmuir, near Stirling, which both sides claimed as a victory. Argyll suffered the heavier casualties but Mar withdrew northward, leaving Argyll in possession of the field, so that symbolically at least the victory was his. James VIII, delayed by illness, storms at sea and poor communications, did not reach Scotland until the end of the year, and then proved himself far too fatalistic to reinvigorate his discouraged supporters. He and Mar both sailed from Scotland in February 1716, leaving the disarrayed Jacobites to fend for themselves.

A third Jacobite attempt took place in 1719, when the Marquess of Tullibardine and Lord George Murray, sons of the first Duke of Atholl, joined a small Spanish force brought to Scotland by the Earl Marischal, which was defeated in Glenshiel. Both the Murray brothers survived to participate in the last and most nearly successful of the Jacobite Risings, in which Lord George Murray distinguished himself as the ablest Jacobite general.

Prince Charles Edward Stuart, son of James VIII and III, born in 1720, dedicated himself from childhood to the recovery of his father's kingdoms, and though brought up in the comforts of the exiled Jacobite court in Rome, attempted to prepare himself for the rigours of military campaigns. Though disappointed of the French help which he had believed he would receive, he sailed for Scotland with a handful of companions, and raised his standard in Glenfinnan on 19 August 1745. Support for him was initially reluctant but he proved himself a far more charismatic leader than his father. His small Highland army won a dramatic victory over the government forces under General Cope on 21 September at Prestonpans, near Edinburgh. One battle had given the Jacobites the mastery of Scotland, and they invaded England and advanced as far as Derby. This was the moment at which the Jacobites came nearest to success, and might have won it by continuing to gamble on the power of the terror they had caused. But lack of a spontaneous rising in England and of reinforcements from abroad led to defeatist counsels forcing a retreat on the reluctant Prince. The Jacobites won another victory over the government forces under General Hawley at Falkirk, on 17 January 1746, but they were decisively defeated by the Duke of Cumberland at Culloden, near Inverness, on 16 April. The Prince survived the battle and the ensuing manhunt, and with the assistance of many Highlanders and Islanders, including Flora MacDonald, escaped to France, with the intention of returning to fight another day. But Jacobitism did not survive Culloden as a viable political cause, and the warlike character of Highland society, already changing, was changed for ever in the aftermath of the Rising.

However, the adventure of Jacobitism made an enormous appeal to the imagination of a Scotland still resentful of the Union and of the eclipse of national identity. Prince Charles Edward's penultimate birthday, 31 December 1787, was hailed by Robert Burns with a Pindaric ode:

> Afar the illustrious Exile roams,
>   Whom kingdoms on this day should hail,
> An inmate in the casual shed,
> On transient pity's bounty fed,
>   Haunted by busy Memory's bitter tale!
> Beasts of the forest have their savage homes,
>   But He, who should imperial purple wear,
> Owns not the lap of earth where rests his royal head:
>   His wretched refuge, dark despair,
> While ravening wrongs and woes pursue,
> And distant far the faithful few
>   Who would his sorrows share![8]

If the Prince, whose reputation had foundered in the self-destructive alcholism of his later years had heard that ode, which is unlikely, he would have appreciated the ensuing verses' invocation of the curse of Heaven on the house of Hanover:

> The base apostates to their God
> Or rebels to their King!

The Jacobite legend inspired a remarkable flowering of poetry and song, in which political resentment could be disguised as nostalgia. The final defeat of Jacobitism was its conversion into mere sentimentalism, from which it is now in process of being rescued by renewed study of its political background, and its reinstatement in the mosaic of eighteenth century history as a serious threat to the Whig supremacy in Hanoverian Britain.

Highlanders had always been formidable warriors but the victories of Highland armies in the seventeenth and eighteenth centuries, under Montrose and Alasdair MacColla, Viscount Dundee, Lord George Murray and Prince Charles Edward Stuart, astonished even adversaries who were well aware of the Highlanders' martial reputation. Despite the fact that the Highland armies of the Civil Wars and the Jacobite Risings were not professional standing armies and despite the fact that they were always short of firearms and ammunition, under inspiring leadership their particular tactics and their ferocity could give them victory over professional soldiers with superior arms and firepower.

Up to the end of the sixteenth century the arms and armour of the Highland warrior were still medieval. His appearance was that of the warrior portrayed in West Highland sculpture. His armour, if he possessed it, was a long mail shirt; his head was protected by a *clogaid*, or conical steel cap; his principal weapon was his great two-handed sword, the *claidheamh mor*, or claymore. Other favoured weapons were the Lochaber axe, a long-handled battle axe with a spike on the head, and the dirk, a long dagger for use in close combat. Even in the late sixteenth century firearms were rare and bows and arrows were still in use as long range weapons. Hand-to-hand fighting with claymores and Lochaber axes was still a battle of single combats performed *en masse*, in which a champion of immense strength could hew through his adversary's mail and deliver the *coup de grâce* with his dirk.

With the early seventeenth century, firearms became commoner and new weapons came into fashion, which were lighter and cheaper; they were easier to provide for larger clan armies and they gave the armies greater mobility. The huge, unwieldy *claidheamh mor* was abandoned in favour of a single-edged broadsword with a basket-hilt (to which the name 'claymore' was transferred, though as an Anglicization of the name of a different weapon, it is a misnomer). The mail shirt was also abandoned and for defence the swordsman carried a targe, a small round shield made of oak boards pegged together, covered in leather and reinforced with metal studs. Prince Charles Edward had an elaborate targe ornamented with the head of Medusa wreathed with serpent-tresses, in chased silver. The targe was slipped on to the left forearm with leather loops.

Lightweight shields and swords made possible the development of the 'Highland Charge', which was used with devastating effect in Montrose's victories, at Killiecrankie, and at Prestonpans and Falkirk. Dr David Stevenson has argued convincingly that the Highland Charge, despite its name, was devised by Alasdair MacColla in the Irish Rising before he brought his army to Scotland and first used in Scotland at the Battle of Tippermuir.[9] The charge of Alasdair's soldiers at the Laney, Co Antrim, on 11 February 1642 began with a single volley of musket fire, then his soldiers threw down their firearms and charged their enemies with the sword. In this way, a small amount of ammunition was used to maximum effect and, in the charge, the soldiers were not impeded by their firearms.

In the ensuing battles in Scotland this simple and effective tactic was used again and again. It was especially effective when used against infantry armed only with muskets, which were laborious to reload. Once the musketeers had returned the Highlanders' single volley they were helpless until they had reloaded, and the charge usually hit them first. They frequently broke and fled, only to be cut down as they ran. Sometimes the musketeers were interspersed with pikemen who were supposed to protect them while they reloaded. But a thrust of an unwieldy eighteen-foot pike could be caught on the Highlander's targe and the staff of the weapon slashed through with the claymore.

Once the enemy had broken and fled the rout became a massacre, in which the swift-footed and lightly-armed Highlanders cut down the fugitives without mercy. Those battles at which the Highland Charge won the day were over very briefly. When the charge had decided the outcome, that was the end of it; the rest was pursuit and slaughter, which ended only in satiation and exhaustion. Even the pipers who had played for the onset played no other tune to halt the pursuit; they too were warriors who, before the charge began, had exchanged their pipes for claymores and charged with the rest.

The Highland Charge required dashing leadership and suitable terrain. It was not attempted in all the battles in which Highlanders fought. It was not used at Auldearn, where Montrose's army was surprised by the enemy, or at Alford, where the Covenanters attacked first. Nor was it used at Inverkeithing, which was a defensive action, in which the Royalists attempted to prevent the Cromwelliam forces from crossing the Forth. But at Tippermuir, Inverlochy and Kilsyth the charge was decisive. Probably the most brilliant victory ever won by the Highland Charge was Killiecrankie where Dundee, with his army drawn up on the heights above the pass, waited until the setting sun had ceased to dazzle his men before charging down on MacKay's forces like an irresistible torrent. At Prestonpans the shock of the charge had the added advantage of an early morning surprise and the fighting lasted only a few moments, before turning to rout, pursuit and slaughter.

After Prestonpans Prince Charles Edward had some reason to believe that his Highlanders would win his war. The Highland Charge possessed one great advantage and that was the power of terror, which was also a cumulative terror, since it had won so many victories. But by this time, without the additional assistance of surprise, the Highland Charge no longer enjoyed the same advantages as in the mid-seventeenth century. Firearms had improved: eighteenth century firelocks were quicker to load than seventeenth century matchlocks. And they were equipped with ring-bayonets, so that a soldier who had no time to reload still held a formidable weapon. On the field of Culloden a preliminary artillery bombardment, accurate musket-fire and disciplined bayonet-drill won the day over a Jacobite army which was demoralized by retreat, half starving, in part exhausted by an attempted night-attack which had failed, and lacking the advantage of the ground. Under these circumstances, the fact that an almost suicidal charge penetrated Cumberland's front line at some points and inflicted casualties was an astonishing feat of resolution and valour. The Highland Charge, like the Jacobite cause, did not survive Culloden, but in its heyday it had been invincible.

131

The Highlanders who took arms in the Royalist and Jacobite armies from the mid-seventeenth to the mid-eighteenth centuries were not like the raw volunteers or conscripts of a peaceful society, the unpromising and sometimes ludicrously incompetent recruits of a Home Guard or National Service. They were men who had been bred to bear arms and who expected to fight in interclan forays. When they were drawn into the larger-scale battles which absorbed the clans from the mid-seventeenth century onwards, their traditions had prepared them to become formidable soldiers. Alasdair MacColla, Montrose, Dundee and Lord George Murray needed only to discipline their natural aptitude and early training. Skill in the handling of weapons was encouraged not only in small-scale forays but, when there was no warfare going on, in the *tainchel*, or organized deer-drive, in which red deer and other game were driven by the clansman for a chief and his hunting guests to slaughter. The third Earl of Atholl's entertainment of James V included a *tainchel*, and so did the entertainment offered to Mary Queen of Scots by the fourth Earl in 1564. On this occasion, some two thousand Highlanders brought together two thousand red deer besides fallow deer and roe for the Queen and her courtiers to shoot. A *tainchel* provided the pretext for the Earl of Mar's gathering in 1715, the inauguration of the Jacobite Rising. A *tainchel* also provided the occasion for competitions in martial skills and other trials of strength; archery, running, wrestling and throwing the stone. These competitions provided the model for some of the events of later Highland Games.

The dress of the Highland soldier from mid-seventeenth to mid-eighteenth century was a shirt of linen made from home-grown flax and a voluminous belted plaid of home-spun and home-dyed wool, woven into a tartan which might be a pattern of local tradition or of the weaver's personal design. At night the Highlander slept in his plaid, wrapping it round himself as a blanket. In the morning he dressed in it, by laying his belt flat on the ground, spreading his plaid lengthwise over the belt, lying down on it with the belt at waist level, and girding it round himself before standing up. The plaid might be bunched round him in haste, or carefully pleated and folded as time and inclination permitted. The chief would wear the jacket, trews and belted plaid, as previously described; the tacksman might wear a short jacket of tartan or plain cloth over his shirt and under his plaid and a pair of leather shoes and gartered woollen stockings; the poor clansman might wear nothing but his shirt and plaid. But, whatever the differences in costume detail and sartorial sense, the plaid was still the garment common to all ranks of society.

The plaid, as an all-purpose upper and nether garment, was appropriately called in Gaelic the *feileadh mor*, or 'great wrap'. In the 1730s a variant was devised, the *feileadh beag*, or 'little wrap'. In this form of Highland dress, which is the direct ancestor of modern Highland dress, the plaid was divided into two parts. The smaller part was stitched into permanent pleats and wrapped around the waist in the form of a kilt, worn at first as short as mid-thigh length and later as long as knee-length. The remainder of the plaid continued to be worn as a wrap or cloak, over the short kilt, shirt or shirt and jacket. The Gaelic name of this costume was Anglicized as 'phillabeg'. The *feileadh mor* was an easy and adaptable costume to wear and carry, but it had its disadvantages: it was bulky to wear when fighting or doing manual work. In battle, Highlanders often threw down their plaids before the charge and fought in their shirts – thus, no doubt, creating a proverb. At Sheriffmuir some of the Highlanders who had left their plaids before fighting were unable to recover them and had to return to their homes to be reclothed. The change from *feileadh mor* to *feiladh beag* had obvious advantages. Many Scots cannot bring themselves to believe that the 'phillabeg' was the brainchild of an Englishman, and also a Quaker, Mr Alan Rawlinson, forgemaster of the Invergarry ironworks, who saw that his workers were encumbered by their great plaids and devised a more versatile costume.[10] However, whether the change from *feileadh mor* to *feileadh beag* was his alone, or a general development suggested by the need to assimilate Highland dress to new activities, or to make it wearable in conjunction with other items of Lowland dress, the 'phillabeg' or kilt became and remains the basic garment of modern Highland dress. The next development would be the kilt made of a particular 'clan tartan' to identify its wearer's clan.

As the clan tartan did not exist during the heyday of clan warfare, the clansman identified himself by wearing a sprig of his clan's chosen plant pinned to his bonnet. The Campbells, for example, wore the wild myrtle, the Gordons ivy, the MacKenzies holly. Up to the sixteenth century most clansmen had probably gone bare-headed, apart from the champion who donned his *clogaid* for combat. Then, a large branch or spray of the clan plant would have been carried before a clan contingent, tied to a lance or a pole. In the late sixteenth or early seventeenth century the Lowland blue bonnet was adopted as the universal headwear of the Highlands and to it a small sprig of the clan emblem could be pinned without difficulty. However, since plants wither and cannot always be found easily, it was a natural development to wear a ribbon cockade in time of war, especially in a war which drew a number of clans together. In the Forty-Five the Jacobites adopted the white cockade and the Hanoverians wore either a yellow or a red cross of ribbon.

Following the Union of 1707 tartan began to be worn as a nationalist symbol: Lowland lairds and their wives and children were portrayed sporting tartan to signify their anti-Union principles. For this purpose, items of tartan clothing rather than full Highland dress were worn. In the mid-eighteenth century, Lowland ladies with Jacobite sympathies frequently wore the white cockade, or a silk tartan 'screen' or shawl around their shoulders. Tartan was sometimes used for men's jackets or greatcoats, and tartan clothes were made for children: tartan frocks for little girls, tartan coats and breeches for small boys. All these diverse uses of tartan are illustrated in many attractive contemporary portraits, family groups and conversation pieces.

The association of tartan with rebellion led to the proscription of Highland dress and all other forms of tartan clothes, under the Dress Act of 1746 (19 Geo II, c.39):

And be it further enacted by the Authority aforesaid, That from and after the First Day of August, One thousand seven hundred and forty seven, no Man or Boy, within that Part of Great Britain called Scotland, other than such as shall be employed as Officers and Soldiers in His Majesty's Forces, shall, on any Pretence whatsoever, wear or put on the Clothes commonly called Highland Clothes (that is to say) the Plaid, Philebeg, or little Kilt, Trowse, Shoulder Belts, or any Part whatsoever of what peculiarly belongs to the Highland Garb; and that no Tartan, or part-coloured Plaid or Stuff shall be used for Great Coats, or for Upper Coats; and if any such Person shall presume after the said First Day of August, to wear or put on the aforesaid Garments, or any part of them, every such Person so offending, being convicted thereof by the Oath of One or more credible Witness or Witnesses before any Court of Justiciary, or any One or more Justices of the Peace for the Shire or Stewartry, or Judge Ordinary of the Place where such offence shall be committed, shall suffer Imprisonment, without Bail, during the Space of Six Months, and no longer; and being convicted for a second Offence before a Court of Justiciary, or at the Circuits, shall be liable to be transported to any of His Majesty's Plantations beyond the Seas, there to remain for the Space of Seven Years.

The Act was not repealed until 1782. The Highlanders bitterly resented the prohibition of their traditional dress, and Gaelic poets wrote laments for it. Iain Mac Codrum's 'Song against the Lowland Garb' also praises the uses of the plaid:

Poor is our night-clothing, to be swathed in folding black coats,
Our legs we cannot stretch, sleep itself forsakes us;
    Better joy of mind, in th' single cloth ten yards long
Which we'd put into the kilt when we rose at morning;
That's the handsome clothing that would keep the wind and rain
    off,
Cursed be now and ever he who forbade its wearing.

There's no better clothing for the summer than the tartan,
Light it is and cheerful when the snow is falling;
    Once it was the clothing of the active heroes
Bitter their complaining since it's taken from them;
The garb that once protected every handsome Gael,
God! 'twas an injustice to decree its abolition.[11]

But the penalties of imprisonment and transportation were heavy. When Doctor Johnson travelled in the Highlands and Islands in 1773 he found that the Act had been 'universally obeyed'. However, the general feeling was that by this time the law was a dead letter. Doctor Johnson commented:

The common people do not think themselves under any legal necessity of having coats; for they say that the law against plaids was made by Lord Hardwicke, and was in force only for his life: but the same poverty that made it then difficult for them to change their clothing, hinders them now from changing it again.[12]

This was a shrewd observation, and it provides the explanation of why, when the Act was rescinded, Highland dress was not readopted as the dress of the ordinary Highlander. During the years of prohibition there had been defiance of the Act in secret by members of the aristocracy who had had their portraits painted in Highland dress. With the renewed fashion for Highland dress in the nineteenth century, and its adoption as Scottish national costume, it did not reappear in the Highlands as the dress of the people. It was too expensive to be worn by those who could not afford some display. In the later nineteenth century when George Washington Wilson, David Octavius Hill and other pioneering photographers recorded scenes of Highland life, there was little tartan to be seen. In these pictures the Highland poor are dressed in clothes of Lowland style, in tweed, serge and flannel. Highland dress had become the costume of the aristocracy and gentry, when they chose to wear it, and of the prosperous middle class who increasingly visited the Highlands and acquired property there. Highland servants and the ghillies of sporting estates wore Highland dress as a livery.

The Stewart Kings of Scots had been severe in their treatment of their turbulent Highland subjects. Alexander, third Lord of the Isles had experienced the severity of James I; the power of the Lordship had been broken by James III and abolished by James IV. There had followed the 'danting' of the Isles under James V, and the anti-Gaelic measures of James VI. It seemed that the Gaels had little reason to love the monarchy. After these experiences, that Highlanders should have been the most loyal and self-sacrificing subjects of the later Stuarts has almost defied explanation.

Two opposing explanations have been offered: on the one hand it has been argued that the patriarchal nature of clan society disposed the clans to support the monarch as the father of his country, the *pater patriae*; on the other hand it has been suggested that a rebellion was no more than a raid on the largest scale, which enabled the Highlanders to plunder the Lowlanders or the English in the grand manner. However, while both sentiment and self-interest may have contributed to Royalism and Jacobitism, neither alone is sufficient to explain Highland support of the House of Stuart. Both sentiment and self-interest are present whenever choices have to be made and in the Jacobite period both were expressed in unequivocal language. For example, Lord Kilmarnock, a notorious bankrupt who was executed for his part in the Rising of 1745, explained his Jacobitism with the words 'For the two kings and their rights I cared not a farthing which prevailed; but I was starving, and by God, if Mahommed had set up his standard in the Highlands I had been a good Muslim for bread and stuck close to the party, for I must eat.' For Kilmarnock's second in command, Laurence Oliphant of Gask, it was different: 'God sent our rightful Prince among us and I followed him.'[13] Between these extremes the Highlanders' reasons for taking arms on behalf of Charles I, Charles II, James VII and II and his exiled successors were continually changing. For many, attachment to the idea of the monarchy may have become increasingly warm as the monarchy itself became more remote and symbolic.

Charles I was little known in Scotland and was not in his lifetime an inspiring figure. His religious policies provoked enormous antagonism in the Lowlands; in the Highlands support for him may have had the negative inspiration that he interfered with the Gaels less than his father had done. Yet Montrose had difficulty in raising Royalist support in the Highlands; from first to last the backbone of his army was Alasdair MacColla's Irish contingent. From the Engagement of 1647 onwards Royalist sentiment strengthened, when it was too late to be of any help to Charles I. His execution redoubled Royalist fervour and the Cromwellian conquest and occupation continued to fuel it.

The Restoration of Charles II was welcomed in the Highlands, as was the reinstatement of Episcopalianism as the established religion. Episcopalian and Catholic clans supported Charles II and James VII, and were natural Jacobites when the Revolution Settlement reinstated Presbyterianism. Many of the Episcopalian clergy refused to take the Oath of Allegiance to William and Mary, and these 'non-jurors' were officially deprived of their livings. However, many of them continued to carry out their spiritual duties and their influence was strongly Jacobite. Episcopalianism was strongest in the north-east, and in the Central Highlands, and it increased in strength during the thirty years in which it was the established religion, 1660–90. After 1707 Episcopalianism became increasingly associated with anti-Unionism, and continued to be the creed of the Jacobites. After 1685 James VII and his exiled successors were Catholic and they naturally enjoyed Catholic support, thus providing their enemies with a useful propaganda weapon.

Catholic clans were the MacDonalds of Clanranald and its cadet branches of Glengarry, Knoydart and Morar, the MacDonalds of Keppoch and the MacNeils of Barra. Branches of the Clan Donald which were not Catholic were Episcopalian. Catholicism was predominant among the Gordons, Chisholms, Farquharsons and the Grants of Glenmoriston, but not their chiefs. Apart from these, in so far as it is possible to generalize, the Jacobite clans were the Stewarts of Appin, the Camerons, Drummonds, Frasers, MacRaes, MacGillivrays, Mac-Beans, Mackintoshes, MacKinnons, MacLachlans and Menzies. Nominally Jacobite, though less consistent in their support, were the MacDonalds of Sleat, the MacKenzies, MacLeods, MacDougalls, MacGregors and Sinclairs. The clans which supported the Union, the Hanoverian succession and the Whig supremacy were the Campbells, Munroes, MacKays, Sutherlands, Rosses, Buchanans and Colquhouns. Yet within these clan alignments there were divisions. As in all civil wars, larger loyalties divided families, or families might divide themselves for reasons of self-interest: a chief might stay at home 'loyal' to the government, and send his son 'out' with the Rising, so that whichever cause won, the clan could claim to have supported it.

Consistency was not found even in the three predominant clans. The Gordons were Royalist, but rivalry between the second Marquess of Huntly and the Marquess of Montrose limited Gordon support for the Royalist cause; Huntly's execution in 1649 was rather for his enmity to the Covenant than for his support for the King. The first Duke of Gordon held Edinburgh Castle for James VII for a year after the Revolution, and died in 1716. His heir, Alexander second Duke of Gordon, as Marquess of Huntly, joined the Earl of Mar in 1715 and was present at Sheriffmuir, after which he retired from the Rising, and the following year surrendered to the Earl of Sutherland, who was employed in suppressing the Rising. The third Duke remained aloof from the Rising of 1745, but his younger brother, Lord Lewis Gordon, fought for Prince Charles Edward and survived Culloden to escape to France, where he died in 1754.

The MacKenzies' support of the Royalist and Jacobite cause was somewhat more fluctuating. The second Earl of Seaforth originally supported the Covenant, but later joined Charles II in exile; his son joined the Earl of Glencairn's rebellion against Cromwell in 1653. The fifth Earl of Seaforth took part in both the Risings of 1715 and 1719. The misfortunes of the MacKenzies in three disastrous enterprises deterred the clan as a whole from supporting Prince Charles Edward though the Earl of Cromartie, chief of the cadet branch of Seaforth, joined him. After the Rising, Cromartie was brought to trial with Lords Kilmarnock and Balmerino and, unlike them, had the good fortune to be reprieved at the last moment. His abject explanation of his support for the Rising was that he had been 'seduced from his loyalty in an unguarded moment by the acts of desperate and designing men'. Lord Kilmarnock's engagingly frank explanation has already been quoted. Lord Balmerino said simply that Charles Edward was 'so sweet a Prince that flesh and blood could not resist following him' and concluded his life with the words 'O Lord, reward my friends, forgive my foes, bless King James, and receive my soul'. Not many adherents of either cause expressed such unambiguous fidelity.[14]

The adherence of the Campbells to the Covenant, the Revolution, the Union, the Hanoverian succession and the Whig supremacy was remarkably steadfast, though not completely unbroken, since the first Earl of Breadalbane (Sir John Campbell of Glenorchy, created Earl of Breadalbane in 1681) joined the Earl of Mar in 1715. Nor did adherence to the ultimately victorious cause preserve the Campbells from occasional disasters: the executions of the eighth Earl and first Marquess in 1661, and of the ninth Earl in 1685. However, the power of the Campbells and their steadfastness in their chosen cause stimulated the western clans who feared the Campbell hegemony to support the Stuarts; this motive, in the opinion of the Highland historian W.R. Kermack, was so much more powerful than adherence to Episcopalianism or respect for the Divine Right of Kings that had the western clans been Moslems or Buddhists it would have aligned them with the Stuart cause (an echo of Lord Kilmarnock's invocation of an alien creed to explain his adherence to a cause for which he cared nothing).[15] Anti-Campbell sentiment was so strong that the execution of the ninth Earl of Argyll probably won for James VII far more Highland support than he deserved for any sympathy which he had shown the Gaels.

That the support for either cause by a particular clan can be expressed in terms of the decision made by its chief illustrates the autocratic power which the chief wielded. General Wade, in the *Report on the Highlands* which he wrote in 1724 described the clansmen as owing their chief 'A Servile and Abject Obedience', so that if a chief decided to join a Jacobite Rising, or sent his son 'out', the clansmen were perforce obliged to go. However, the chief was not a complete autocrat; the greatest men of the clan, his own relatives, would act as his council, and in such an important matter as a Rising might incite him to join it, or endeavour to restrain him. But once the decision had been reached there was no consultation of the clansmen. By 1745, however, the memory of previous Jacobite defeats and, in particular, of the losses and suffering which had resulted from defeat in 1715, made some clansmen reluctant to show the automatic obedience which their chiefs expected. These might be 'forced out' by the threat of burning their houses or 'houghing' (hamstringing) their cattle; the consequence was that clansmen who left their homes so reluctantly sought the first opportunity to desert. MacDonald of Barisdale tried the pleasanter method of bribing his clansmen out with offers of free whisky but desertion followed when supplies ran out.

The Jacobite armies were continuously fluctuating, as new recruits were gained, as reluctant ones deserted, or as men paid return visits to their homes to leave their plunder or bring supplies to their families. In consequence, historians have found it difficult to estimate Jacobite numbers. In 1724 General Wade estimated the total military power of the Highlands at 22,000 men, of whom some 10,000 might be expected to support the Government. On this reckoning, even some years after the Rising of 1715, the advantage still lay with the Jacobites. The Earl of Mar's army may have reached 12,000 at the maximum but Prince Charles Edward's army in 1745 never exceeded 8,000 and by some estimates never exceeded 6,000.[16] W.R. Kermack sensibly remarked that 'doubtless from first to last a good many more Highlanders fought under these commanders than were at any one time serving with their standards'.[17] But the smaller numbers involved in 1745, and the incidence, however limited, of 'forcing out', suggests that enthusiasm for the Jacobite cause had reached its zenith in 1715, and declined thereafter.

Jacobitism gained overtones of nationalism in 1707 when the Union of Parliaments threatened the extinction of Scotland's national identity, for the exiled Stuarts as Scotland's ancient royal line provided a focus for nationalist sentiment. The Hanoverian succession in 1714 enhanced the legitimist fervour of the Jacobites, and Gaelic Jacobite poetry is suffused with hatred of the Hanoverians as a dynasty of usurpers. The reprisals taken on the Jacobites after Culloden led the poet Alasdair Mac Mhaighstir Alasdair to contrast the brutalities committed in the name of George II with the fatherly care which he imagined would characterize James VIII:

> O, thin's the string, King George,
>   On which thou'st harped to win three realms;
> And false the Act which clad
> Thee with the kingship over us;

Full fifty folk and more
   Have better claims, and truer blood
Than thou, in Europe's continent.
Remote and bent and weak
   The female branch from which thou camest,
Far distant on the tree . . .

The child that's not his own,
   Though it were cut in twain
Its pain affects him not,
His heart untouched, unmoved,
And likewise would it be
   If every Briton suffered death
For no cause at all;
Since he owns not the child,
   The man who's not its father is
Unmoved to clemency.

Hasten, O kindly James,
   Thou art our King and earthly sire,
Under the holy, heavenly One;
Pity the folk, be kind,
And since thou own'st the child,
   Put end to gallows and to axe
By which we lose our heads;
Put thy flock into fold,
   Allow no more our harrying
O'er hill and mountainside . . .[18]

Alasdair followed this poem with a *Brosnachadh do na Gaidheil* (An Incitement to the Gaels), urging them to make ready to fight for Prince Charles Edward again. But the defeat of the Rising of 1745, despite its initial promise, had demonstrated to any possible European allies the narrow base of Jacobite support even within the Highlands. After the expulsion of the Prince from France in 1748 the decline of Jacobitism was irreversible.

After the Restoration, with the dissolution of the Cromwellian Union, England and Scotland once again had separate military establishments, until the Union of 1707. Charles II's popularity in the Highlands owed something to the withdrawal of the English garrisons, the dismantling of the fort at Inverness and even more to the restitution of the heritable jurisdictions, which survived until 1747.

A renewed effort to discipline and demilitarize the Highlands followed the Revolution. In 1690 the Williamite General MacKay rebuilt the Cromwellian fort of Inverlochy, replaced its earthworks with stone walls, and renamed it Fort William. In 1713 a barracks was built at Inversnaid on Loch Lomond. After the Rising of 1715 the Ruthven Barracks was built near Kingussie and the fort of Inverness was rebuilt and named Fort George. Another fort, built at the Kilchuimin at the head of Loch Ness, was later enlarged and renamed Fort Augustus and in 1722 the Bernera Barracks was built in Glenelg, on the Sound of Sleat. All these forts and barracks and also Duart Castle, Isle of Mull, were occupied by regular troops, who formed in effect an army of occupation.

In 1724 General Wade was appointed Commander-in-Chief in Scotland; to him fell the hitherto unachieved task of disarming the Highlands. The defeat of the Rising of 1715 had been followed by a disarming act which had been widely disobeyed; a second act of 1725 gave Wade wider powers, whereby weapons which had not been surrendered in obedience to the first act could be searched for and seized. For these purposes, isolated garrisons were of little use, so between 1725 and 1739 Wade built a network of roads to facilitate troop movements. Wade's roads which covered 250 miles and included 42 bridges, linked Inverness to Fort William, through the Great Glen; led from Inverness by Dalwhinnie and Blair Atholl to Dunkeld, and from Crieff to Aberfeldy, Dalwhinnie and Fort Augustus. The stretch between Dalwhinnie and Fort Augustus included a magnificent feat of engineering, the series of hairpin bends by which the road ascended to 2,500 feet to cross the Pass of Corrieyairack. This in 1745 proved of great assistance to the advance of Prince Charles Edward.[19]

During the reign of William and Mary some independent companies of Highland soldiers had been raised from clans which accepted the Revolution regime, to assist in keeping order in the Highlands, but all had been disbanded by 1717. General Wade requested their revival and accordingly four new companies were raised in 1725, and two more were added in 1729. They were collectively known as 'the Watch', 'the Highland Watch', or in Gaelic *Am Freicaedan Dubh* ('the Black Watch'). They owed their Gaelic name to their dark blue, black and green tartan, a perfect night camouflage, a uniform which distinguished them from the *Saighdean Dearg*, the English 'Redcoats' of the regular army.[20] In 1739 Wade was deprived of his Highland soldiers by a Government order that the six existing companies should be expanded to ten and formed into a regular regiment of foot. In 1740 they duly became the 43rd regiment of the line (later renumbered as the 42nd), always known as the Black Watch. In 1743 they were marched to London, where they mutinied at the rumour that they were to be sent to the American Plantations.[21] However, they were destined for Europe. At the Battle of Fontenoy in 1745 they fought with conspicuous valour in one of the last actions which witnessed the Highland Charge. After their return from the Continent, during the last phase of the Jacobite Rising, they were stationed in the south of England, in readiness to resist the anticipated French invasion, which did not take place.[22]

Meanwhile General Wade had been promoted Field Marshal and appointed Commander-in-Chief in England. In the hope that he would defeat the Jacobites a new verse was added to the Hanoverian National Anthem:

> God grant that Marshal Wade
> May by thy mighty aid
> Victory bring.
> May he sedition hush
> And like a torrent rush
> Rebellious Scots to crush.
> God save the King.

Wade led an army to intercept Prince Charles Edward's invasion of England, and was outmanoeuvred, a muted ending to his distinguished career. The man honoured as the conquering hero was the Duke of Cumberland, whose name was forever disgraced by the atrocities which he ordered after his victory at Culloden.

After the defeat of the last Jacobite Rising the Highlands ceased to be a theatre of war and became a reservoir of military manpower. The failure of France to send assistance to the Jacobites in 1745 led some Highland chiefs to blame Prince Charles Edward, who had always assured them of its imminent arrival, and others to blame the perfidy of the French in failing to support him. Both views led to complete disillusionment concerning French or any other foreign support for a

143

future rising. Such disillusionment opened the way to reconciliation between erstwhile Jacobites and the British Government: Jacobite chiefs and chieftains who had fought against the Hanoverians could mend their fortunes by fighting for them in foreign fields; and clansmen, who had no profession but that of arms, and no prospects but those of starvation or stagnation in the demilitarized and overpopulated Highlands in the later eighteenth century, were willing to follow them. In the second half of the eighteenth century and the opening years of the nineteenth there were plenty of opportunities: in the Seven Years' War; in America, first against the French and then in the American War of Independence; in India; in the West Indies; and in the Napoleonic Wars.

The first of the Highland regiments with Jacobite antecedents was Fraser's Highlanders, raised by the Master of Lovat, the eldest son of the villainous and devious Simon Fraser, eleventh Lord Lovat, who had been executed for his support of the Rising of 1745. Lord Lovat might have deserved to have lost his head for many reasons but steadfast Jacobitism would not have been the best of them; however, it was certain that his son had been reluctant to be sent 'out' with the clan. Through the good offices of the third Duke of Argyll, young Lovat was offered the command of the first of the Highland regiments raised for service in America, in 1756. Some 600 of his recruits were raised from the Lovat estates, and 800 from surrounding districts.

According to a recent historian of the Highland regiments, between 1725 and 1800 thirty-seven units of Highlanders were raised for British service. This excluded twenty-six regiments of fencibles, whose terms of service were for home defence; but the fencibles 'generally showed a willingness to fill up the thinning ranks of regiments serving abroad'.[23] Highland regiments were frequently raised, disbanded, re-embodied, and renumbered, according to the exigencies of war, so that the history of all of them is an intricate story. However, of the twenty Highland regiments raised between 1777 and 1800, nine remained on the military establishment in 1820. These were: Lord Seaforth's Highlanders, raised 1778 (78th, and later 72nd); the Perthshire Highlanders, raised 1789 (73rd); the Highland Regiment of Foot, raised 1787 (74th); the Stirlingshire Regiment, or Abercromby's, raised 1787 (75th); The Highland Regiment of Foot, raised 1793 (78th); the Cameronian Volunteers or Cameron Highlanders, raised 1783 (79th); the Argyllshire Highlanders, raised 1794 (98th, and later 91st); the Gordon Highlanders, raised 1794 (100th, and later 92nd);

the Sutherland Highlanders, raised 1800, (93rd).[24]

When the earlier Highland regiments were recruited the Dress Act was still in force and the fact that it excluded military personnel disposed many young Highlanders who were reluctant to abandon Highland dress to enlist in the regiments. When Highland regiments were first recruited the kilt was worn by all ranks, though later many variations of dress were introduced, often for climatic reasons in regiments serving abroad. In most of the Highland regiments the sombre tartan of the Black Watch was accepted as the standard military sett, though it was differenced with fine overchecks of red and white in the case of the Seaforth Highlanders, and yellow in that of the Gordon Highlanders. Colonel Alan Cameron of Erracht, who raised the Cameron Highlanders, came of Jacobite stock and objected to his men wearing the Government tartan, or any variant of it. The regimental tartan was designed by his mother, a daughter of MacDonald of Keppoch, and was based on a sett associated with her family; it is known as Cameron of Erracht, and is one of the few tartans with a clear provenance.

By some historians the Highland regiments are seen as victims of a cynical British Government, deployed in the most insalubrious theatres of war with complete disregard for their losses. On the other hand, they have been seen as the means of preserving Highland traditions of military honour, Highland dress and Highland music, and of exporting them, in a period during which they were suffering repression at home, and might have been extinguished. While the British Government might have been indifferent to Highland losses, the Highlanders found both military pride and cultural identity in their regiments. The survival of pipe music, in particular of *Ceol Mor*, is associated with the Highland regiments.

As a result of the battle honours won by the Highland regiments in the late eighteenth and early nineteenth centuries: 'In place of doubt there grew up, particularly around the kilted regiments, an aura of heroism and romance. In the popular interest and enthusiasm surrounding Wellington's army, and especially the battle of Waterloo, the Highlanders assumed in the eyes of the British public an entirely new status . . .'[25]

The metamorphosis of the Highlander from Wild Scot to national hero was complete.

THE HIGHLANDS
TRANSFORMED

God and Sanct Petir was gangand be the way
Heiche up in Ardgyle quhair thair gait lay.
Sanct Petir said to God in a sport word
'Can ye not make a heilandman of this horss tourd?'
God turnd owre the horss turd with his pykit staff,
And up start the helandman blak as ony draff.
Quod God to the helandman 'Quhair wilt thow now?'
'I will doun in the lawland, Lord, and thair steill a kow'.[1]

Ho! Ho! Ho! the foxes!
Would there were more of them,
I'd give heavy gold
For a hundred score of them!

My blessing with the foxes dwell,
For that they hunt the sheep so well!

Ill fa' the sheep, a grey-faced nation,
That swept our hills with desolation!

Who made the bonnie green glens clear,
And acres scarce and houses dear;

The grey-faced sheep, who worked our woe,
Where men no more may reap or sow . . .[2]

'I have lived to woeful days,' said an old Argyllshire chieftain in 1788, whose words were reported by Sir Walter Scott, 'when I was young the only question asked concerning a man's rank was how many men lived on his estate; then it came to how many black cattle it could keep; but now they only ask how many sheep the lands will carry.'[3]

This was a succinct summary of the changes which he had witnessed in his lifetime, assuming that his span had more or less matched the century. It indicated a change in the character of a Highland chief, which had converted him from a warlord into a landlord. It also implied that the land had been depopulated in favour of the sheep. There was some truth in this, though like most truisms it was an oversimplification. Perhaps it would have been truer to say that though in the past the measure of a chief's rank or status had been the number of men living on his land, the number of cattle would always have been the measure of his wealth.

Cattle and people had coexisted in the Highlands since Neolithic times. The early Celts had assessed their wealth in terms of their cattle: so many cattle could provide a ransom or a dowry, or define the value of an object. Celtic tribes increased their wealth by stealing their neighbours' cattle and the deeds of valour which warriors performed in the course of cattle raids were matters for pride. One of the ancient epics of the Gaels, the *Tain Bo Cualnage* ('The Cattle Raid of Cooley') concerned the theft of a marvellous bull from the herds of Medb or Maeve, Queen of Connaght, and the ensuing warfare.[4] The cattle raiding which continued in the Highlands down to the middle of the eighteenth century was rendered heroic by its association with the deeds of bygone heroes. The old Argyllshire chieftain quoted by Scott was not lamenting that Highland chiefs had taken to keeping cattle, which they had always done, he was lamenting that they had taken to trading in cattle instead of 'lifting' them. In his eyes, a chief's status suffered when his cattle were counted to assess his rank, while his warriors were counted no longer, since trade had made them obsolete. With the coming of sheep the situation seemed even worse, for the men had become superfluous population.

The old cattle of the Highlands were called 'black cattle' because black was the predominant colour, but it was not the only colour, for the cattle could also be russet, brown or dun, though black was always preferred. Their coats were thick and shaggy, and glossy when they were in good condition, and their long sweeping horns were admired for 'a clear, green and waxy tinge'. They were no bigger than present day Channel Island cattle, but their small size was considered suitable for their terrain. According to a description dating from 1811, 'Heavy cattle cannot seek their food in bogs and marshes, leap over ravines, rivers and ditches, or scramble through rocks, and in the faces of cliffs and precipices, like the present breed, which is almost as active and nimble as a chamois goat.'[5] Black cattle might be required to do all these things, when being hastily driven across country in the course of a raid. The Highland cattle of today, though descendants of the black cattle, are much more massive beasts and the predominant colours are now russet and brown but their shaggy coats and splendid horns suggest the appearance of their ancestors.

The immense importance of cattle to the Highlanders is suggested not only by the epics, folk tales and clan traditions in which they figured but also by the superstitions connected with them and the charms and spells which were used to help their recovery from diseases. When cattle were sick or injured they were sometimes thought to have been shot by the fairies with 'elf-bolts'. These were flint arrow heads but as the Highlanders knew nothing of their remote ancestors they imagined a supernatural origin for these ancient weapons. An 'elf-bolt' might be mounted in silver as a charm, to fend off the harm which others, in the hands of the fairies, might inflict. The Highlanders' belief in the magical properties of stones led them to impute to certain remarkable pebbles or crystals the power to cure diseases of both people and cattle. The Stewarts of Ardvorlish possessed a famous *Clach Dhearg* ('Red Stone'); the Stewarts of Ardsheal a rock-crystal globe mounted in silver; and the Campbells of Glenorchy an oval crystal, perhaps once part of a reliquary, set in silver and surrounded with pieces of coral. These charms were dipped in water, to the accompaniment of a prayer or incantation, and the water was then believed to possess healing properties.[6] Fire could also protect and heal. At Samain (1 November) and Beltainn (1 May), eighteenth century Highlanders still lit festal fires and on the latter festival drove their cattle between them, to protect them from evil spirits. If the disaster of a murrain, or cattle plague, occurred, all the household fires throughout the affected area would be extinguished, and a 'need-fire' kindled by friction of wood; from this new fire all the hearths were rekindled, and from this rite the recovery of the cattle was expected.

The value of the cattle on the whole ensured their good treatment; those who stole them might drive them hard to secure possession of them, but thereafter they took care of them. Rare examples of cruelty to cattle, such as 'houghing' them or 'puttin furth of thair ene' were reported to the Privy Council and these were probably occasioned by malice against the owners; normally the complaints to the Council, of which there were many concerning cattle, were simpy of theft. Cattle theft was so commonplace within the Highlands, along the Highland foothills and in the adjacent parts of the Lowlands that a satirical Lowland Scots poem of the sixteenth century represented the Highlander as a cattle thief from the moment of his creation.

Many cattle raids, especially those on a small scale, were committed under cover of darkness, but larger forays of the heroic kind could be ostentatious and provocative. For example, in 1592 Stewart of Ardvorlish with some confederates was accused of driving off 160 head of cattle 'with twa bagpypis blawand before thame'. The Battle of Glenfruin, between the MacGregors and Colquhouns, was provoked by the MacGregors' theft of 600 cattle. Cattle raiding remained ineradicable, not only because of ancient traditions of which no clan was ashamed, but because 'broken men' like the MacGregors depended on it for their livelihood. In the late seventeenth and early eighteenth centuries some chiefs and chieftains took advantage of the situation by running protection rackets. They levied 'blackmail' (reputedly the first application of this ill-omened word) in return for which they guaranteed to prevent the theft of cattle or to assure their return. Rob Roy MacGregor and his nephew MacGregor of Glengyle levied quarterly payments from the 'heritors' (landowners) of the Lennox, to protect their cattle; MacDonald of Barisdale received an income from Ross-shire, Strathglass and the Aird; MacDonald of Lochgarry from Strath Errick, and Cluny MacPherson from the whole of the country between Loch Ness and Dundee.[7] The Independent Companies were supposed to suppress cattle raiding but there was an unsavoury rumour that some of their captains employed half of their men to raid the cattle and the other half to return them to their owners. If there was any truth in this it implied that genuine cattle raiding was on the decline.

Alongside unlawful cattle raiding, lawful cattle trading developed, though the two were long intermingled. Cattle intended for markets were uplifted from their breeding grounds and driven to market by the raiders. This problem was reported by General Wade in 1724. To protect the cattle trade, drovers were exempted from the Disarming Act which followed the rising of 1715 and which Wade's best efforts failed to enforce. In 1725 General Wade issued 230 licences to 'foresters, drovers and dealers in cattle', permitting them each to carry a gun a sword and a pistol, and similar licences were granted during and after the rising of 1745.

Cattle trade between Scotland and England had existed during the Middle Ages in spite of the incredible difficulties caused by constant warfare and the discouragement of the Scottish government, which tended to see the export of livestock as more likely to cause hardship in Scotland than to generate prosperity. Trade gradually became easier following the Union of Crowns of 1603. After the Restoration positive encouragement was given to cattle breeding and droving, and drovers themselves began to be recognized as 'part of the commercial life of the country and as forming a body of men engaged in an honourable trade'.[8] But the troubled times which continued until the defeat of the rising of 1745 ensured that drovers had to continue to carry arms, and be prepared to use them. The change from raider to drover could be a short step; perhaps a change of occupation in one man's lifetime, or within one family a change between one generation and the next. Similar qualities were required of both raider and drover: familiarity with the ways of cattle, intimate knowledge of the countryside, and readiness to face loneliness and hardship.

The Highlands contain little agricultural land, and plenty of grazing. As the population increased food production became increasingly problematical, while there was always a plentiful supply of cattle which could be brought into good condition by the end of the summer but which could not be fed over the winter. By exporting their cattle in the autumn the Highlanders were able to buy extra supplies of oats and barley, the very means of subsistence which their own increasingly subdivided lands could no longer provide. In the course of the eighteenth century the Highland economy became dependent on the cattle trade.

All over the Highlands and throughout the Isles during the summer months deals were arranged. Drovers toured the remotest areas, often announcing their arrival through notices given out in church. In this way the poorest clansmen who owned only a few beasts were enabled to sell them locally or entrust them to a drover who would negotiate for them at a cattle sale or 'tryst'. There were trysts at Broadford in Skye, at Muir of Ord at the head of the Beauly Firth and at Pitmain in the upper valley of the Spey. At these trysts the greater cattle dealers would buy from the lesser ones, or arrange with drovers to take their cattle on to the bigger trysts at Crieff in the Highland foothills of Perthshire, or at Falkirk. In the first half of the eighteenth century the greatest of the trysts was at Crieff; in the second half the balance had shifted in favour of Falkirk, to convenience the increasing number of English cattle dealers who came north to do business. By 1777, 30,000 head of cattle were sold at Falkirk at three sales in August, September and October; by 1850 the number had grown to 150,000.[9] Thenceforward there was a steady decline, accelerating in the last years of the nineteenth century. The cattle trade with England had dwindled so much by the turn of the century that the Falkirk Tryst was held for the last time in 1901, though as late as 1916 Highland drovers could be seen driving a few cattle to market in Stirling.[10]

In the eighteenth century bringing the cattle from the remotest breeding grounds to the local trysts involved dangerous journeys, even without the additional threat of having the cattle stolen. Cattle from the Outer Hebrides were ferried across the Minch in small boats, a hazardous voyage whose success depended on choosing fair weather. One of the last surviving drovers, whose reminiscences were given to the historian Dr Eric Cregeen, described how a thick layer of birch branches would be laid in the bottom of the boat before the cattle were loaded; he was not describing the Minch crossing but something similar would have been required wherever cattle had to be ferried.[11] The half-wild cattle were easily frightened by the sound of their own hooves clattering on boards and this sound often caused a stampede if cattle were obliged to cross a wooden bridge. Highland cattle were strong swimmers and, where possible, swimming them was found easier than loading them on to boats or herding them across bridges. Cattle would swim from Skye to the mainland at Kyle Rhea, they would swim across the arm of a sea loch, or the narrowest part of an inland loch, or they would cross a river by swimming it or by plunging through a ford. The cattle would be driven into the water by the drovers' dogs, and urged on by wild cries which made them fear to turn back. If the water were deep an armed drover would hold his pistol in his teeth, raise his gun above his head in one hand, seize a cow's tail with the other, and be pulled across loch or river by the swimming cow.

Overland the drove roads followed the easiest routes, broad straths or narrow watercourses, along which the long lines of beasts moved like rivers themselves, spreading out where the land permitted, massing close together through narrow gorges. The slow plodding or crowded pounding of their hooves has left its own marks on the landscape. When the cattle moved over hard, high ground the routes existed in the drovers' knowledge rather than in features of the landscape. At night the drovers sought grassy areas to rest the cattle.

An upland meadow, a natural hollow, the floor of a corrie, or some other suitable area would become a recognized 'stance' or resting place. Having been much manured, erstwhile stances are often identifiable by their vivid greenness. Beside the stance the drovers would lie down to sleep in the open air, wrapped in their plaids, instinctively aware even in sleep of the movements of the cattle. The restless animals could not simply be ignored at night; on the early days of a journey they might attempt to break away and make for home; later they might be disturbed by the proximity of strange cattle as more beasts were added to the drove; at any time they might be excited by bright moonlight. When a large drove was attended by a number of drovers, one might be set to watch while the others slept, but the drovers were so accustomed to nights in the open that even when they came to a stance with an inn beside it where some might find a night's lodging, there were many who were loath to sleep under a roof.

When the cattle left the natural drove routes for man-made roads it was necessary to shoe them if they faced a long journey. Since cattle have cloven hooves each shoe was formed of two small crescents of iron, each fixed by three hammer-headed nails, so that each cow required eight shoe-plates and twenty-four nails. But sometimes, to save both time and expense, only the outer edge of the hoof was shod. There was a busy cattle-smithy at Trinafour, on the main route to Crieff from the north; and at Kennethmont, Aberdeenshire, a famous smith named Robert Gall could boast of having shod seventy cattle in a day. Drovers who undertook the long journey from Crieff or Falkirk into England would need to have repairs done at roadside smithies, and some drovers carried a stock of replacements for cast shoes.

Most of the Highland cattle bought by English dealers were driven to the rich meadows of Norfolk where they were fattened up before being driven on to London and sold at Smithfield. The drovers followed the Great North Road (now the A1), which in the eighteenth century had in places broad stretches of grass on either side, on which the cattle could walk and graze. They would turn east at Grantham and go by way of Spalding and Wisbech to the Norfolk grasslands.[12] There the drovers' responsibility ended; they left the cattle and returned to Scotland by mail coach, by boat, or in the later nineteenth century, by train.[13] In England their route is marked by the names of inns at which they halted: the 'Drover's Inn' at Boroughbridge and at Wetherby; the 'Drover's Call' between Gainsborough and Lincoln; the 'Highland

Laddie' at Nottingham and at St Faith's near Norwich. Drovers, like sailors and gypsies, were touched with the romance which attends the wanderer but, unlike most wanderers, they were respected for being responsible for the wealth of others. For the most part they discharged their responsibility honourably, for the continuance of the trade depended on it.

The drovers of the late eighteenth and early nineteenth centuries often wore 'a course plaid of plain brown and white chequer', which would have been woven of undyed wool. Towards the end of the nineteenth century drovers were described as 'dressed usually in homespun tweeds which smelt of heather and peat smoke . . .'.[14] Some drovers, who were prosperous enough to have ponies, loaded them with home-made goods to sell on their journeys. In the late nineteenth century drovers were seen passing through Liddesdale in the Borders, knitting stockings as they went along. No clearer illustration of the change from a warlike to a peaceful society could be found than the contrast between the armed drovers of the eighteenth century and the strolling knitters of the nineteenth.

An obvious aspect of the transformation of the Highlands in the second half of the eighteenth century and the first half of the nineteenth was the gradual displacement of cattle by imported breeds of sheep. Yet there had always been a great many sheep in the Highlands, perhaps as many sheep as cattle. But while cattle had represented wealth and had been raided and traded for profit, sheep had been kept principally to supply basic needs, wool for clothing, milk and cheese which provided a high proportion of the Highlanders' diet. Chiefs and tacksmen might own large flocks of sheep but even the poorest Highlanders needed to keep a few.

The old Highland sheep are thought to have been descendants of the flocks of the Neolithic pastoralists. Dr I.F. Grant, who founded Am Fasgadh, the Highland Folk Museum, Kingussie, sought unsuccess-fully to find some examples of the breed, and feared that it had become extinct.[15] The Soay sheep, originating from the St Kilda archipelago and currently enjoying a revival of popularity, are of a different breed. The old Highland sheep were very small, only some fifteen to twenty pounds in weight. They might be any colour from near-black to pure white: brown, beige, cream and often parti-coloured. All but the darkest had white faces and pink noses, and their heads carried four or six horns. The sheep had a downy undercoat and a scattered topcoat of long silky hair. This spun into a hard, strong yarn. It was woven into a material known as 'hard tartan', which was extremely durable but rather comfortless, as the selvedge of the material was abrasive. It is a well-known story that Queen Victoria, when reviewing Highland soldiers, noticed that the men's knees were scratched by the edges of their kilts. She ordered that their uniform kilts should be woven in future of the soft worsted tartan which was being produced by commercial woollen mills. The wool of the old Highland sheep was not only hard, it was also scanty, partly because the little animals were regarded as delicate and were taken indoors at night, so there was no climatic incentive for a thick coat to develop. Sheep were treated by Highland families as domestic pets, cosseted as far as possible, and given names; but there was little food to spare for them over the winter and as a result of poor nutrition they were only capable of lambing on alternate years. Highlanders did not expect to eat mutton. After a lifetime of lambing, milk production and near starvation in winter, when death came the sheep were too emaciated to be edible. Their skins could be sewn together to make sacks, or stretched tight on frames and pricked with holes to be made into sieves. Their horns could be made into drink horns or powder horns or spoons; nothing of a sheep was wasted.

In about 1750 the discovery was made that sheep could be wintered out, not only surviving but thriving. The traditional story was that a Perthshire innkeeper had bought a few black-faced Linton sheep from the Borders and, since he was a drunkard, neglected to take them indoors. Their surprising survival encouraged enterprising flockmasters to make the same experiment deliberately and the sheep continued to thrive. Whether this story is true or not, a decade or so later sheep farmers from the Borders were leasing large tracts of land in Perthshire and breeding Linton sheep. Gradually their enterprise extended into Argyllshire, Inverness-shire, Ross-shire, Sutherland and Caithness. Commercial sheep farming was slower to reach the Hebrides and was not established in the Long Island until the mid-nineteenth century.[16] The Linton sheep had denser coats than the old Highland breed, but their wool was coarse. By the end of the eighteenth century the commercial woollen mills were demanding a finer type of fleece, which led to the introduction into the Highlands of Cheviot sheep and Leicester sheep. These were the breeds castigated by the poet Duncan Ban MacIntyre as:

> . . . a grey-faced nation
> That swept our hills with desolation

and their role in depopulating the Highlands will be discussed later in this chapter.

Besides cattle and sheep the Highlanders had always kept goats. But goats are destructive feeders and were probably far more responsible for deforestation in the Highlands than had ever been realized. When improving landlords in the later eighteenth century began replanting trees and introducing exotic species, goats became unpopular, and on many estates tenants were forbidden to keep them. As a result, many goats were turned loose and became wild; flocks of wild goats survive in several parts of the Highlands and in Galloway today. Pig keeping was never popular with the Highlanders, many of whom had an almost Hebraic horror of eating pork. This may derive from an ancient Celtic taboo, for among the Celts pigs had been sacred to the god Moccus, whose name is said to be commemorated by the Isle of Muck.

The horses and ponies used by the Highlanders were a native breed characterized by their grey or dun colour. Island ponies were smaller and lighter than mainland ones, which had probably been enlarged by cross breeding, though the predominant colours survived. The more stalwart animals were capable of pulling a plough and all were used to pull the wheelless carts or sleds with wooden runners which in trackless areas were used to bring in harvests or loads of peat or seaweed. Highland ponies were also used as both saddle and pack animals and would have been used by the mounted drovers. On the sporting estates of the nineteenth century they were loaded with the dead stags shot by deerstalkers and in this role they often appear in the Highland scenes painted by Landseer. Unlike the old Highland sheep, they were expected to fend for themselves and as a result were extremely hardy. The tiny Shetland ponies, which became so popular as children's first mounts in the Victorian period, are an entirely separate breed, believed to be aboriginal.

The Highlanders lived in the closest intimacy with their domestic animals, for Highland houses were shared by beasts and people. It seemed a primitive arrangement to sophisticated visitors to the Highlands, but it had obvious advantages: warmth was enhanced by being shared and it was preferable to attend to a calving cow or a

155

lambing ewe under the same roof than to struggle outside to attend to it in wild weather.

The design of houses varied over different areas of the Highlands and Isles, but a common trait was the adaptive use of local materials. It was said that if a local community acted together a new house could be built within a day. Stones for drystone walls could be found everywhere; timbers were the most valuable materials. On the west coast and in the Isles shipwrecks often provided building timbers and even such useful additions as complete doors. A typical Highland house would have double drystone walls and a roof supported on timber 'couples'. These might be formed of naturally bent branches, or of straight tree trunks or ships' timbers placed to form inverted V-shapes. The bases of the couples would be lodged against the lower courses of the inner wall. The crossing or summit of the couples would support the rooftree, laid lengthwise. An infilling of smaller branches or laths would support the thatch, which might be of sods, heather, straw or bracken. The thatch might be held in place by ropes of heather, the ends knotted with stones to assist in weighting it down. To some roofs a fringe of heather twigs was added to encourage the rainwater to run off. The space between the two thicknesses of drystone wall was infilled with sand or earth which could also absorb rainwater and help to keep the interior of the house dry. Thatching material was often bound into neat little bunches which overlaid one another like birds' feathers, attractive in effect and helping to create a watertight roof.[17]

A coupled house could be extended to any length required. A MacGregor chieftain who lived in one in the late fifteenth century must have had a substantial dwelling in which to entertain his clansmen and the bard who honoured him. As late as 1728 the minister of Carron, Easter Ross, lived in a coupled house 100 feet long:

> First there was a room called 'the chamber'. It had a fireplace, glazed windows, and a box-bed which formed the partition between it and the next room. In it the family sat and took their meals and any guests slept in the box-bed. The next two rooms were bedrooms for the family. Beyond that was the room used by the servants with the fire in the middle of the floor and the byre was beyond that.[18]

More modest houses accommodated the human inhabitants at one end and the animals at the other. The fire, often of peat, was in the centre of the house and a hole in the roof was intended for the escape of the smoke. But frequently the smoke failed to escape and filled the house, and rain dripped in, blackened by soot as it fell. *Snighe* was the Gaelic name for this inky liquid. An improvement was the introduction of the 'hanging chimney'. The hearthstone was laid against the wall and a wooden structure was placed above it, the upper end narrowed to form a chimney, the lower end widened to provide a smoke-hood above the fire. Eighteenth and nineteenth century travellers usually thought Highland houses insufferably squalid, but Dr I.F. Grant was a guest in one of the last to remain inhabited in the 1930s, and saw a beautiful interior: 'The rag rugs and the curtains of the box bed were all of subtle shades of faded red harmonizing with the glowing peat fire and contrasting with the warm darkness of the roof.'[19]

In Lewis a different type of house was built, which consisted of rooms divided into animal and human living quarters linked by little passage ways, all within an immensely thick surrounding wall. This construction recalls the prehistoric dwellings of Skara Brae. Within the entrance was a small room called the *fosgalen*, which might contain a quern for grinding corn and a stall for calves or lambs; a short passage led to a byre and living room, divided by a turf or wood partition; beyond, another passage led to a barn, which might also contain extra sleeping quarters. Little apertures in the surrounding wall prevented it from becoming completely airless and from time to time a hole had to be made in the wall of the byre to remove cattle droppings.

Highland houses were built in communities known as 'townships', often built by a group of local tenants who held their lands jointly from either a chief or a tacksman. In either case their conditions of tenure would require of them both rents – whether in kind or money – and onerous services. They did not enjoy security of tenure, but could be moved by the chief at will. This was not a threat as long as the chief wished to maintain a large following of armed clansmen; things changed to the tenants' disadvantage with the pacification of the Highlands in the eighteenth century. Townships grew in a random fashion. Houses were built as they were required and they seldom faced in one direction as in an urban or village street. When Highlanders moved, either willingly or under duress, they usually carried away their rooftrees and couples, leaving the drystone walls of the houses to rejoin the land. Thus the ruins of old Highland houses have either disappeared or require an expert eye to identify them.

The lands of a Highland township were worked on the principle of a commune, and the inhabitants were described by a late seventeenth century writer as a 'commonwealth of villagers'. The efficiency of the whole depended upon the capacity of the inhabitants to work together, and upon the honesty of their dealings with one another. It was observed that though cattle theft was common in the Highlands, theft of personal belongings was almost unknown.

Of the land pertaining to each township, part was retained as the 'mensal land' of the chief; part might be granted hereditarily by the chief to such office-holders as the Bard, the Harper or the Physician, who held their lands rent-free; part was held or rented nominally by the tacksmen, who sublet portions of the land to the tenants (unless, as previously mentioned, they leased it jointly from their chief). Some of a tacksman's tenants might be 'bowmen', who cared for a proportion of a tacksman's cattle and the pasture to maintain them; others were 'steel-bowmen', to whom the tacksman supplied both stock and agricultural implements. There were subsidiary grades of tenantry: 'cottars' and 'acremen', who, in return for small parcels of land for cultivation and grazing worked both for the tacksman and the subtenants. The humblest class of township inhabitants were the *scallags*, or farm servants, who provided four days' work a week for the tacksman, in return for which they received a small bit of agricultural land and grazing for one cow and her 'followers' (her calf or calves) and a weekly allowance of food while at work, four pairs of shoes a year, and a yearly wage of £1.

The subtenants' services to chief or tacksman included work with their horses in ploughing, harvesting and carrying corn to the mill, and personal manual work, such as spreading manure on the fields, cutting peats and repairing dykes. The labour services were all the more onerous for being in many cases nonspecific; sometimes tenants might be required to perform extra services such as bringing home a new millstone. Another heavy due was the obligation to provide subsistence contributions for local dignitaries or craftworkers whose work prevented them from farming themselves: the teacher, the smith, the tailor. After all this, the subtenants' labours and the fruits of those labours sustained themselves and their families.

Each township was unique. The Gaelic landmeasure was the *davach*, but this was a measure of productivity rather than of size. East of Drum Alban a *davach* was divided into four 'ploughgates', theoretically the area a team of horses or oxen was capable of ploughing but in practice a landmeasure which included both arable and pasture. In the western Highlands a quarter of a *davach* was a *ceathramh*, which means simply a quarter. The average township occupied one ploughgate or *ceathramh* or, in the Hebrides, a 'pennyland' and by the eighteenth century each of these landmeasures was supporting an ever-increasing number of people.

The arable land of each township was divided into 'infield' and 'outfield'. The infield was kept fertile with most of the manure of the farm and domestic animals, and was planted with crops of oats and barley, and a smaller quantity of flax, for linen. The outfield was 'tathed' by making enclosures on it with turf banks, enclosing the cattle within them for several successive nights, and then cropping these areas for so long as they remained fertile, so that different patches of the outfield were cropped successively. In the Hebrides, seaweed was also used to fertilize the land. Patches of cultivable land too small, or steep or stony for the township's plough team were dug with a *cas chrom* or footplough.

The agricultural land of the townships was divided into strips, so that each of the joint-tenants held an assortment of strips intermixed among the rest. The strips were reallocated, either annually or at agreed intervals, so that everyone from time to time had the use of better or poorer land. By the eighteenth century, in most parts of the Highlands, the reallocation had become a rarer event; in some places it did not occur, whereby tenants could receive the impression that continuous occupation had given them possession of the land, which unhappily for them proved not to be the case. The strips of farming, with their different crops of oats, barley and flax, divided by weed-grown ridges, made the township farms look 'like a piece of striped cloth'. This style of farming was known as 'run-rig', which may have been derived from the Gaelic *Rouin Ruith* ('division run'), though different terms were used in different areas of the Highlands and the Isles.

The arable land of the township and the common pasture land beyond it would be separated by the 'head dyke', a drystone wall or a turf dyke, to keep the cattle from the crops. It was a line of demarcation rather than an effective barrier and the children and young people of the township, night and day, were employed in watching the cattle and protecting the precious crops from their determined depredations.

In the late spring and early summer the cattle were driven from the township pastures to hill grazings which might be many miles distant. Here were the *airidhean* ('shielings'), stone huts in which the people lived while the cattle fattened on summer grass. The men cut peats, while the girls and women made cheese and butter; these would supply warmth and sustenance through the coming winter. At the end of summer, people and cattle returned to their townships: the people to bring in the harvest, the cattle to be gathered by the drovers, and driven to Crieff, Falkirk, and on into England.

Every activity was accompanied by singing. Men sang as they rowed *berlinns* and *lymphads*, or later, smaller boats from island to island; women sang as they reaped crops or 'waulked' (thickened) cloth and as they wove or spun. James Boswell commented that as he and Dr Johnson approached the shores of Raasay 'The music of the rowers was succeeded by that of the reapers'. Perhaps the most familiar impression of the Highland worksong is in a famous poem by Wordsworth:

> Behold her, single in the field,
> Yon solitary Highland lass,
> Reaping and singing by herself –
> Stop here, and gently pass.
> Alone she cuts and binds the grain
> And sings a melancholy strain.
> Oh listen! for the vale profound
> Is overflowing with the sound . . .

The remarkable thing about this poem is that the Highland lass was working alone. Work songs were intended to give the time to a band of workers but so ingrained was the habit of working in time to a song that the solitary reaper could not help singing even though she worked alone.

On light summer nights at the shielings, or on dark winter nights in the townships, the Highlanders told and retold the old stories which their remote ancestors had brought from Irish Dalriada. They told the old tales of Deirdre and Naiose, and of Fionn and Osgar and Oisin. They talked of the Fienne, now imagined as giants. They pointed out landmarks which located the stories: three standing stones which had supported Fionn's cauldron, or a green hollow in which Fionn's favourite white cow had lain down to rest. The heroic past and the supernatural present were all around them. They pointed out green mounds which they called *sitheans*, or fairy hills. These might be Neolithic burial mounds or Mesolithic shell middens, but to the

160

James V, who voyaged to Orkney and the Western Isles.

James VI, who promulgated the Statutes of Iona.

John Graham of Claverhouse, Viscount Dundee, the victor of Killiecrankie.

Prince James Francis Edward Stuart, to the Jacobites 'King James VIII and III'.

Prince Charles Edward Stuart in 1745.

An unknown Highland Chief, wearing the *feileadh mor*, the version of Highland dress which was the forerunner of the kilt.

A young woman of the Clan Matheson. McIan's rendering of the traditional Highland woman's dress described by Martin Martin. The boy is shown wearing *cuarans* or buskins of red deerskin.

Flora MacDonald wearing a tartan dress of fashionable cut.

Neil Gow, the Highland fiddler, wearing tartan breeches and stockings. He is shown similarly dressed, playing the fiddle, in David Allan's painting 'The Highland Wedding'.

Crofters planting potatoes in Skye. The men are using the *Cas Chrom*.

Crofters outside their houses in Cromarty.

A nineteenth-century deerstalker at rest.

Winter sports: skiers on the Glenshee ski-lift.

Highlanders they were the dwellings of the fairies, sinister beings who were known as the *daoine sith* ('Men of Peace'), because they were thought to be malevolent and dangerous, to be placated by being spoken of politely, just as the ancient Greeks had called the dread Furies the Eumenides ('Kindly Ones'), in the hope of placating them.

In the Highland townships each house in turn, or certain special houses, would be specified as the place where the ceilidh or storytelling was to be held. The *Fer an Tigh* ('Man of the House') acted as host, and invited each storyteller to speak in turn, or each singer to perform. With the transformation of the Highlands in the eighteenth century, these traditions faded, but fortunately the stories and songs were written down before the oral tradition had failed.

No society is ever static, but from the beginning of the eighteenth century to the middle of the nineteenth Highland society changed with unprecedented rapidity. The kin-based Celtic society of the Highlands, modified by feudalism, had produced a form of clanship which chiefs and clansmen alike believed to be based on immemorial tradition, though in reality the clans attained their greatest power and cohesion only in the sixteenth century. By the late seventeenth century the clan system was already under threat and it was disintegrating before the defeat of Jacobitism in 1746. The anonymous author of a pamphlet entitled 'The Highlands of Scotland in 1750' believed that there had been a noticeable decline of the 'Clannish Spirit' between the Glorious Revolution of 1688 and the Jacobite Rising of 1745. Symbolically, the last interclan battle, between the MacDonalds of Keppoch and the Mackintoshes at Mulroy, was fought in 1688. Thenceforward, government attempts to pacify the Highlands were continuously exerted. Though General Wade's disarming measures following the defeat of the Jacobites in 1715 appeared unsuccessful, the very much smaller forces recruited by Prince Charles Edward in 1745 suggest that overall Highland society had grown more peaceful in the intervening years. Thereafter the martial spirit of the Highlanders found a new outlet in the Highland regiments and clan armies ceased to exist. The decline and ultimately the disappearance of the 'clannish spirit' was the natural result, since the clans in their heyday had been essentially military organizations.

The Highland chiefs and chieftains of the late eighteenth century have been blamed individually and collectively for failing to defend the cultural and social traditions of the Gaels, or for seeking to defend or extend their own prosperity with complete disregard for their clansmen's welfare, while the clansmen have often been represented as the helpless victims of avaricious landlordism. But the transformation of the Highlands was not as simple as that: both chiefs and clansmen were responding to new economic and social pressures which, in the nature of things, were imperfectly understood.

The pacification of the Highlands was followed by a dramatic increase of population. In 1750 an unofficial but probably fairly accurate estimate gave a population of 337, 038, and the first official census of 1801 returned a figure of 381,576. By 1841 the figure had risen to 472,487.[20] The subsistence economy of the Highland townships was incapable of responding to rapid population growth such as this; either new methods of production had to be found, or the population had to provide for itself elsewhere. In a static and conservative society the result was widespread misery and dislocation.

A population of some 300,000 at the beginning of the eighteenth century is believed to have been static for some time, though this would be hard to prove. In a violent society a high birthrate was required to maintain population, the more so as there was also a high rate of infant mortality. Adam Smith's shocking estimate was that many Highland women bore more than twenty children and perhaps successfully reared no more than two. Pacification alone did not account for the sudden population growth. Young men of military age joined the Highland regiments and met their deaths in foreign wars instead of being killed on their home ground. But after the atrocities which followed Culloden there were no more massacres of noncombatants. The population growth was rather due to a lower level of mortality in normal conditions.

As early as 1715 inoculation against smallpox was practised in the Highlands, possibly as a development of folk medicine. A detailed account of the method dates from 1765:

I am assured that in some remote Highland parts of this country it has been an old practice of parents where children have not had the smallpox to watch for an opportunity of some child having a good mild smallpox that they may communicate the disease to their children by making them bedfellows of those in it and by tying worsted threads with the pocking material around their wrists.[21]

In 1774 Dr Johnson observed that on the Isle of Muck the disease had been 'disarmed . . . of its terrour' when the laird himself inoculated eighty of the inhabitants (half the population), charging them two shillings and sixpence each.[22] Whether or not many lives were saved by primitive methods of inoculation, by the end of the eighteenth century there was general faith in its efficacy.

Probably more effective in keeping alive people at the margin of subsistence was a simple improvement in nutrition, the introduction of the potato. First grown in South Uist in 1743, potatoes were soon introduced to Skye and thence to the mainland.

> Within thirty years of its acceptance in South Uist and Skye, the potato had become a staple and essential article of almost every Highlander's diet . . . and as in Ireland, the multiplication of the inhabitants was, in part at least, a consequence of this sudden, substantial, easy, but unreliable addition to the food supply.[23]

It was unfortunate that the population growth occurred when it was least desirable to the owners of the land; when chiefs no longer required a clan army, the last thing they wished for was a growing mass of unprofitable tenantry. Even had the chiefs retained the qualities which medieval bards had celebrated they would have been unable to preserve the lifestyle of the clans. At the beginning of the eighteenth century Martin Martin in his *Description of the Western Islands of Scotland* characterized MacNeil of Barra as the pattern of a chief, a true father of his people:

> When a tenant's wife . . . dies, he then addresses himself to Mackneil of Barray [sic], representing his loss and . . . desires that he would be pleased to recommend a wife to him, without which he cannot manage his affairs, nor beget followers to Mackneil . . . Upon this representation Mackneil finds out a suitable match for him; and the woman's name being told him, immediately he goes to her, carrying with him a bottle of strong waters for their entertainment at marriage, which is then consummated.[24]

MacNeil likewise found husbands for the widows of his clan, provided livestock for those whose cattle had died, and took the aged and infirm into his own household and maintained them for the rest of their lives. Such exemplary paternalism already seemed to be a survival of antique virtue. As the eighteenth century progressed MacNeil had few imitators. The general belief in a blood relationship between chief and clansmen faded and with it the chief's sense of paternal responsibility. However imperfect clan relationships may have been in reality, the myth that all chiefs had once behaved like MacNeil simultaneously created nostalgia for the past and fuelled resentment against chiefs who behaved like normal commercial landlords.

The metamorphosis of chief into landlord had been long in preparation. James VI's Statutes of Iona had introduced legislation intended to Anglicize Gaelic chiefs, by obliging them to send their sons or daughters to be educated in England or in the Lowlands. The legislation was at first resented, so that in the short term the results were slight; but in the long term the magnetic effect of the English court as the centre of power and the importance of an English education as the entrée to it were decisive. With increasing frequency Highland chiefs attended the English court, sent their sons to be educated at English schools and universities and married their daughters to English noblemen. One of the most influential marriages in Highland history was that of the Countess of Sutherland to the Marquess of Stafford. By education, by the pursuit of ambition through military or diplomatic service, in politics and by marriage, Highland chiefs or scions of the Highland aristocracy were introduced to different lifestyles and more luxurious standards of living, which they wished to imitate in their own homes. New buildings and their furnishings, clothes and small items of luxury all had to paid for and to the Highland chief ready money was in short supply. In the past, rents paid in kind had provided the raw materials for the bountiful hospitality on which the prestige of a Highland chief was founded; but these rents did not pay for a journey to Whitehall, for residence in London, or for the rebuilding or modernization of a castle. These aspirations demanded larger rents, paid in money.

Economic and social pressures would have converted Highland chiefs from warlords into landlords but political pressures dated the change. As early as 1599 James VI in *Basilikon Doron*, the book of advice which he wrote for his son Prince Henry, condemned heritable jurisdictions and advised his son whenever they fell vacant to 'dispone them never heritably againe'. The greater heritable jurisdictions, suppressed under the Commonwealth, were revived at the Restoration. They were finally abolished in 1747, after which the Highland aristocracy, now devoid of both armies and jurisdictions, became in the natural course of events an aristocracy of landlords.

The eighteenth century was an age of agricultural revolution; 'improvement' is too weak a word for its metamorphic changes in the use and appearance of the land. In the Highlands new farming methods were being introduced before 1745; by the end of the century they were widespread.

The second Duke of Argyll (1703–1743) introduced new systems of land tenure on his estates. With the advice of Duncan Forbes of Culloden, who acted as his commissioner, he systematically eliminated the tacksmen and leased farms to former subtenants who thenceforward held lands directly from Argyll on written leases and for a specified term of years. After the defeat of the Rising of 1745 a similar policy was followed by the Crown Commissioners who administered the annexed estates of exiled Jacobite chiefs. Thenceforward large-scale landowners terminated leases to their tacksmen, redeemed wadsets, and divided their lands into moderate-sized farms which they let to incoming farmers on fixed-term leases, on condition of their introducing agricultural improvements. The first and essential improvement was the levelling of the old 'rigs' and their dividing 'baulks', high ridges bristling with thistles and weeds, which had added to the striped effect of the old 'run-rig' system of farming. This levelling was often a condition of new leases, and it was followed by reorganization of field systems, introduction of crop rotation, and of new crops, such as turnips and hay, which provided adequate feed for livestock over the winter.

At the same time new land was brought into cultivation. On the floors of many straths ground was drained and converted into rich meadows. This eliminated the need to move cattle to high grazing grounds around the old shielings and some landowners divided these grazings into small crofts for the subtenants removed from former townships. Thus, over half a century, the appearance of many Highland straths and their neighbouring uplands changed completely: in the place of striped 'infields' and randomly patched 'outfields' appeared neat patterns of rectangular fields of different colours, according to their crops. Marshy valleys became green meadows, often surrounding handsome farmhouses. The haphazard group of drystone houses in the old townships were often replaced with a few neat cottages with mortared walls. The use of mortar was in itself an innovation in Highland houses; until the eighteenth century it had been used almost exclusively in building castles and churches.

Agricultural improvement displaced many subtenants, for one remaining power of Highland landlords was their power to remove their tenants at will. In some instances new and attractive accommodation was provided for them, in the form of planned villages, many of which survive and bear witness to the taste of their creators. The elegant little town of Inveraray, planned by the second Duke of Argyll to replace the old town partly burnt by Montrose, was built over the second half of the eighteenth century. Grantown-on-Spey was founded by Sir James Grant in 1766, and Tomintoul by the fourth Duke of Gordon in 1779. Other examples are Kenmore in the Perthshire Highlands, Plockton, Kyleakin, Poolewe and Ullapool on the West Coast, and Tobermory on Mull. For the most part the inhabitants of planned villages were intended to gain their livelihoods through cottage industries or fishing, supplemented by their crofts or gardens. Ullapool and Tobermory were both founded by the British Fisheries Society in 1788;* Sir James Grant intended Grantown to be a centre for linen manufacture. Tomintoul was apparently less industrious. According to the Revd John Grant in 1790: 'Tammtoul [*sic*] . . . is inhabited by thirty seven families, without a single manufacture . . . All of them sell whisky and all of them drink it. When disengaged from this business the women spin yarn, kiss their inamoratos, or dance to the discordant sounds of an old fiddle . . .'[25]

For more than half a century there was an assured livelihood for Highlanders in the kelp industry. Kelp, a golden seaweed which grows on the shores of the West Coast and the Western Isles, was burned to produce an alkali used in bleaching linen, and in glass and soap manufacture. Like many other Highland innovations kelp burning had been introduced before 1745 and increased enormously in the second half of the century, with the expansion of the industries in which it was used. An alternative source of alkali was the similarly produced barilla,[26] which was imported from Spain, but a duty was levied on it, and supplies were interrupted during the Napoleonic Wars, so that the price of kelp rose from £1 to £20 per ton. Owners of kelp-producing estates attracted labour by providing coastal crofts for kelp-burners. Though kelp-gathering, burning and ash-collecting was hard labour

---

* The fifth Duke of Argyll was the governor of the Society.

the industry provided a steady livelihood until supplies of barilla were imported again. The bottom fell out of the kelp market when the duty on barilla was removed in 1825, and brought destitution to those who had relied on kelp.

It also starkly illuminated the reality of the overpopulation which existed all over the Highlands; these coastal crofts had been supporting more people than their official tenants. It was typical of the Celts that they did not want to send their children out into the world to seek their own living; they preferred to share with them the existing opportunities of employment. When the industry failed the crofts were overcrowded with idle hands, threatened with starvation by the first failure of their potato crop. A similar situation existed in many inland straths, where holdings were described as having been 'frittered down to . . . atoms'.[27] The agricultural revolution distributed the farming population to some extent, providing a better standard of living for some, and dislocation and hardship for others. But it was the pastoral revolution of commercial sheepfarming which ejected surplus population, often with unnecessary inhumanity, in the notorious 'Highland Clearances'.

It is probably impossible to make a noncontroversial statement on the Clearances, for they have generated a vast and polemical literature. However, the basic fact was that the introduction of commercial sheepfarming from 1760 onwards led large scale sheep farmers from the Borders and the Lowlands to offer Highland landlords rents far in excess of those which they received from their existing tenants. For example, a shieling in Glengarry had been let to local tenants for £15 a year, but a sheep farmer was able to offer a rent of £250 for it. The tenants having been evicted, the rental of the Glengarry estate increased between 1768 and 1802 from £700 to over £5,000.[28] It was next to impossible for existing tenants to convert to sheepfarming, even by clubbing together to raise a competitive rent, for sheep themselves required investment of capital. At the end of the eighteenth century a flock of 600 sheep cost £376.[29] It was beyond the scope of most tenants to make the change even had they wished, but for the most part their limited experience prevented their even imagining the attempt. However, there were the rare exceptions. A great sheepmaster named Cameron, in Lochaber, who was a crofter's son, grazed 60,000 sheep on eleven farms, having amassed his initial capital as a drover.[30]

The Sutherland Clearances have been seen as a paradigm of the whole movement, with the first clearance of Kildonan in 1813, and the clearances of Strathnaver in 1814 and 1819 providing shocking examples of brutality committed against tenants who were reluctant to leave their homes. The irony of the whole tragic episode was that the evictions and house burnings to enforce them occurred within the framework of a policy of estate management and social engineering which the remote proprietors intended to be beneficial.

In 1785 Elizabeth, only surviving child of the seventeenth Earl of Sutherland, and Countess in her own right, married George Granville Leveson Gower, second Marquess of Stafford, who was created Duke of Sutherland in 1833, the year of his death. The Countess of Sutherland inherited between 800,000 and 1,000,000 acres, most but not all of Sutherland. Subsequent acquisitions increased her estates to 1,500,000 acres. Her husband inherited the great wealth of the Gower family and was bequeathed the fortune of his uncle, the canal-building Duke of Bridgewater. On his death, the diarist Charles Greville described him as 'a leviathan of wealth; I believe the richest individual who ever died'.[31] His fortune made it possible to apply the latest theories of improvement to the Sutherland estates, the intention being that the estates should yield profit while a tenantry facing starvation should become prosperous through new means of livelihood. The Staffords 'abhorred the many examples of wholesale evictions in the Highlands. These they regarded as the antithesis of their own policies.'[32] The metamorphosis of Sutherland was managed by the Staffords' commissioner, James Loch, who was implicitly trusted by the remote grandees who employed him and inflexible in his determination that the tenants should be forced to leave their homes and take a new livelihood, for their own good. Unconsulted, they were removed from the inland straths and settled on small crofts on the coast, to earn their living by the unknown and dangerous activity of fishing. Loch was insistent that the crofts should not be large enough to support them without recourse to fishing; they were to be forced to become industrious. Fishing stations at Helmsdale, Brora and Port Gower were intended to become new centres of coastal prosperity. The Sutherland Clearances resulted in the uprooting of some 10,000 people from the inland straths, far more than could make a living on the coasts, where prosperity proved more elusive than Loch had expected. As an effort at social engineering the experiment was a failure and it earned the 'Great Lady of Sutherland' a legacy of public hatred.

Fierce condemnations of the Sutherland Clearances were published in *Gloomy Memories of the Highlands of Scotland* (1857) by Donald MacLeod, of Strathnaver,[33] and in *Memorabilia Domestica* (1889) by the Revd Donald Sage. He described the immediate aftermath of the Strathnaver clearance of 1819:

> Of all the cottages the thatch and roofs were gone . . . the flames of the preceding week still slumbered among their ruins and sent up into the air spiral columns of smoke; whilst here a gable and there a long wall, undermined by the fire burning within them, might be seen tumbling to the ground, from which a cloud of smoke and then a dusky flame slowly sprang up . . . nothing could more vividly represent the horrors of grinding oppression.[34]

Some Highland landowners were more successful in introducing sheepfarming while making provision for their tenantry. A little earlier the fifth Duke of Argyll (d. 1806) established many sheep farms on his estates and at the same time introduced a wide variety of local industries. His enterprises included the development of Oban, with fishing, tanning and brewing, and the founding of a spinning school and a carpet factory at Inveraray. According to a modern historian 'Perhaps no man worked harder to build a modern economy with a variety of employment opportunities in the Highlands.'[35] However, in the depression which followed the end of the Napoleonic Wars, the sixth Duke was obliged to sell the Glenmorvern estate, in the Morvern peninsula, which was converted to sheepfarming, the tenants being evicted by the new proprietor, in 1824. Other landowers, less enterprising but conscientious towards their tenants, impoverished themselves in attempting to support the tenants in their traditional way of life. Clanranald was finally forced to sell the last of his estates in South Uist in 1838. Lord MacDonald's lands in Skye and North Uist were handed over to the management of trustees, who carried out the clearances he had resisted, in 1851.

In the second half of the nineteenth century many more Highland estates changed hands, when sheepfarming was no longer profitable, and landlords who had evicted their tenants were themselves forced out by economic pressures. Frequently the new owners were English aristocrats or industrialists, who were not looking for a profitable investment.

'To them,' wrote Professor Gordon Donaldson, 'a Highland estate . . . was a status sybol, it provided them and their guests with deer-stalking, game-shooting and salmon fishing, and on it they were prepared to spend lavishly. But deer forests required if anything fewer hands than sheep farms, and they led to further depopulation. Sometimes the removal of tenants did no more than rectify the previously grossly inflated population, but sometimes almost stripped an area of people altogether.'[36]

From the 1730s onwards there was continuous emigration from the Highlands. Often the emigrants were the most able and enterprising people who, seeing no opportunities of a better life in their own country, were bold enough to try their fortunes overseas.

In 1732 three Highlanders took grants of land in the Cape Fear district of North Carolina and one of them, Gabriel Johnston, became its Governor. Their influence drew more Highland emigrants to the region. In 1739 eighty-five families from Argyll, under the leadership of five former tacksmen, a total of 350 persons, settled there. These were the small beginnings of a Gaelic settlement. After the end of the Seven Years' War in 1763 soldiers who had served in the Highland Regiments in America were offered land grants, and they too settled there. By 1775 there were some 12,000 Highlanders in North Carolina, who formed a Highland colony, speaking Gaelic and wearing Highland dress. In 1771, after a 'black winter', 700 MacDonalds emigrated from Skye, and more followed in 1773. When Dr Johnson and James Boswell were in Skye in 1774, Boswell described the mood which the emigration had created:

> We had again a good dinner and in the evening a great dance . . . a dance which I suppose the emigration from Skye has occasioned. They call it 'America' . . . It goes on till all are set a-going, setting and wheeling round each other . . . It shows how emigration catches till all are set afloat. Mrs Mackinnon told me that last year when the ship sailed from Portree for America the people on the shore were almost distracted when they saw their relatives go off; they lay down on the ground and tumbled and tore the grass with their teeth. This year there was not a tear shed. The people on the shore seemed to think that they would soon follow.[37]

The outbreak of the American War of Independence in 1775 brought a temporary pause. But the war ended in 1783, and a severe

170

winter, bringing famine conditions in the Highlands gave impetus to a renewal of emigration.

By the opening of the nineteenth century emigration had become a business enterprise in which unscrupulous contractors crammed as many passengers as possible on board their ships, with little regard for their sanitary conditions or their safety. In 1801 over three thousand people were crowded aboard eleven ships which sailed from Fort William. In 1802 the victims of the second Glengarry clearance sailed for Nova Scotia. In 1803 came the settlement on Prince Edward Island, Canada, organized by Thomas Douglas, fifth Earl of Selkirk, which brought 800 Highlanders from Skye, Argyll, Ross and Inverness. Selkirk's second settlement, in the Red River Valley, Manitoba, had a heroic struggle for survival between 1811 and 1815, but was eventually successful.[38]

Selkirk's enterprises received little official support, as the Government had become anxious at the scale of emigration from the Highlands. In 1801 the great engineer Thomas Telford was appointed to report on the transport problems of the Highlands, with a view to finding a solution to them, part of his remit being to enquire into the causes of emigration and the means of preventing it. The result of the report was his commission to build a new system of roads and bridges in the Highlands and to construct the Caledonian Canal, with the excellent intentions of providing employment, encouraging industry, facilitating transport, and preventing emigration. The canal, Telford's most beloved project, was opened in 1822 and fully completed in 1847; but it was a failure in that it never carried the volume of traffic which it had been expected to generate. After the roads had served their initial purpose in providing employment, they may in fact have had the opposite effect to that which had been intended: they may have facilitated emigration from the Highlands, not beyond the seas, but to Lowland farms and industrial cities, where Highlanders were increasingly seeking work.

In the years following the Napoleonic Wars economic depression and the climate itself seemed to conspire to worsen the lot of the Highlanders. After 1820 food shortages became more frequent. In 1835 and 1836 the summers were so remarkably cold, wet and stormy that the crops failed. In 1836 there was a widespread failure of the potato crop on the West Coast and so much rain fell that the peat was too sodden to cut, causing a fuel crisis for the following winter. In 1845 an even more widespread potato blight led to starvation. The

Government provided £10,000 in relief and committees of private individuals raised another £80,000, an early example of the modern disaster fund. The relief money was used to provide meal, potatoes and blankets. In 1847 a Board of Destitution was set up, which organized the employment of Highlanders on another road-building project, the results of which were given the sombre name of 'Destitution Roads'.

As early as 1826 a Select Committee on Emigration had reported that there were areas of Scotland with redundant population, able-bodied members of which should be removed to the colonies. The hardships of the next two decades seemed to demonstrate the dangers of overpopulation. The Earl of Selkirk's old idea of the benefits of assisted emigration now gained official approval. In 1851 the Sherriff-Substitute of Skye founded the Highlands and Islands Emigration Society. The following year it was transformed into the Society for Assisting Emigration from the Highlands and Islands of Scotland, with the Under-Secretary at the Treasury, Sir Charles Trevelyan as its chairman, and Prince Albert as its patron. Between that date and its dissolution in 1859, it assisted 5,000 people to emigrate from the Highlands and Islands.

Up the middle of the nineteenth century population growth counteracted the attrition of emigration, but from then onward the population of the Highlands and Islands began an absolute decline from which it has never recovered. It has been estimated that between 1850 and 1950 the Highland population declined by at least 100,000.[39] For many people one of the chief attractions of the Highlands is their emptiness, their appearance of being unaffected by the more damaging activities of humanity. It requires a perceptive eye to discern that in many places the emptiness is not that of natural wilderness but of depopulation. The poet Helen B. Cruickshank, who described herself as a 'nonconformist' shooting guest, perceived the human tragedy imperfectly concealed by the beauty of the deer-forest:

> You promised I should see the golden eagle;
> Speckled brown adders basking in the sun;
> Proud antlered stags and herds of red hinds leaping
> Across great rocky corries rainbow-spanned;
> Peat mosses where three thousand feet on high
> The luscious scarlet averens are glowing;
> Pools where the otter stalks for salmon flesh;
> Heron, grey on a green sky, solemn floating.

But these I saw while you to butts were striding
Guided by servile gillies to your sport.
Fast-rooted bracken where the corn once ripened;
Roofless and ruined homesteads by the score;
Once-fertile gardens, mildewed, choked with weed,
Hemlock and nettle where the children played.

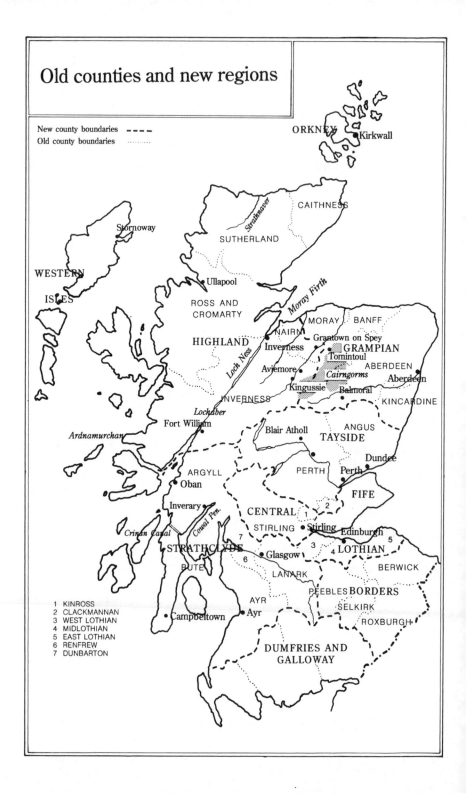

Old counties and new regions

New county boundaries — — — —
Old county boundaries ....

ORKNEY
Kirkwall

CAITHNESS

SUTHERLAND

Strathnaver

Stornoway

WESTERN

ISLES

Ullapool

ROSS AND
CROMARTY

Moray Firth

HIGHLAND

MORAY   BANFF

NAIRN

Grantown on Spey

Inverness

GRAMPIAN

Loch Ness

Tomintoul

INVERNESS

Aviemore

Cairngorms

ABERDEEN

Aberdeen

Kingussie

Balmoral

KINCARDINE

Lochaber

Fort William

Blair Atholl

ANGUS

TAYSIDE

Ardnamurchan

Dundee

PERTH   Perth

ARGYLL

Oban

FIFE

Inverary

CENTRAL

2

Crinan Canal

Cowal Pen.

STIRLING   Stirling

1

Edinburgh

5

STRATHCLYDE

7

3

LOTHIAN

BUTE

Glasgow

6

4

LANARK

BERWICK

PEEBLES BORDERS

AYR

SELKIRK

Campbeltown

Ayr

ROXBURGH

1 KINROSS
2 CLACKMANNAN
3 WEST LOTHIAN
4 MIDLOTHIAN
5 EAST LOTHIAN
6 RENFREW
7 DUNBARTON

DUMFRIES AND
GALLOWAY

8

THE HIGHLANDS DISCOVERED

If I had my home on Iona, and lived there upon melancholy as others do on their rents, my darkest moment would be when, in that wide space that is concerned with nothing but cliffs and seagulls, a curl of steam would suddenly appear, followed by a ship, and finally by a gay party in veils and frock coats, who would look for an hour at the ruins and graves and three little huts for the living, and then go away.[1]

The Highlands attracted the interest of countries beyond their immediate neighbours in the mid-seventeenth century, when they became a theatre of war in which some of the decisive conflicts of that troubled century were fought. From the beginning of the eighteenth century, as they grew more settled (apart from the violent though brief disturbances of the Jacobite Risings) increasing numbers of travellers visited the Highlands and Western Isles and made them known to the wider world. A modest start was made by Martin Martin, who wrote in his *Description of the Western Isles of Scotland* (1703), 'The modern itch after the knowledge of foreign places is so prevalent that the generality of mankind bestow little thought or time upon the place of their nativity'.[2]

As a native of Skye and a graduate of the Universities of Edinburgh and Leyden he was well qualified to describe the place of his own nativity to modern travellers and to attempt to redirect their interest from the familiar scenes of the Grand Tour of Europe to the little known wilderness on their own doorstep. Martin Martin had no great eye for scenery, for the appreciation of savage grandeur would be awakened later in the century by the new perceptions of the Romantic

Movement. But he was in embryo an archaeologist, a naturalist and an anthropologist. His informal reportage of his tour provided valuable basic comments for later scholars in all these disciplines. He described the greatest megalithic monument of the Western Isles, the stone circle and associated avenues at Callenish, Lewis, and included in his book a diagram of this 'Heathen Temple'. He wrote of animals, birds, plants, marine life, and of methods of agriculture and fishing; he described the diet and folk medicines, the superstitions and religious practices of the people of the Western Isles; he recorded the incidence of 'Second Sight' among them, and cited many examples of it.[3]

Contemporaneously the Welsh savant, Edward Lluyd, Keeper of the Ashmolean Museum, toured the Celtic lands on a wider scale, and in a more scientific spirit, gathering archaeological, botanical, historic and linguistic material. In the Highlands and Isles of Scotland he visited Kintyre, Knapdale, Lorn, Mull and Iona, collecting Gaelic manuscripts and making drawings of ancient monuments. His sketches of these were published in his great work *Archaelogia Britannica* (1707). In common with other eighteenth century intellectuals both he and Martin Martin believed that megalithic monuments were temples of the Druids, an idea which has been ridiculed in the twentieth century, but in the eighteenth, which had not discovered the time-scale of prehistory, represented an advance on the beliefs of the local populations, to whom megaliths, in the context of folk tales, might be victims of sorcery, warriors or lovers turned to stone, or even the tethering post of Fionn's dog.[4]

Dr Johnson, on his way to the Western Isles with James Boswell, commented on a 'druidical circle' near Banff, but interest in antiquities was not his chief reason for undertaking this famous tour. He had read Martin Martin's book and shared his interest in 'Second Sight', concerning which he made his own enquiries and remained respect-fully agnostic. But he had thrown himself with characteristic vigour into one of the great literary debates of the age, the Ossianic controversy, and in his travels he sought and found confirmation of the views he had already formed upon it.

'Ossian' had brought the Highlands to the attention of the rest of Britain and of Europe in a way that Martin's travels and Lluyd's researches, and the works of a handful of other travelling intellectuals would never have done. In brief, the great cult of Ossian originated in the claim of James MacPherson (1736–96) to be the translator of ancient Gaelic epic poems. His English prose works, published as

Fragments of Ancient Poetry (1760), *Fingal* (1761) and *Temora* (1763) were claimed to be translations of the Gaelic bard Oisin or Ossian, dated by MacPherson to the third century of the Christian era. He presented Ossian to a willingly credulous public as the equal of Homer and Virgil, though his style, at least in this 'translation' was turgid and bombastic:

> Now I behold the chiefs in the pride of their former deeds. Their souls are kindled at the battles of old . . . Their eyes are flames of fire. They roll in search of the foes of the land. Their mighty hands are on their swords. Lightning pours from their sides of steel. They come like streams from the mountains; each rushes roaring from his hill. Bright are the chiefs of battle in the armour of their fathers, gloomy and dark their heroes follow, like the gathering of the rainy clouds behind the red meteors of heaven . . .[5]

In this style MacPherson narrated stories of romantic love, mistaken identity, heroic combat and untimely death.

This now inexplicable best seller must have appealed to ths spirit of the age, which found in it confirmation of the myth of the Noble Savage. In French, German and Italian translations 'Ossian' retained his popularity for some sixty years and provided inspiration for many artists and composers. Ossian aroused in Napoleon a devotion which has been compared with Hitler's devotion to Wagner; it was his campaign pocket book and his solace on St Helena. He commissioned Ingres to paint *Le Songe d'Ossian* for the ceiling of his bedchamber in the Quirinal Palace in Rome, though his final defeat prevented his enjoying the finished work. There were several Ossianic operas, including *Les Bardes, ou Ossian*, by Lesueur, the teacher of Berlioz, performed before Napoleon in 1804.[6] Schubert composed Ossianic songs, setting the words of a German translation in 1815, and Ossian inspired Mendelssohn's journey to the Hebrides with his friend Klingemann in 1829. As is well known, Mendelssohn's publisher urged him to take advantage of popular taste by calling his *Hebrides* overture 'Fingal's Cave'.

Mendelssohn and Klingemann were not pioneering travellers like Martin Martin, who had voyaged to far-flung St Kilda, or Edward Lluyd, nor even unusually adventurous travellers like Johnson and Boswell, for by the late 1820s the cult of Ossian had created tourism in the Highlands and Isles. Then the immense success of Sir Walter

Scott's narrative poems *The Lady of the Lake* (1810) and *The Lord of the Isles* (1815) had encouraged hundreds more visitors to tour the Highlands and make steamer trips to view the ruins of Iona and the columned sea cave of Staffa. No doubt many tourists found their appreciation of its strange splendour heightened by reading Scott's verses describing it:

> And the shy seal had found a home,
> And weltered in that wondrous dome,
> Where, as to shame the temples deck'd
> By skill of earthly architect,
> Nature itself, it seem'd, would raise
> A Minster to her Maker's praise!
> Not for a meaner use ascend
> Her columns, or her arches bend . . .
> Nor doth its entrance front in vain
> To old Iona's holy fane,
> That Nature's voice might seem to say
> 'Well hast thou done, frail child of clay!
> Thy humble powers that stately shrine
> Task'd high and hard – but witness mine!'[7]

Klingemann was sensitive enough to imagine the resentment an impoverished islander might have felt at the sight of fashionably dressed tourists disembarking from their steamer to view the ruins of 'old Iona's holy fane' and then departing again with the freedom conferred by prosperity.

While Ossian continued to charm the Continent his spell faded in Britain, where MacPherson was discredited by his inability to produce an original Gaelic text for Ossian's epics. Dr Johnson's contempt for a translator without a text played an influential part in the ruin of Ossian's reputation. Johnson's discovery on his tour of the Western Isles of general illiteracy among the Gaelic-speaking population confirmed his belief in the non-existence of ancient Gaelic manuscripts, but he appreciated the existence of oral tradition and admitted that it contributed a genuine element to MacPherson's work: 'He had found names, and stories, and phrases, nay, passages, in old songs, and with them has blended his own compositions, and so made what he gives to the world as the translation of an ancient poem'.[8]

MacPherson, in fact, had more substantial foundations than

Johnson supposed, if not what he claimed. But Johnson disposed of MacPherson to his own satifaction, and ultimately to that of most other people, though there remained a hard core of MacPherson partisans who continued to believe in Ossian's epic for reasons of Gaelic patriotism.[9]

As Ossian faded from popular imagination another hero took his place, to ensure that the Highlands would retain their attraction as a theatre of romantic interest. The new hero was Prince Charles Edward Stuart. When Dr Johnson published his *Journey to the Western Isles* (1775) the defeat of the Jacobite Rising of 1745 was still a delicate topic and his allusions to it were tactful. James Boswell, who published his own account of his tour with Johnson ten years later, was able to be more outspoken. He described the meeting in Skye between Dr Johnson and Flora MacDonald, and included an account of the escape of 'the Grandson of King James II', in which Flora's role had made her a popular heroine. Boswell's book was a milestone in the metamorphosis of Charles Edward from a defeated invader into a mythic hero. The Prince was still alive when Boswell wrote, surviving as an elderly drunkard who had alienated most of his supporters and embarrassed all of them. But after his death early in 1788 he was immediately resurrected as 'Bonnie Prince Charlie' and apotheosized in nostalgic songs and poems. Genuine Jacobite songs which had been remembered and sung in secrecy were revived, and sometimes reworked, to become part of the popular repertoire. Jacobitism, as a half-secret expression of nationalism, was reborn as a romantic cult which inspired a new outpouring of poetry and song. James Hogg's 'Bonnie Prince Charlie' is an example of the extravagantly romantic neo-Jacobite style:

> Cam ye by Athol, lad wi' the philabeg,
> Down by the Tummel, or banks o' the Garry;
> Saw ye our lads, wi' their bonnets and white cockades
> Leaving their mountains to follow Prince Charlie?
> > Follow thee! Follow Thee! Wha wadna follow thee?
> > Lang hast thou loved and trusted us fairly:
> > Charlie, Charlie, wha wadna follow thee,
> > King o' the Highland hearts, bonnie Prince Charlie?

Sir Walter Scott made the Rising of 1745 the setting of his first novel *Waverley* (1814) which he subtitled ''Tis Sixty Years Since'. It was enormously successful, for its theme chimed with the nostalgic mood of the period. Scott had an intensely romantic sense of the past, yet he supported the Parliamentary Union of 1707; his novel dramatized the conflict of emotions and ideas for many readers who probably thought and felt as he did. Scott had made his reputation as a poet, and feeling that fiction was a lesser form of art, he did not admit his authorship of the Waverley novels until 1827, by which time it was an open secret.

In 1822 he was regarded as the doyen of experts on Scottish history and an anxious Lord Provost of Edinburgh requested him to organize historical pageantry for the state visit of King George IV. Scott seized the opportunity to devise a pageant of reconciliation. Jacobite Highlanders had invaded Edinburgh in the army of Prince Charles Edward in 1745; in 1822, he resolved, loyal Highlanders should parade in Edinburgh in honour of George IV. Detestation of the Union had been the inspiration of a great deal of Jacobite support; acceptance of it was suitably expressed by Highland pageantry in honour of the Hanoverian King. Highland dress, which had been prohibited from 1746 to 1782 as the dress of a resistance movement, provided a splendid symbol of reconciliation, and George IV played his part by wearing Highland dress at a levee held at Holyroodhouse on 17 April 1822. A commemorative portrait was painted by Sir David Wilkie. The significance of the symbolism was not apparent to everybody. One observer commented contemptuously that 'a tartan fit had come upon the city'; another thought it inappropriate because the Highland clans 'had always constituted a small and almost always an unimportant part of the Scottish population . . .'. But these dissentient voices were ignored in a national upsurge of enthusiasm for Highland dress.[10]

The prohibition of it following the defeat of the Rising of 1745 had been regarded generally as unjust, the more so because it extended to the Highland clans which had supported the Hanoverian Government. By 1822 the romantic appeal of 'Bonnie Prince Charlie' and his archetypal supporter, the 'lad wi' the philabeg' made the erstwhile forbidden costume seem all the more glamorous. However, apart from the tartan dress provided by Highland landowners to dress their followers for the royal visit, or as liveries thereafter, Highland dress did not reappear among the dwindling population of the Highlands. It was revived among the gentry and the middle class and adopted throughout these classes in the Lowlands as an aspect of the 'Celtic Revival' which owed its first inspiration to the cult of Ossian, and its continuance to the cult of 'Bonnie Prince Charlie' and the lasting popularity of the poems and novels of Sir Walter Scott.

Scott's orchestration of neo-Jacobitism in honour of George IV had the surprising effect of translating what might have been an ephemeral fashion for tartan into a lasting national symbol. And with the adoption of Highland dress as the national costume of Scotland arose the myth that the clan tartans had provided an immemorial identification system for Highland clans and, even less credibly, for Lowland families. The belief took root very rapidly, encouraged by a number of books of dubious historical validity.

In 1831 James Logan published *The Scottish Gael, or Celtic Manners preserved among the Highlanders*, which listed existing tartans ascribed to Highland clans (not Lowland families) and stimulated demand for more information and more tartans. In 1845 Logan produced *The Clans of the Scottish Highlands* with beautiful colour plates by R.R. MacIan. In these illustrations MacIan showed chiefs and clansmen dressed for the most part in authentic styles of Highland dress from the Middle Ages to the nineteenth century but he was misleading in so far as he backdated the existence of clearly differentiated clan tartans.

In 1842 appeared an even more controversial work entitled *Vestiarium Scoticum; from the Manuscript formerly in the library of the Scots College at Douay*, with an Introduction and Notes, by John Sobieski Stuart. Here was a curious echo of MacPherson and Ossian, for Sobieski Stuart claimed the authority of a manuscript which he likewise was unable to produce. The *Vestiarium Scoticum* listed tartans of Highland Clans and 'Lowland Houses and Border Clans' supposedly dating from sixteenth century. Predictably, it generated a furious controversy. In 1845 it was followed by *The Costume of the Clans* by John Sobieski Stolberg Stuart and Charles Edward Stuart. The author, or soi-disant editor, of the *Vestiarium* and his younger brother, who had started life as John and Charles Hay Allen, claimed to have been informed that their father Thomas Allen was in truth the legitimate son of Prince Charles Edward Stuart and his wife Princess Louise of Stolberg. The infant was handed to an English admiral (the boys' real or putative grandfather) to save it from a Hanoverian assassination plot. The brothers surely believed the tale, for it inspired their life's work, though in the *Vestiarium Scoticum* and in *The Costume of the Clans* imposture and genuine scholarship were inextricably blended. For the interested reader, the question is thoroughly discussed in John Telfer Dunbar's *History of Highland*

Dress (1962), the most scholarly and least biased book on a controversial subject. Many Highland and Lowland tartans have no provenance other than the Sobieski Stuarts' works, but they bear lasting testimony to the brothers' artistic skill. And indeed, by the last decade of the twentieth century a tartan invented in the middle of the nineteenth has gained a respectable antiquity.

Much of the tartan woven to be worn in honour of George IV's state visit had been made by the firm of Wilson of Bannockburn, Stirlingshire, an old-established firm which wove the regimental tartans. From this date onwards the evolution of many clan tartans can be traced in Wilson's pattern books. Here it may be seen that new tartans were frequently created on demand, or tartans previously designated simply by a number were given the name of a clan or a family.[11] The mid-nineteenth century was an era simultaneously of invention and definition, but this fact was denied even as the process was taking place.

The existence of ancient clan tartans was already an article of faith by the time Queen Victoria made her first tour of Scotland in 1842. She described her reception by Lord Breadalbane at Taymouth in her Journal:

> The house is a kind of castle built of granite. The *coup d'oeil* was indescribable. There were a number of Lord Breadalbane's Highlanders, all in the Campbell tartan, drawn up in front of the house, with Lord Breadalbane himself in a Highland dress at their head, and a few of Sir Neil Menzies' men (in the Menzies red and white tartan), a number of pipers playing, and a company of the 92nd Highlanders, also in kilts . . . It seemed as if a great chieftain in olden feudal times was receiving his sovereign.'[12]

This was the beginning of Queen Victoria's long love affair with the Highlands. In 1848 she and the Prince Consort took a lease of Balmoral, which a few years later they bought and rebuilt as a large castle in the 'Scottish Baronial' style. Indoors Queen Victoria created the Scottish Victorian style which was widely imitated, though in a subsequent revulsion against Victorian taste it was sneeringly labelled 'Balmorality'. There were curtains and carpets of Royal Stewart and Dress Stewart tartan, sofas and chairs upholstered in Dress Stewart poplin, and other curtains in thistle patterned chintz. The choice of tartan was an allusion to the Queen's Stewart ancestry and to her emotional attachment to Jacobitism, now safely consigned to the Romantic past. In her Journal on 12 September 1873, the Queen wrote:

> I feel a sort of reverence in going over these scenes [of Prince Charles Edward's fugitive wanderings] in this most beautiful country, which I am proud to call my own, where there was such devoted loyalty to the family of my ancestors – for Stuart blood is in my veins, and I am now their representative . . .[13]

Victoria was sufficiently secure on her throne to forget or ignore the existence of a multitude of possible legitimist claimants more substantial than the Sobieski Stuarts.

In her appreciation of the Highlands the Queen expressed the by now well established romantic taste for wild scenery, over which she enthused in her Journal, emphasizing her pleasure by quoting from Scott's poems and noting Prince Albert's comparisons between Swiss and Highland landscapes. The Queen explored extensively, accompanied by members of her family and household, supposedly incognito, on foot and on horseback, in carriages and pony chaises, with a disregard for the weather which would astonish more comfort-loving modern tourists. Everything about the Highlands charmed her: Highland dress, Highland scenery, Highland dancing, Highland games, Highland sports. Highland dances were performed at court balls, even in England; the royal family patronized Highland games by attending the Braemar Gathering; the Queen enthused over Prince Albert's prowess at deer stalking.

Sir Edwin Landseer, as an unofficial painter laureate, publicized the royal family's life in the Highlands. In 1854 he exhibited at the Royal Academy a picture entitled *Royal Sports on Hill and Loch*, a highly theatrical scene which shows Queen Victoria being handed ashore by a kilted Prince Albert, after a boat trip on Loch Muich. The tartan rug spread over the gangplank, the crouching ghillies gazing at the Queen as if at a heavenly apparition and the irrelevant dead stags arranged in the foreground, all lend artificiality to what was, after all, a representation of an informal occasion.

Landseer's paintings provided acceptable publicity for the Queen's family life, of which she herself chose to reveal something by publishing two volumes of selections from her Journal, *Leaves from the Journal of Our Life in the Highlands* (1868), which covered her life at Balmoral with Prince Albert and *More Leaves from the Journal of A Life in the Highlands* (1884), which treated of her life in Scotland after her widowhood. The second volume exposed her to some ridicule for her fulsome references to her favourite Highland servant John Brown, and her imprudent dedication of it to his memory.[14] But both books were best sellers, both for the charm of their simple but far from naïve style, and for the glimpses which they provided of the secret world of royalty.

As early as 1849 the Revd Thomas MacLauchlan wrote:

> Much as we rejoice in our beloved Sovereign's visits to our country, we fear that they may hasten the consummation of making our Highlands a great deer forest by inducing a large number of our English aristocracy to flock to them for the purpose of sport.[15]

Economic pressure caused by the reduced profits from sheep farming led many Highland landowners to convert their estates to deer forest. But undoubtedly the Queen and Prince Consort's acquisition of Balmoral created a fashion for the purchase of Scottish property among those who could afford it. Queen Victoria herself admired the dignity and courtesy of the Highlanders who lived on her estate, or whom she encountered on her Highland tours; it would have shocked her to imagine that her enthusiasm for the Highlands encouraged a trend which was detrimental to its population.

Paradoxically the discovery of the Highlands by the outside world occurred at the same time as the progressive extinction of traditional Highland life. Eighteenth and early nineteenth century travellers were aware that they were observing and describing a vanishing society. But fortunately the so-called 'Celtic Revival' stimulated by outside influences was paralleled by an entirely native initiative which ensured that Gaelic culture did not disappear together with the society which had nurtured it.

This genuine Celtic revival, or Celtic preservation movement, owed much to the efforts of two Highland Societies. In 1778 the Highland Society of London was founded by twenty-five Highland gentlemen resident in London, part of its expressed intention being the preservation of the 'martial spirit, dress and music of the Highlands'. It also undertook charitable work, founded a Gaelic Chapel in London, and was influential in securing the repeal of the Act forbidding the wearing of Highland dress. The Society took an active part in the Ossianic controversy, and in 1807 published a Gaelic version of 'Ossian'; but this was a translation of MacPherson's English works into Gaelic, which further served to demonstrate the lack of an original text. In 1781 the Society encouraged the revival of *piobaireachd* by organizing piping competitions which were held for three consecutive years at the Falkirk Tryst. The Society continues to present gold medals for piping, in contests held at the Oban and Inverness Highland Gatherings.

In 1784 the Highland Society of Scotland was founded in Edinburgh. It later became the Royal Highland and Agricultural Society of Scotland, with predominantly agricultural interests, but between 1784 and 1844 an important aim was 'the preservation of the language, poetry and music of the Highlands'. The Society appointed its own bard, piper, and 'Professor of Gaelic'. In 1784 it took over the supervision of the piping contest inaugurated by the London Society and transferred it from Falkirk to Edinburgh, where it was held together with Highland dancing and recitations of Gaelic poetry.

In 1797, after the death of James MacPherson, the Highland Society of Scotland encouraged by its secretary, the novelist Henry MacKenzie (1745–1831), undertook an investigation of MacPherson's claims and of the survival of ancient Gaelic poetry in general. In the course of the investigation it amassed a collection of Gaelic manuscripts which were later deposited in the Advocates' Library, Edinburgh. These included the manuscript of the *Dean of Lismore's Book*, which had been acquired by MacPherson and included Ossianic poems. This had been MacPherson's most substantial source and Dr Johnson had not known of its existence when he condemned MacPherson as having been wholly reliant on oral tradition. However, when the Society published its findings in 1805, it reached the honest and scholarly conclusion that while a corpus of Gaelic poetry survived, MacPherson had manipulated his sources in accordance with his own ideas: there was no single epic such as he had claimed to have translated. The Society continued to encourage the search for genuine survivals.

Highland music, dancing and traditional sports continued to be encouraged by the organization of Highland Games or Gatherings. In 1800 a charitable society was founded at Braemar and later became the Braemar Highland Society, which in 1832 held its first Highland Games. This event gained enormous publicity and popularity when

Queen Victoria began to attend it in 1848, inaugurating a tradition of royal patronage. From 1788 a 'Northern Meeting' was held at Inverness, a week of balls, dinners and other social events, attended by the northern Highland gentry. From 1840 onwards Highland Games became an important part of the occasion. Oban became the scene of the Argyllshire Gathering and Highland Games were established as annual events in many parts of the Highlands, and also in the Lowlands and in distant parts of the world, wherever there were communities of Highland emigrants and their descendants. From the Aboyne Games derives a particularly attractive women's costume for Highland dancing, the 'Aboyne Dress'. (Though young girls often wear kilts in Highland dancing competitions, many experts on Highland dress disapprove of girls or women wearing the kilt, an essentially masculine garment). Highland gatherings, of their very nature, encouraged the wearing of Highland dress, but sometimes direct encouragement was given in the form of a competition for 'the best dressed Highlander, at his own expense'.[16]

The games themselves derived from traditional trials of strength: throwing the hammer, 'putting' the stone, tossing the *cabar* (tree trunk). There would be other contests, not specifically Highland in origin, such as wrestling and tug-of-war. The cultural events of Highland Gatherings were and are competitions in piping and Highland dancing.

In the second half of the eighteenth century *piobaireachd* was kept alive by the Highland regiments. In the Highlands at large the knowledge and practice of it was dying out. Many of the great pipers of the past, the MacCrimmons, the Rankins and their pupils, had been unlettered men. They had passed on their music by a system called *canntaireachd*, a vocal, syllabic notation, the oral tradition of music.[17] If the knowledge of *canntaireachd* failed, the knowledge of *ceol mor*, the 'great music' of the past would be lost with it. The Highland Societies encouraged the publication of *ceol mor* in standard musical notation. Three pipe tunes were included in the *Collection of Highland Vocal Airs* by the Revd Patrick MacDonald of Kilmore (1784). In 1822 the bagpipe maker Donald MacDonald, of Edinburgh, who had been encouraged by the Highland Society of Scotland to collect pipe music, published *Ancient Martial Music of Caledonia*. Another important publication was the *Collection of Ancient Piobaireachd* by Angus Mackay of Raasay (1848). A century later the Piobaireachd Society had published twelve volumes of Archibald Campbell's *Kilberry Book of*

Ceol Mor. In the meantime the pipe music of the Highland regiments had undergone a change. Up to the middle of the nineteenth century the pipers attached to the Highland regiments had been paid by the officers and had received no recognition from the War Office. From 1854 onwards pipers were officially attached to their regiments and were formed into pipe bands; thenceforward their characteristic music was the regimental march. However, this did not imply that *ceol mor* was necessarily neglected in the Highland regiments, for the pipe majors of the regiments have been among its most noted exponents.

Traditional Highland dancing was probably likewise saved from desuetude and oblivion through the research encouraged by the Highland Societies and the competitions organized at Highland Games. The origins of Highland dancing had long been forgotten, though Celtic tribes and early Highland clans must have had their characteristic dances. All primitive societies dance, first for ritual and later for festivity. A hint that Highland dancing is very ancient is the survival of *port-a-beul* ('mouth music'), wordless song to provide accompaniment for dancing. Solo dances for men, *Dannsa a'Chlaidnimh* ('sword dance') and *Dannsa na Biodaig* ('dirk dance'), and sword dances for two, three or four men may have a remote ancestry in the pre-battle dances of Celtic warriors; and it is natural to see a fertility or courtship ritual as the origin of a *Dannsa nan Pòg* ('dance of kisses'). The primitive origin was also suggested by the popularity of dancing out of doors. In the eighteenth and nineteenth centuries *Dannsa a rathaid* ('road dancing') was often performed on moonlit nights at a crossroads or on a bridge.[18]

Playing music for dancing was considered beneath the dignity of pipers. By the beginning of the eighteenth century such popular dances as 'reels' and 'Strathspeys' were usually played on the fiddle, so-called from the Gaelic *fidheall* ('violin' or 'viol'). The earliest named composer of a Strathspey was James MacPherson, an outlaw who was hanged in 1700; he played his own composition 'MacPherson's Rant', and then smashed his fiddle, at the foot of the gallows. More fortunate composers of popular reels and Strathspeys were Niel Gow (1727–1807) and his son Nathaniel Gow. Niel, who was particularly admired as a performer, was the subject of a fine portrait by Sir Henry Raeburn, which shows him seated playing his fiddle, dressed in a dark coat and waistcoat and tartan breeches and hose. He appears in the same costume in a delightful painting of a Highland wedding on the Atholl estate in 1780, by David Allan. Highland dances and their music have retained their popularity to the present day. In the second half of the nineteenth century the accordion was introduced as an alternative to the fiddle to accompany the dancing.

Highland dancing is enthusiastically performed at Highland balls, whether at the grand 'Subscription Balls' which take place at the larger Highland Gatherings or at the 'Caledonian Balls' organized by Highland Societies throughout the world. These occasions are also displays of the modern version of Highland dress for evening. The women's costume is a white evening dress, with a long silk tartan sash passed over the left shoulder and secured there with a brooch. The men's costume shows more variation:

> It is no uncommon sight to see together on the same ballroom floor a dancer in the full panoply of the eighteenth century, with kilt and jacket in two different tartans; another wearing a plain velvet doublet with lace jabot and cuffs; and a third exhibiting the most modern version of all, a short black coat and bow-tie.[19]

A fairly recent development of clan tartans has been the differentiation of 'dress' and 'hunting' tartans, the dress tartans being woven in brighter colours. Not all clan tartans exist in two versions, but when they do it is customary to wear the dress tartan in the evening.

The revival of Highland music and dancing encouraged by the Highland Societies also helped to raise awareness of other aspects of Gaelic culture which in the later nineteenth century were in decline and might have been in danger of extinction but for the efforts of a handful of dedicated enthusiasts. The *iorrams*, or rowing songs, and the *orain luadhaidh*, or chorus songs to accompany agricultural work or the fulling of cloth were falling out of use. Miss Frances Tolmie (1840–1926), a native of Skye, collected the words and music of Gaelic songs, from old people who still remembered them, throughout the Western Isles. They were published by her collaborator, Miss Lucy Broadwood, editor of the *Journal of the Folksong Society*. Mrs Marjory Kennedy-Fraser (1857–1930) began to study Gaelic music in 1882, and published her collection *Songs of the Hebrides* in 1909. Many of these songs had been given her by Miss Tolmie. However, Mrs Kennedy-Fraser was responsible for popularizing Gaelic songs. After the First World War 'in magnificent and archaic costume [she] sang her songs to crowded audiences in the larger cities'.[20]

The nineteenth century saw a great upsurge of interest in folktales throughout Europe. The brothers Grimm published their *Household Tales* in 1812–15, and these were translated into English in 1823. In 1859 G.W. Dasent, who had been encouraged by Jacob Grimm to study Scandinavian mythology, published *Popular Tales from the Norse*. These works inspired John Francis Campbell of Islay (1822–1885) to collect Gaelic folktales, and in 1860–62 he published *Popular Tales of the West Highlands*. J.F. Campbell was fortunate in having the encouragement of the eighth Duke of Argyll and the assistance of an able team of collectors. John Dewar, a woodman on the Argyll estate, and Hector Urquhart, a gamekeeper, directed to help Campbell by the Duke, took down stories in Gaelic from the lips of the storytellers, at a period when a few professional storytellers still survived. Another collaborator was Hector MacLean of Ballygrant, Islay, who both collected stories and helped prepare J.F. Campbell's work for publication.[21]

Another great Gaelic folklorist was Alexander Carmichael of Lismore (1832–1912), whose particular interest was pre-Reformation religious poetry, a remarkable amount of which still survived in oral tradition. He collected hymns and prayers, and also charms and incantations in which Christian and pagan elements were inextricably interwoven. A selection from the great mass he had collected was published as *Carmina Gadelica* (two volumes, 1900), and later scholars have produced a further four volumes from his material. An example from one of the later volumes is a Prayer to the Virgin, which conveys both the spirituality and the poetry of Gaelic piety:

> The Virgin was seen coming, the young Christ at Her
> breast, angels bowing in submission before Them, and the
> King of the Universe saying it was fitting.

> The Virgin of ringlets most excellent, Jesus more surpassing
> white than snow, melodious Seraphs singing Their praise,
> and the King of the Universe saying it was fitting.

> Mary Mother of miracles, help us, help us with Thy
> strength; bless the food, bless the board, bless the ear, the
> corn, and the victuals.

> The Virgin most excellent of face, Jesus more surpassing
> white than snow, She like the moon rising over the hills,
> He like the sun on the peaks of the mountains.[22]

It has proved, and is proving, more difficult to preserve the most important of all aspects of Gaelic culture, the Gaelic language itself. James VI's Statutes of Iona (1609) had initiated a Government policy of eliminating the Gaelic language in the interests of national unity. From that date onwards the policy was systematically pursued and a series of education acts endeavoured to establish the ascendancy of English. An Act of the Privy Council of 1616 declared that there should be a school in each parish, to ensure that 'the youth be exercised and trayned up in civilitie, godlines, knowledge and learning, that the vulgar Inglishe toung be universallie plantit, and the Irishe language [Gaelic] whilk is one of the cheif and principall causis of the continewance of barbaritie and incivilitie amongis the inhabitantis of the Ilis and Heylandis, may be abolisheit and removit'. Successive Acts of Parliament of 1633, 1639 and 1646 continued this policy, and attempted not wholly successfully to make financial provision for the schools and schoolmasters. The anti-Gaelic policy was pursued whether the polity of the Church of Scotland was Episcopalian or Presbyterian. After the Revolution of 1688 an Act of Parliament granted the rents of the bishopric of Argyll to the Synod of Argyll in 1695, for the purpose of 'Erecting of English Schools for rooting out of the Irish Language, and other pious uses'. However, Highland parishes were very large, and the progress made by the parochial schools was slow. It was to supplement their efforts that the Society in Scotland for Propagating Christian Knowledge was founded in Edinburgh in 1709, its declared intention being 'the further promoting of Christian Knowledge and the increase of piety and virtue within Scotland, especially in the Highlands, Islands and remote corners thereof, where error, idolatry, superstition and ignorance do mostly abound, by reason of the largeness of the parishes and scarcity of schools'. Regrettably the SSPCK was convinced that its aims would be furthered by the continuance of the elimination of Gaelic through the use of English in all its schools. By 1715 the Society had founded twenty-five schools; the number had grown to one hundred and fifty by 1750. It concentrated on remote locations, and in 1711 even established a school on St Kilda.

Fortunately the revival of interest in Gaelic culture in the 1760s led to a rethinking of this policy. In 1767 the SSPCK permitted teaching in its schools to be conducted in Gaelic. In the same year the Revd James Stuart (1701–1789) minister of Killin, published his translation of the New Testament from Greek into Gaelic. He then set to work on the

Old Testament, which was published after his death, in 1801. The Gaelic scriptures were greatly valued by Gaelic speakers who were able to read their own tongue, but of course there were many Gaelic speakers who remained illiterate.

The Revd Dr Norman MacLeod (1783–1862) recognized that the survival of Gaelic depended on the survival of literacy, and to encourage it he founded Gaelic periodicals in which he himself wrote many contributions to provide his readers with 'every kind of useful information' previously 'locked up in English books'.[23] He wrote and published articles on history, geography, current affairs, science and religious issues, besides book reviews and original essays. His periodicals, *An Teachdaire Gaelach* ('The Gaelic Courier', 1829–31) and *Cuairtear nan Gleann* ('Pilgrim of the Glens', 1840–43) created a popular Gaelic readership and stimulated future Gaelic publishing ventures. His efforts on behalf of Gaelic, and his involvement in relief work in the Highlands during the hardships of the 1840s won him the title of *Caraid nan Gaidheal* ('Friend of the Gaels').

The Chair of Celtic Studies was founded in the University of Edinburgh in 1882 and has been held by a succession of distinguished Gaelic scholars. In 1891 *An Comunn Gaidhealach* ('The Highland Association') was founded in Oban and the following year established the national Mod (modelled on the Welsh Eistedfodd), a competitive festival of Gaelic speech, literature and vocal and instrumental music. From 1905 onwards local Mods were also established. In 1937 the Scottish Gaelic Text Society was founded, to publish authoritative editions of Gaelic works in verse and prose and in 1968 *An Comunn Leabhraichan* ('The Gaelic Books Council') was set up in the Celtic Department of the University of Glasgow to administer the Gaelic Books Grant awarded by the Scottish Education Department to the University to subsidize the publication of new and original works in the Gaelic. In the course of the twentieth century a number of Gaelic periodicals have come and gone, the most enduring to date having been *Gairm*, which began publication in 1952.

The success or otherwise of these and other ventures towards the paramount purpose of maintaining Gaelic as a living language can be measured to some extent in the figures of the decennial population census. The Gaelic Society of Inverness, founded in 1871, acted as a Gaelic lobby in both political and cultural matters, and was instrumental in securing the incorporation of a Gaelic census from 1881 onwards:

THE GAELIC-SPEAKING POPULATION OF SCOTLAND, 1881–1981

Year	Population of Scotland	Gaelic-only speakers	Gaelic-only speakers as % of population	Gaelic- and-English speakers	Gaelic- and-English speakers as % of population
1881	3,735,573	231,594	6.2		
1891	4,025,647	43,738	1.1	210,677	5.2
1901	4,472,103	28,106	0.6	202,700	4.5
1911	4,760,904	18,400	0.4	183,998	3.9
1921	4,573,471	9,829	0.2	148,950	3.3
1931	4,588,909	6,716	0.1	129,419	2.8
1951	5,096,415	2,178	0.04	93,269	1.8
1961	5,179,344	974	0.01	80,004	1.5
1971	5,228,965	477	0.009	88,415	1.7
1981	5,035,315	no data	—	82,620	1.6

Source: Census data

The table illustrates the unhappy fact that the speaking of Gaelic has steadily declined, both numerically and proportionately to the population of Scotland. However, the census figures do not reveal certain shifts of emphasis which have occurred: for example, although the *Gaidhealtachd*, or Gaelic speaking area has steadily shrunk, some Gaelic speaking groups have been established in Lowland areas, especially in cities, from which Gaelic had previously died out. This results from the efforts of such societies as *An Comunn Tir nam Beann* ('The Society of the Land of the Mountains') to keep Gaels together and to keep their language alive. It will be noticed from the table that the census of 1971 recorded the existence of 477 monoglot Gaelic speakers, whereas the census of 1981 returned no data on this. It is possible that no monoglot Gaelic speakers remain; if any survive, they will be a handful of the very old. Obviously the pressure to get on in the world includes the pressure to learn English. A writer on Scottish traditions commented in 1967:

It is easier to lose Gaelic than to acquire good English; and often it is found that the Gaelic speaker who is a good English speaker is sufficient of a linguist to care about his own language and to appreciate its virtues and values. It is often the less literate and less intellectual Gael who, in his impatience with the burden, as he

192

thinks it, of two languages, sacrifices his own, his birthright, and will have nothing to do with it.[24]

The last decennial census of this century and the first of the next will indicate the chances for the survival of Gaelic; it will depend upon the transmission of enthusiasm for it to the young. Official prejudice against the teaching of Gaelic in schools theoretically ended in 1878 when school boards were for the first time permitted to pay the salary of a teacher of 'Gaelic, drill (i.e. physical education), cooking or any other special subject'. The Education Act of 1918 went further and actually recommended the teaching of Gaelic in Gaelic-speaking areas but it was not until after the Second World War that better provision began to be made for teaching Gaelic language and literature and for the use of Gaelic in teaching other subjects. It is to be hoped that a more sympathetic official attitude to the use of Gaelic in schools will assist the language not only to survive but to expand again.

The general revival of interest in Gaelic culture belatedly extended to interest in the welfare of the Gaels themselves.

In 1882 there was a widespread failure of the potato crop. Wild weather destroyed the cereal crops, cattle prices fell, fishing catches were poor. But no longer could the plight of the crofters be solved by the old panaceas of emigration, an injection of relief, or a disaster fund. The crofters had a vigorous champion in John Murdoch (1818–1903), who had edited a newspaper, the Inverness-based *Highlander*, from 1873 to 1881. He had been associated with Irish Nationalism, and was a tireless and effective anti-landlord campaigner. The cause of land reform was also supported by Professor John Stuart Blackie (1809–1895), Professor of Greek in the University of Edinburgh, who had been instrumental in establishing the Chair of Celtic Studies. He was an influential figure both in the revival of Gaelic and in Gaelic politics. The cause of the crofters was also supported by the energetic Gaelic Society of Inverness.

Encouraged by eloquent and politically active supporters, the crofters demanded more land for cultivation and security from eviction, backing their demands with rent strikes and land-raids in the so-called 'Crofters' War'. Since every reform movement finds it advantageous if it represents its desired innovation as a return to the past, the crofters based their demands on a new-found belief in a golden age before the existence of landlords, when the land had belonged to the people. A Gaelic poet, John MacLean of Balemartin, Tiree, wrote of his own island:

> Before a Duke* came, or any of his people
> Or a kingly George from Hanover's realm,
> The low-lying isle with its many shielings
> Belonged as a dwelling to the children of the Gael.[25]

Even though the golden age was imaginary, the appeal to natural justice of the crofters' cause won it much public sympathy. In 1883 a commission chaired by Lord Napier was appointed to enquire into the condition of the crofters. It collected a vast amount of evidence that their conditions of tenure were profoundly unsatisfactory; but it was yet more unsatisfactory that no Government action followed. Meanwhile a Highland Law Reform Association (later re-named the Highland Land League) was founded and it provided candidates for the Highland constituencies for the General Election of 1885. The Third Reform Act of 1884 had enfranchised the crofters, so that they were able to send four 'Crofters' Party' members to Parliament. In 1886 Gladstone's Liberal administration passed the Crofters' Holdings Act. The legislation applied to the 'Crofting Counties' of Argyll, Inverness, Ross and Cromarty, Sutherland, Caithness and the Northern Isles, and defined a crofter as a tenant of an agricultural holding known as a croft, registered as such and paying a certain annual rent. The holding was not to exceed thirty acres (later increased to fifty acres), though most crofts were much smaller, and the tenancy included pasture rights in common. The Act granted crofters security of tenure, permitted the bequest or assignation of crofts, appointed fixed rents, arranged for outgoing tenants to receive compensation for improvements, and made arrangements for enlargement of holdings. The Government also set up a Crofters' Commission to oversee the working of the Act. In the words of Professor Gordon Donaldson: 'The crofter, in short, received the advantage of ownership without its liabilities, and landlords, it seems, were permitted to exist principally so that they could shoulder half the rates and pay compensation to outgoing crofters.'[26]

However, this reversal in the landlords' fortunes did not appear to

---

* i.e. Duke of Argyll.

crofters an adequate compensation for the Clearances, and there was widespread dissatisfaction that the Crofters' Holdings Act had not extended to a large-scale redistribution of land. Furthermore, the Act did nothing to help the landless cottars, whose poverty was even greater than that of the crofters had been. After the passing of the Crofters' Holdings Act many cottars carried out land raids and built themselves houses to signify their determination to continue to occupy the land they had seized. In Lewis in 1886 disaffected cottars vented their anger by raiding the estate of Park, which had recently been converted from sheep farm to deer forest, for letting to shooting tenants, and they slaughtered deer to reduce its attraction as a letting property. In 1897 the Congested Districts Board was set up to attempt to solve such problems by making more land available and by sponsoring schemes to help provide employment. In 1911 it was superseded by the Board of Agriculture which introduced new land settlement projects and these included buying large farms, breaking them up into crofts and distributing them. From 1911 onwards, permanent residence was no longer required of a crofter so that many tenants sought a more profitable livelihood, often in the fisheries of the north and east coasts, or in the Merchant Navy. In a curious reversal of former conditions, 'the trouble came to be not absentee landlords but absentee crofters, who abandoned cultivation and used the land only to graze sheep'.[27] The crofters' position was a great deal more secure than it had been but the economic conditions of crofting continued to present intractable problems, which a new Crofters' Commission, set up in 1955, had the unenviable task of tackling. In 1968 it recommended that crofters should be given full rights of ownership. The Crofting Reform (Scotland) Act of 1976 gave the crofters the opportunity of acquiring the ownership of their crofts at a price based on the rental value, rather than the current market price of the land.

Many of the sporting estates, the deer forests and grouse moors, created in the mid-nineteenth century continued to be managed as they had been in the reign of Queen Victoria up to the First World War. From the mid-nineteenth century onwards shooting lodges were built all over the Highlands, varying in size from simple cottages to large 'Scottish Baronial' houses capable of accommodating the tenant's family, guests and servants. Dr I.F. Grant, in a fascinating book of history and memoirs, *Along a Highland Road* (1980), has much to say of this now vanished way of life. She cites the example of a great landowner, Alfred, twenty-eighth chief of Mackintosh, whose estates included eight grouse moors. Mackintosh lived at Moy Hall, Strath-dearn, near Inverness, where his guests included King George V and Queen Mary. Mackintosh 'kept the shooting of Moy in his own hands. He was very skilful in the placing of the butts and the management of the drives and was an acknowledged authority on grouse shooting'.[28] His other moors were let to shooting tenants.

The popularity of grouse shooting dated from the second decade of the nineteenth century, when the flintlock muzzle-loading guns of the period demanded superb marksmanship for any success at all and bags were necessarily small. The sport became easier in the 1820s with the introduction of the percussion cap. In 1860 the introduction of the double-barrelled breech-loading shotgun made possible the enormous bags which delighted the sportsmen of the late Victorian and Edwardian periods. Up to the 1890s the sportsmen walked up the game, preceded by their pointers or setters, and shot over the dogs. If ladies were present at the shoot they usually followed on ponies. With the development of less cumbersome and voluminous country clothes they began to walk with the guns, and would then stand behind their companions while the shooting took place. A later development was the employment of beaters to drive the birds over a line of butts in which the sportsmen awaited them.

The shooting tenants of the late nineteenth centuries were 'largely soldiers, members of the higher branches of the Law and Colonial Services, and business people with much the same or a rather more affluent style of living'.[29] They rented the grouse moor for some nine or ten weeks, and occupied the shooting lodge with their own staff of domestic servants. The keeper was the most influential local person-age and the need for ghillies, domestic servants and beaters provided some local employment. This way of life, dependent on increasingly anachronistic social rituals, began to die a natural death between the two World Wars, when few families, either of proprietors or of tenants, were able to maintain the outdoor or indoor staffs upon whom the organization depended. Grouse shooting retains its popularity, but frequently the shooting is let to syndicates of sportsmen, often for short periods throughout the season, or even for single drives. Dr Grant, who remembered the last days of the ancien regime, deserves the last word on the matter:

When I think of the tutoring in the proper use of a gun that the boys of a family received from a keeper, I feel sorry for the game, beasts

196

and birds, of the present day, so apt to be the quarries of ill-trained sportsmen . . . Roads are made over the moors to convey urbanized tycoons up to the very butts . . . I hear there are further plans for the commercialization of sport to enable deep-pursed visitors to indulge their blood lust, which makes me feel sick.[30]

A strong body of opinion would now like to see the end of shooting for sport and the elimination of sporting estates. But the state intervention required to bring about such an end and the consequent revolution in the use of the land at present covered by sporting estates appear unlikely.

Throughout the twentieth century, however, the Highlands as a whole have been subjected to unprecedented state intervention, some of it beneficial, much of it inevitably controversial. Two examples, which have affected both the appearance of the land and the life of the people, have been the founding of the Forestry Commission and the North of Scotland Hydro-Electric Board.

The Forestry Commission was set up in 1919. Vast amounts of timber had been felled during the First World War, and part of the Commission's purpose was the replacement of stocks against future necessity. The Commission took over the Crown Forests and was also empowered to acquire land by compulsory purchase. An unhappy consequence of this has been described by a recent writer on the Highlands:

The crofters in the area of Roy Bridge . . . were among those thus affected. In 1959 the Forestry Commission acquired land in this area for the Inveroy and Glenspean forests. This involved taking over land on which crofters grazed sheep . . . many felt that they were thus reduced to the stage where they could no longer earn their living on the land remaining to them and were forced to turn to the Forestry Commission for work . . . Although provided with work and a regular wage, as well as the offer of housing in the neat Forestry commission villages to be found in many parts of the Highlands, this . . . did not always satisfy those who had been uprooted by these latter-day Clearances.[31]

By the mid-1950s the Forestry Commission was the largest landowner in the Highlands, possessing some one and a half million acres, much of it previously unplantable land which modern methods of arboriculture have brought under cultivation. In the years following the Second World War the Forestry Commission was criticized for its over-enthusiastic planting of the fast-growing Sitka spruce, which covered the landscape with huge areas of darkly monotonous coniferous forest. However, recent planting has paid more attention to variety, and to the inclusion of native trees. A new 'Great Caledonian Forest' is taking the place of its long-vanished predecessor, and providing a habitat for such endangered species as the Scottish wild cat and the pine marten. The task of preserving the wild life of the Highlands is chiefly that of the Nature Conservancy, founded in 1949. In 1951 it formed the Ben Eighe Nature Reserve, which contains one of the last remnants of the ancient forest, with native plants and animals; in 1964 it created the Cairngorms National Nature Reserve, a habitat for peregrine falcons and golden eagles, wild cats, red and roe deer, and the rarer game birds such as ptarmigan and capercailzie. In 1990 the proposal was made by the Scottish Office that the Cairngorms should be designated a 'World Heritage Site', a status already enjoyed by St Kilda, from which the indigenous population was evacuated in 1930, unable any longer to sustain its incredibly harsh and primitive way of life.

The North of Scotland Hydro-Electric Board was set up in 1943, under the inspiration of Tom Johnston, Secretary of State for Scotland in Churchill's Second World War coalition Government. Its commission was to develop water-power in the Highlands, so as to bring both economic advantage and social improvement to the area. The area under the authority of the Hydro-Electric Board lay north of a line drawn from the Clyde to the Tay, and this was omitted from the national scheme when electricity was nationalized under the postwar Labour Government in 1947. The board supplied both industrial and domestic consumers, and for the latter provided power and light even in the remotest parts of the Highlands and the Isles. In bringing comfort to everyday life in these areas the introduction of hydro-electric power was the greatest step forward which had ever occurred. For the most part the Board's installations were created with sensitivity to the preservation of the landscape, the most remarkable example being the creation of a subterranean pump-storage system in a vast artificial cavern beneath Ben Cruachan. The processions of pylons bearing transmission lines across the Highlands are a necessary evil, their majestic ugliness accepted for the sake of the benefits they have brought. Between 1954 and 1962 the Hydro-Electric Board experimentally developed a peat-fired power station at Altnabreac, Caithness, which was one of its few failures. By the 1980s it had successfully pioneered grass and grain drying, and fish conservation, in addition to attracting into its area thirty-three new industries, estimated to have provided 16,000 new jobs.[32]

In 1965 the Highlands and Islands Development Board was established under Harold Wilson's Labour Government. It was intended to provide assistance to a great variety of projects for the economic and social development of the Highlands and Islands, including industries, fisheries, agriculture and tourism. At the outset industry was seen as the means of bringing prosperity to the region:

The Board's initial strategy was directed towards what it termed 'growth centre policy', that is, concentrating manufacturing industry at one or two more points to minimize the high costs involved in establishing it in a remote area, to achieve economies of scale and to limit the effects of industrialization. The area around the Moray Firth was chosen. The biggest single project was the Aluminium smelter at Invergordon, representing a huge investment of capital but without the hoped-for mass employment.[33]

The Board has been more effective in assisting, by means of grants and loans, many enterprises which increase prosperity within their immediate areas without disrupting the local way of life.

In many parts of the Highlands such enterprises as fish-farms and smoke-houses (which produce smoked salmon, smoked trout, smoked venison and other delicacies), woollen and tweed mills, craft workshops, local museums, small hotels and restaurants, all help to provide employment. One thing which all such enterprises have in common is dependence on the tourist industry and also, in appropriate concerns, on mail-order arrangements.

The discovery of the Highlands by the outside world occurred through the invention and development of tourism, and a phenomenon which began as adventurous exploration by a few has grown to become an annual invasion by overwhelming numbers. The first tourists, as mentioned earlier in this chapter, were attracted to the Highlands by 'Ossian', by the poems and novels of Sir Walter Scott and by the romantic appeal of the Jacobite legend. Queen Victoria's annual visits to Balmoral set a fashion for visiting the Highlands in the second half of the nineteenth century, when railways and steamers made the

Highlands and Islands increasingly accessible. Many visitors to the Highlands in this period were sportsmen less affluent than those who rented the shooting lodges. They found accommodation at Highland inns, which have been charmingly described by Michael Brander, who is surely acquainted with surviving examples:

> Catering primarily for sportsmen rather than travellers, these inns were generally sited near good stalking, fishing or shooting. Inside they were varnished a dark brown, which grew darker with each passing year and were furnished with comfortable leather arm-chairs for the tweed-clad, often kilted sportsmen who visited them. On the walls were hung glass cases with record trout and salmon and heads of exceptional deer shot in the vicinity. Glass cases containing stuffed wild cats, martens, capercailzie and ptarmigan or other fauna of the Highlands were another favourite decoration. Along the walls the bound volumes of Punch steadily accumulated year by year to provide reading material for the sportsmen on the Sabbath when all other forms of occupation were strictly forbidden.[34]

Neither this form of tourism nor this style of accommodation has entirely disappeared, though those who enjoy them cannot fail to have a sense of visiting another era.

Tourism in the Highlands did not alter a great deal up to the First World War: tourists arrived in the area by train and usually reached remoter destinations by pony trap. Thenceforward, the sportsmen relied on their feet, and the guidance of their ghillies.

Between the two World Wars skiing, mountaineering and walking increased in popularity and brought more visitors to the Highlands. The development of more reliable and cheaper motor cars brought the discovery of the Highlands within the range of people who wanted to enjoy beautiful scenery and places of historic interest without physical exertion. This, essentially, was the beginning of modern tourism. Its development was interrupted by the Second World War, when travel was restricted, petrol was rationed and access was forbidden to some areas of the Highlands and Isles, which were set aside for military purposes. The most famous and the most sinister example was the island of Gruinard, which was sprayed with anthrax germs as an experiment in chemical warfare, and remained unvisited until 1988.

After the war, from the mid-1950s onwards, tourism took off, facilitated by road improvements, ferries and road-bridges, and the expansion of air travel. The decline of the railways, following the regrettable Beeching Report of 1963, threw an extra burden on the Highland roads, which are intolerably overloaded at the height of the tourist season, with cars, motor-coaches and caravans. The popularity of winter sports has created a second tourist season, with the sports centre at Aviemore as an international resort.

In response to tourism, and further to encourage it, the Highlands have developed a network of tourist attractions: Forest Parks and Nature Reserves; Nature Trails and Farm Parks; Open-air Museums and Visitors' Centres. There are also numerous caravan parks and tourist villages of self-catering cottages. These are profitable and well-run enterprises, which bring to the Highlands visitors far outnumbering the local population. Tourism creates prosperity, but paradoxically tends to destroy what it seeks to discover: unspoilt places and communities unaffected by the stresses of the modern world. This is not a problem limited to the Highlands or indeed to any country, it is a worldwide problem, compounded by overpopulation and ease of travel. Remoteness does not convey inviolability anywhere in the world and from the tourists' point of view the Highlands possess the advantage of being apparently remote but very easy of access.

Yet despite saturation by tourism, the discovery of the Highlands is not yet complete. The prehistory of the Highlands and Isles still holds many mysteries; there is much to be discovered concerning the enigmatic Picts. When present-day tourists visit the latest discoveries of archaeology they are participating in a continuous process of revelation.

NOTES AND REFERENCES

CHAPTER ONE: THE HIGHLANDS AND ISLANDS IN PREHISTORY

1 Richard Feachem, *Guide to Prehistoric Scotland* (2nd edn, p. 15).
2 'The constantly recurrent motif of antiquity is that of forest clearance; throughout Scottish prehistory echoes the sound of the woodman's axe, its blade of flint, stone, bronze, iron . . .' (Stuart Piggott, *Scotland before History*, p. 11).
   This was only the beginning:

> The biggest effect man has exerted on the history of the Highlands has been in the destruction of the ancient forest – the Great Wood of Caledon. This has happened within historic time, partly between AD 800 and 1100 and then from the 15th and 16th centuries till the end of the 18th. Even our own day cannot be exempt from this vast tale of almost wanton destruction, for the calls of the two German wars have been ruthless. Even after the war [the Second World War], in the name of scrub clearance, natural oakwood has been cleared (F. Fraser Darling and J. Morton Boyd, *The Highlands and Islands*, p. 66).

   The desperate attempts of modern environmentalists to prevent the destruction of the last rainforests have highlighted, it is to be hoped not too late, the heedlessness with which the destruction of the world's most valuable resource still continues.
3 If these were not religious symbols, they could have been status symbols, a concept which is surely as old as that of possession itself: 'Objects of prestige are with us today, as fur coats or expensive cars; perhaps more comparable with the useless jadeite axe-blades are diamonds, or the bars of gold in our national vaults, which we endow with unreal or talismanic values.' (Piggott, *Scotland before History*, p. 31)
4 Maes Howe, Orkney Mainland, is a passage grave, but it is different from all the other examples and has been described as 'representing a standard of design and workmanship which is not otherwise known to have been reached in Neolithic Britain – or indeed in any place N and W of the Mediterranean' (Richard Feachem, *Guide to Prehistoric Scotland*, p. 50). This Orcadian Mycenae suggests the existence of a local chief or king powerful enough to command craftsmen of exceptional skill and organize the acquisition and movement of materials on a grand scale.

5 Clothing made of furs and skins must have been the earliest form of clothing to have been invented, long predating textiles:

> It is likely that the making of adequate skin garments, cut and sewn with sinews, may well go back to a remote period of prehistory, even into the later Paleolithic. The tailored garment, in fact, and the use of trousers as a warm leg covering, are likely to be contributions to our comfort from the Mesolithic north, rather than what were to become the centres of ancient civilization in more southern and warmer regions, where the early invention of woven cloth gave rise to the simpler hot-weather clothing of the type of toga, burnous, dhoti and sarong. (Piggott, *Scotland before History*, pp. 25–6).

However, the idea that textiles were unknown in Skara Brae may require to be revised, in view of the discovery, in 1989, of a rock-cut tomb only a quarter of a mile from the prehistoric village, containing 'up to three square feet of 4,000 year-old cloth – probably woven flax . . . The cloth, originally used to hold cremated human remains, is about 1,500 years older than any other textiles discovered'. (*The Independent*, 21 July 1989, report by David Keys, Archaeology Correspondent.)

6 This is the theory propounded by Professor Alexander Thom, in *Megalithic Sites in Britain* (Oxford, 1967), and *Megalithic Lunar Observatories* (Clarendon Press, 1971).

7 The discovery of a crannog in Loch Olabhat, North Uist, excavated by Ian Armit of the University of Edinburgh, has pushed the invention of crannogs much farther back into prehistory. This crannog was a stone 'artificial island' with a timber and wattle perimeter fence and a wooden causeway forty yards in length connecting it to the shore of the loch.

> The island was constructed in around 3500 BC out of 20,000 cubic feet of stone and was occupied for at least 300 years . . . Hundreds of other artifical islands were constructed in lakes in Scotland and Ireland in prehistoric times. All served as platforms for small settlements – but Loch Olabhat is 2,500 years older than any of the other sites identified. (*The Independent*, 30 December 1989, report by David Keys, Archaeology Correspondent).

8 Boudicca led the revolt of the East Anglian Iceni against the Roman occupation of Britain in AD 60. Tacitus makes her address her soldiers with a speech beginning 'We British are used to woman commanders in war ...' (Tacitus, *Annals of Imperial Rome*, translated by Michael Grant, 1956, p. 330).

Dio Cassius left an indelible impression of a Celtic warrior queen in his famous description of Boudicca:

> She was very tall, in appearance terrifying, in the glance of her eyes
> most fierce, and her voice was harsh; a great mass of the tawniest hair
> fell to her hips; around her neck she wore a large golden necklace; and
> she wore a tunic of divers colours over which a thick mantle was
> fastened with a brooch. This was her invariable attire. (Grant Uden,
> They Looked Like This (1965), p. 18)

Though the historian lived over a century after Boudicca, his description
may be derived from authentic memories of her; his description of her
Celtic dress and ornaments is accurate.

9 It was Lucan in *Pharsalia* who mentioned three Celtic gods, Teutates,
Taranis and Esus, and early commentaries on his text have amplified
Lucan's information:

> Here Taranis is stated to have been propitiated by burning, while to
> Teutates victims were drowned, and to Esus they were hanged . . .
> There is the possibility . . . that these three modes symbolized the
> elements of earth or vegetation (Esus: hanging), fire (Taranis:
> burning), and water (Teutates: drowning). The drowning sacrifice is
> depicted on one of the panels of the great silver basin from Gundestrup
> in Denmark, itself a votive offering in a peat bog, but in manufacture of
> Celtic origin (T.G.E. Powell, *The Celts*, pp. 181–2).

10 The word *nemeton*, implying a sacred wood, is well distributed in place-
names throughout Celtic lands:

> Some examples are Drunemeton, the sanctuary and meeting place of
> the Galatians in Asia Minor . . . and Nemetodurum, from which is
> derived the modern name of Nanterre. In Britain there was a place
> Vernemeton in Nottinghamshire, and in Southern Scotland a Medione-
> meton. In Ireland *fidnemed* meant a sacred wood . . . and the eleventh-
> century cartulary of the Abbey of Quimperlé refers to a wood called
> Nemet, thus showing the continuity of Celtic tradition in Brittany
> (Powell, *The Celts*, pp. 166–7).

The Drunemeton of the Galatians was an oakwood, which may contain
the key to the meaning of the word 'druid':

> Druid as a word is considered to derive from words meaning
> 'knowledge of the oak' . . . Pliny compared the word to the Greek one for
> an oak tree *[drus]*, and seems to imply that its connection with oak was

intended. The connection between the druids and the oak is indeed explicit in Pliny's account of the cutting of mistletoe from an oak tree by the druids . . . If the oak, principally but not exclusively among trees, was the symbol of deity, 'knowledge of the oak' would be apposite for those who mediated with the supernatural (Ibid., p. 183).

11 Tacitus, *Agricola*, translated by H. Mattingly (revised edn 1970), p. 81. Tacitus is not only projecting himself into the mental world of the enemy, he is using his dramatized Calgacus as a mouthpiece of his own castigation of Roman covetousness.

CHAPTER TWO: PICTS AND SCOTS

1 Kenneth H. Jackson, 'The Duan Albanach', *Scottish Historical Review* 36 (1957, p. 131).
2 'The case for a pre-Celtic language lurking behind these inscriptions is not proven. Many of the inscriptions are agreed to be illegible due to careless inscribing and later weathering, and the number of clearly legible inscriptions is not sufficient to provide a corpus which would identify the nature of the language beyond doubt.' (Alfred P. Smyth, *Warlords and Holy Men*, p. 58)
3 There were 'Northern Picts' and 'Southern Picts', divided by the enormous territorial barrier of the Mounth (the Cairngorms). Possibly there was a High King and subsidiary kings of each group:

> This in turn is confirmed by reference to Talorgen son of Drustan, a king of Atholl, who was drowned by the Pictish overlord, Oengus son of Fergus (Unuist son of Urguist) in 739. If one concedes there was a tribal king in Atholl, then why not in Circinn (Angus and the Mearns), Fortriu (Strathearn and Menteith), Fife, Ce (Mar and Buchan), Fidach (Moray and Ross), and Cait (Caithness and southeast Sutherland), those seven ancient regions of Pictland as described in 'De Situ Albanie' and in the 'Pictish Chronicle'? Indeed the 'De Situ Albanie' informs us that each of the seven Pictish kingdoms (*septem regna*) was ruled by a king who was himself the overlord of seven under kings! (Ibid., p. 69).

4 The supposed matrilinearism of the Picts has been the subject of a vast controversy. Anthony Jackson in 'Pictish Social Stucture and Symbol Stones' argues in favour of a form of matrilinearism. Alfred P. Smyth in *Warlords and Holy Men* demands 'a radical appraisal of the matrilinear thesis' – and provides one, in his second chapter 'Picts: The Last Men on Earth, the Last of the Free' (pp. 36–83).

5 'Irrespective of the origins of the symbols themselves there is the problem of why put them on stone, and why in pairs? It is likely that the actual erection of the monuments took place within a relatively short space of time. The reason for saying this is that the symbols display a striking similarity all over Pictland and they display a remarkable technical mastery of stone cutting. This may be put down to itinerant stone-masons who executed these monuments for the lineage heads . . . Where an alliance was based on a new marriage arrangment then the bridewealth symbol could be added . . . In the centralizing and unifying period of Pictish history the leading lineages may have set the fashion, indeed they may have compelled it. There was more to setting up such stones than pure whim: they would have played an essential part in the unification of the Picts' (Jackson 'Pictish Social Structure and Symbol Stones', p. 136).

6 'If as has been argued the symbols stood for political alliances between lineages, their function would be lost under their Scottish overlords . . . The sudden collapse of the Picts in the face of the Scots might have been due to the prior collapse of their old kinship network – the kingpin of their society.' (Ibid., pp. 138–40).

7 Myles Dillon and Nora Chadwick, *The Celtic Realms*, p. 95.

8 Ibid., p. 107.

9 David Stewart of Garth, *Sketches of . . . the Highlanders of Scotland*, 2nd edn, 1822, vol 1, p. 95.

10 McGregor, *The Dean of Lismore's Book*, p. 17.

11 Dillon and Chadwick, op.cit., p. 108; T.G.E. Powell, *The Celts – The Ritual Year*, pp. 144–50.

12 Ibid., pp. 196ff.

13 Smyth, pp. 124–5.

14 Those who are interested in the 'Easter Controversy' will find a very clear exposition of the differing methods of calculating the date of Easter in Marjorie O. Anderson *Kings and Kingship in Early Scotland*, Appendix I 'Easter Tables', pp. 215–18.

15 An aprocryphal medieval Irish account of the circumstances which prompted Adomnan to introduce the Law of Innocents recounts: 'Now Ronait, Adomnan's mother, saw a woman with an iron reaping hook in her hand, dragging another woman out of the enemy host with a hook fastened in one of her breasts. For men and women went equally to battle at that time. After this, Ronait sat down and said "You shall not move me from this spot until you exempt women forever from being in this condition"'. (Smyth, op.cit. p. 135).

16 Ibid., p. 136.

17 'This is the legend apparently referred to . . . in OSC[*Old Scottish Chronicle*, extant in a manuscript copied at York about 1360], and it involves the treacherous massacre of the Pictish King and his magnates at

Forteviot or Scone. The motif from the ninth century onwards is international. It appears in the story of Hengist and Vortigern as told in the 'Historia Brittonum' of 830, in Widukind's account of the Old Saxons, in the foundation legend of Kiew Rus, and elswhere. In these cases it is used to explain the supersession of one ruling group by another, and while in each instance we may accept that such supersession occurred, we may also reject this account of how it happened. The tale is a derivative of oral historiography not only as a simplistic compendium of all the violent events which constituted the supersession, but also in its finality which denies any hope of the appearance of legitimate heirs to the older regime.' (M. Miller, 'The Last Century of Pictish Succession', *Scottish Studies*, 23 (1979), p. 50).

CHAPTER THREE: GAEL, NORSE AND NORMAN

1 Bjorn Cripplehand, poet to Magnus Barelegs, King of Norway, on the King's expedition to the Western Isles in 1098 (Smyth, p. 141).
2 An account of Blathmac's death was written by Walafrid Strabo, Abbot of Reichenau, in southern Germany (838–849):

'Blathmac was an Irish warrior and aristocrat turned monk, who settled on Iona in a deliberate attempt to seek martyrdom from the Vikings . . . According to Walafrid, Blathmac had foreknowledge of a Viking attack and advised those monks who lacked courage to take to their heels 'by a footpath through regions known to them'. The Vikings struck at dawn and slaughtered all Blathmac's followers who had chosen to stand by him. Blathmac was spared on condition he revealed the whereabouts of Columba's shrine and on refusing to divulge this information 'the pious sacrifice was torn limb from limb' and the Northmen began to dig feverishly in their greed for monastic loot. There is much in this account which is sustained from records of Viking atrocities elsewhere. The mutilation of Blathmac may well have marked out his martyrdom for special attention by Christian annalists in Ulster and even in Reichenau (Smyth, pp. 147–8).

3 Translated by Kuno Meyer (Dillon and Chadwick, p. 133).
4 *Laxdaela Saga*, translated by Magnus Magnusson and Hermann Palsson (1967), p. 49.
5 *Orkneyinga Saga*, translated by Hermann Palsson and Paul Edwards (1978), p. 215.
6 Ibid., p. 29.
7 Ibid., p. 37.

8 The Christian convert, or perhaps first generation Christian, in John Buchan's haunting poem belongs to an earlier period, and his conflict is between Roman Paganism and Christianity; but the poem hints at the conflict experienced in all ages by those who embrace a new religion, but cannot bring themselves wholly to relinquish the old:

WOOD MAGIC

I will walk warily in the wise woods on the fringes of eventide,
  For the covert is full of noises and the stir of nameless things,
I have seen in the dusk of the beeches the shapes of lords that ride,
  And down in the marish hollow I have heard the lady who sings,
And once in an April gloaming I met a maid on the sward,
  All marble-white and gleaming and tender and wild of eye;
I, Jehan the hunter, who speak, am a grown man, middling hard,
  But I dreamt a month of the maid, and wept I knew not why.

Down by the edge of the firs, in a coppice of heath and vine,
  Is an old moss-grown altar, shaded by briar and bloom,
Denys, the priest, hath told me 'twas the lord Apollo's shrine
  In the days ere Christ came down from God to the Virgin's womb.
I never go past but I doff my cap and avert my eyes –
  (Were Denys to catch me I trow I'd do penance for half a year.) –
For once I saw a flame there and the smoke of a sacrifice
  And a voice spake out of the thicket that froze my soul with fear.

Wherefore to God the Father, the son, and the Holy Ghost,
  Mary, the Blessed Mother, and the kindly Saints as well,
I will give glory and praise, and them I cherish the most,
  For they have the keys of Heaven, and save the soul from Hell.
But likewise I will spare for the Lord Apollo a grace,
  And a bow for the lady Venus – as a friend but not as a thrall,
'Tis true they are out of Heaven, but some day they may win the place;
  For gods are kittle cattle, and a wise man honours them all.

9 *Orkneyinga Saga*, p. 75.
10 Ibid., p. 76.
11 I.F. Grant, in *Highland Folk Ways* describes the dyeing process:

> As a rule the wool to be dyed and the dye plant are put into the dye pot in layers of about equal quantities and, if necessary, each layer is sprinkled with a mordant. Then the pot is filled with water ... The brew is then boiled and the worker stirs it with a stick and every now and then raises a bit of the wool to see if the right shade has been reached. The

dyeing is often done in the open air. There are no formal receipts and the worker goes by experience, taking handfuls of wool and dye plant and pinches of the mordant as she fills the pot . . . A dullish yellow is easily got from birch leaves or bog myrtle or heather. The colour is much improved by the addition of alum as a mordant . . . The real expert can get a brilliant clear yellow from heather in flower . . . I have been told that staghorn moss was used as a mordant before the introduction of alum . . . (pp. 229–30, 231).

12 *Birlinn Chlann Raghnaill – the Galley of Clan Ranald*, translated by Hugh MacDiarmid, *Collected Poems* (1962), pp. 438–9.

13 Kenneth M. Jackson, 'The Duan Albanach', *Scottish Historical Review*, 36 (1957), p. 133.

14 W.R. Kermack has given the following description of hereditary abbacy:

On the death of the founder [of a monastery], both his spiritual and his temporal rights passed to his coarb (comarba, 'co-heir') who succeeded him as abbot . . . Marriage, however, was not unlawful for the Celtic clergy, so that there was a tendency for the position of coarb to pass in direct descent; and eventually the coarb of the founder of a monastery was simply the possessor of the land of the monastery, who bore the title of abbot even although he might be a layman (*The Scottish Highlands*, p. 33).

15 G.W.S. Barrow, *Kingship and Unity: Scotland 1000–1306*, p. 148.

16 'There is a list of 666 Cistercian houses in a British Museum manuscript, arranged under the years in which they were founded . . . under the year 1160 there is an entry 'de Sconedale' which probably refers to Saddell' (A.L. Brown 'The Cistercian Abbey of Saddell, Kintyre', *Innes Review*, 20 (1969), p. 132). If 'Sconedale' is indeed Saddell, then Somerled would have been the founder; but the earliest documents connected with Saddell are charters issued by Ranald. Perhaps Somerled initiated the foundation, but died (1164) before it was fully organized. It seems reasonable, therefore, to give credit to both father and son.

17 Not all churches dedicated to Celtic saints are survivals of early dedications; many are later dedications resulting from a revival of interest in the Celtic church during later centuries (Barrow, p. 72).

18 I.F. Grant and Hugh Cheape, *Periods in Highland History*, pp. 47–53.

19 Barrow, p. 155.

CHAPTER FOUR: THE LORDSHIP OF THE ISLES

1 *The Dean of Lismore's Book*, pp. 95–97. This poem of lament for the decline of the Clan Donald is headed 'The author of this is Gilliecallum

Mac an Olla'. He is identified by John Bannerman as 'Gille-Coluim Mac an Ollaimh, clearly a court poet to the Lord of the Isles and probably a Beaton' (Bannerman 'The Lordship of the Isles' in Jennifer M. Brown (ed.), *Scottish Society in the Fifteenth Century*, p. 235).

> 'The [Beaton] family held lands near one of the mansions of the Lord of the Isles at Kilchoman in the south west of Islay and another branch was settled in Mull at Pennyghael on Loch Scridain where their herb garden is said to be traceable. The respective branches of the family bore the honorific titles of An t'Ollamh Ileach and An t'Ollamh Muileach, the term *ollamh*, doctor or professor, being reserved only for a very few of the professional classes' (Grant and Cheape, pp. 81–2).

2 W.D.H. Sellar 'The origins and ancestry of Somerled', *Scottish Historical Review*, 45 (1966), p. 128. '. . . in 954/962 a fleet of "Somarlidiorum" were slain in Buchan. However by the end of the tenth century it appears as a personal name . . .'

3 The curiosity of two brothers being called by the same name is explained by the fact that Robert III had been christened John, but John was considered an ill-omened name for a Scottish king after the unhappy example of John Balliol. Accordingly, John Stewart sought to avert the omens by assuming the prestigious name of Robert. His subjects, however, referred to him unofficially as 'John Faranyeir (John of Yesteryear)' (Ranald Nicholson, 'Scotland: The Later Middle Ages', p. 204).

4 Quoted and translated by Derick Thomson in *An Introduction to Gaelic Poetry*, pp. 30–31. Thomson explains the alphabetic aspect of the poem as 'working its way through the alphabet with couplets each giving four epithets beginning with the same letter, all in praise of the Clan Donald, as though one were to say in English:

> Be angry, be ardorous,
> be ape-like, be athletic;
> be bloody, be blustering,
> be bear-like, be barbarous.

This gives some notion of the movement and tone of the Incitement . . .'

5 There are several versions of this ballad; the version quoted is in *The Edinburgh Book of Scottish Verse* (1910), pp. 223–7.

6 Quoted from 'National Spirit and Native Culture' by John MacQueen, in Gordon Menzies (ed.), *The Scottish Nation* (1972), pp. 64–5. There is a less striking translation by the Revd Thomas McLauchlan in *The Dean of Lismore's Book*, pp. 99–100:

Thou head of Diarmad O'Cairbre,
Though great be thy trouble and pain,
I grudge thee not all thou hast suffered,
Although it be painful to tell . . .

7 'History of the MacDonalds' in J.R.N. MacPhail (ed.), *Highland Papers* vol. 1 (Scottish Text Society, 1914), p. 24.
8 Bannerman, op.cit. p. 222.
9 Quoted by Derick Thomson in *An Introduction to Gaelic Poetry*, p. 34.
10 Ibid., p. 38; Grant and Cheape, p. 82.
11 Grant and Cheape, p. 100.
12 Thomson, op.cit. p. 37.
13 Bannerman, op.cit., p. 232.
14 *The Dean of Lismore's Book*, p. 97.

CHAPTER FIVE: THE CLANS IN THE AGE OF FORAYS

1 i) A memorandum presented by Colin, fourth Earl of Argyll to King James V's Council, June 1531 (Gordon Donaldson, *Scotland: James V to James VII*, p. 51).
ii) *Clann Ghriogair air fogradh* – Clan Gregor outlawed (Grant and Cheape, *Periods in Highland History*, p. 136).
2 John Major, *A History of Greater Britain*, pp. 48–9.
3 David Stevenson, *Alasdair MacColla and the Highland Problem in the Seventeenth Century*, p. 17.
4 W.D.H. Sellar, 'The earliest Campbells – Norman, Briton or Gael?', *Scottish Studies*, 17 (1973), passim.
5 Grant and Cheape, p. 135.
6 The 'Letters of Fire and Sword' issued against the Clan Chattan in 1528 contains the following passage:

And thairfore it is our will, and we charge straitlie and commandis yow . . . ye pass all at anys . . . upon the said Clanquhattane, and invaid thame to thair uter destructioun, be slauchtir, byrning, drowning, and uthir ways; and leif na creatur levand of that clann, except preistis, wemen, and barnis . . . and als that ye tak the wemem and barnis of the said clan to sum partis of the sey, nerrest land, quhair schippis salbe forsene on our expressis, to saill with thame furth of our realme, and land with them in Jesland Zesland, or Norway; becaus it were inhumanite to put handis in the blude of wemen and barnis . . . (Gordon Donaldson, *Scottish Historical Documents*, pp. 104–105).

7 Donaldson, *Scotland: James V to James VII*, p. 232.

8 Ibid., p. 234.

9 Ibid., p. 228.

10 Andrew Knox, Bishop of the Isles (Ibid. p. 230).

11 Ibid., pp. 230–31.

12 Thomson, *An Introduction to Gaelic Poetry*, p. 106.

13 Ibid., p. 109

14 Ibid., pp. 110–11.

15 Grant and Cheape, pp. 132–3.

16 Gordon of Rothiemay, 'A History of Scots Affairs' cited by J. Telfer Dunbar in *A History of Highland Dress*, p. 35.

CHAPTER SIX: THEATRE OF WAR

1 Iain Lom MacDonald, 'The Battle of Inverlochy' (1645) in Derick Thomson, *An Introduction to Gaelic Poetry*, pp. 120–22.

2 John Roy Stewart, 'The Battle of Culloden' (1746).

3 Lindsay of Pitscottie, *Historie and Cronicles of Scotland* edited by Aeneas J.G. Mackay in 3 vols, Scottish Text Society 1899–1911, vol. 1, pp. 335–8.

4 Antonia Fraser, 'Mary Queen of Scots', p. 80.

5 Samuel Johnson, *Journey to the Western Isles*, pp. 34–5.

6 C.H. McIlwain (ed.), *Political Works of James I*, Harvard, 1918, pp. 269ff.

7 Frank McLynn, *The Jacobites*, p. 92.

8 Robert Burns, 'Birthday Ode for 31st December, 1787', in Anthony Hepburn (ed.), *Poems and Selected Letters*, with an introduction by David Daiches, Collins, 1959, pp. 254–5.

9 David Stevenson, *Alasdair MacColla and the Highland Problem*, pp. 82–4; David Stevenson, 'The Highland Charge' *History Today*, August 1982, pp. 3–8.

10 J. Telfer Dunbar, *History of Highland Dress*, p. 13.

11 John (or Iain) Mac Codrum, 'A Song against the Lowland Garb', in John Lorne Campbell, *Highland Songs of the Forty-Five*, pp. 249–53.

12 Samuel Johnson, *Jouney to the Western Isles*, p. 46.

13 McLynn, pp. 82, 88. John Daniel, a Jacobite who joined the Duke of Perth's regiment in England said 'The first time I saw this loyal army was betwixt Lancaster and Garstang; the brave Prince marching on foot at their head like a Cyrus or Trojan hero, drawing admiration and love from all who beheld him, raising their long-dejected hearts, and solacing their minds with the happy prospect of another golden age.' (p.88)

14 Lord Balmerino also said, shortly before his execution, in praise of the Prince: 'I must beg leave to tell you the incomparable sweetness of his nature, his affability, his compassion, his justice, his temperance, his patience, and his courage are virtues seldom to be found in the person. In

short he wants no qualifications requisite to make a great man.' (Ibid.).
McLynn goes on to comment:

> Charles Edward's personality remains an enigma. Few historical
> figures have been fated to shine so brightly for a brief period, only to be
> totally eclipsed thereafter . . . Charles Edward was too rough-hewn a
> character to fit easily into polite society. He was fluent in French, Italian
> and English – the last of which he spoke with a slight foreign accent –
> but by no stretch of the imagination could he be considered an educated
> man, especially by the stiff standards of the eighteenth century. For all
> that, he was, two centuries of adverse propaganda notwithstanding, an
> intelligent man with a quick understanding. His weaknesses were not
> primarily ones of intellect but of temperament and character. (pp. 197,
> 201)

15 W.R. Kermack, *The Scottish Highlands*, p. 135.
16 Ibid., p. 138.
17 Ibid., p. 133.
18 Alasdair Mac Mhaighstir Alasdair 'A Song Composed in the Year 1746', in
   John Lorne Campbell, *Highland Songs of the Forty-Five*, pp. 95–105.
19 Bruce Lenman, *Jacobite Clans of the Great Glen*, p. 99.
20 Bruce Lenman and J. Telfer Dunbar disagree on this interpretation.
   Lenman, op.cit. p.100 gives the explanation followed by the author;
   Dunbar, op.cit. p. 156 believes the Black Watch were so called because
   they kept watch over black cattle and prevented 'blackmail'.
21 Three deserters were shot: Samuel MacPherson, Malcolm MacPherson,
   and Farquhar Shaw. Dunbar, p. 171, describes prints of them. A print of
   Farquhar Shaw was subsequently altered by the addition of a white
   cockade and a few other minor details of costume, and was sold as a print
   of Prince Charles Edward Stuart.
22 Lenman, p. 181.
23 I.F. Grant, 'Along a Highland Road'.
24 Diana M. Henderson, *Highland Soldier*, p. 5.
25 Ibid., p. 8.

CHAPTER SEVEN: THE HIGHLANDS TRANSFORMED

1 George Bannatyne, (1568), *The Bannatyne Manuscript* edited by W. Tod
  Ritchie, Scottish Text Society New Series, no. 23, 1928.
2 Duncan Ban MacIntyre (1724–1808), 'A Song of Foxes'.
3 Sir Walter Scott *The Highland Clans, with a particular account of Rob Roy
  and the MacGregors* (1856), p. 36, cited in A.R.B. Haldane, *The Drove
  Roads of Scotland*, p. 197.

4 Myles Dillon and Nora Chadwick *The Celtic Realms*, p. 155: 'The name Medb means "intoxication', and it is now scholarly opinion that Medb was not a historical Queen but a goddess. Her consort in the epic is King Ailill, but she is credited with many consorts. Possibly the King had to be considered to be the husband of the goddess in order to hold authority.'

5 James MacDonald, *General View of the Agriculture of the Hebrides* (1811), cited in Haldane, p. 236.

6 Grant and Cheape, *Periods in Highland History*, pp. 6–6. Religion and magic combined in the incantations which accompanied the dipping of the charms in water. One quoted by these authors invokes St Bride, the Virgin Mary, the Trinity, Apostles and Angels, and concludes:

> A blessing on the gem and a blessing on the water
> A healing of bodily ailments to each suffering creature.

7 W.R. Kermack, *The Scottish Highlands*, pp. 147–8.

8 Haldane, p. 19.

9 I.F. Grant, *Highland Folk Ways*, pp. 69–70.

10 Eric Cregeen, 'Recollections of an Argyllshire Drover', *Scottish Studies*, 3 (1959), *passim*.

11 Ibid. The drover was Mr Dugald MacDougall (1866–1957), the last of three generations of drovers. He took his cattle from Argyll to the Falkirk Tryst. He told Dr Cregeen that it was a matter of pride to take care of the cattle on the journey and bring them in good condition to the Tryst.

12 Haldane, op.cit. p. 180. In 1750 some 20,000 Highland cattle were counted on the Wisbech road. About thirty years ago the author was told that Highland Cattle used to be unshod beside a certain inn near the A1, and that in an adjacent field it was still possible to find cattle shoes. Doubtless this field would have been used as a sort of 'shoe pool', as the shoes would have been too valuable to throw away. Unfortunately this place was never properly identified to the author.

13 Haldane has the following footnote on the drovers' dogs (op.cit. pp. 26–7):

> Some years ago the late Miss Stewart Mackenzie of Brahan, Ross-shire, informed a friend that in the course of journeys by coach in the late autumn from Brahan to the South during her childhood about the year 1840 she used frequently to see collie dogs making their way north unaccompanied. On inquiring from her parents why these dogs were alone, Miss Stewart Mackenzie was informed that these were dogs belonging to drovers who had taken cattle to England and that when the droving was finished the drovers returned by boat to Scotland. To save the trouble and expense of their transport the dogs were turned loose to find their own way north. It was explained that the dogs

followed the route taken on the southward journey being fed at Inns or Farms where the drove had 'stanced' and that in the following year when the drovers were again on the way south, they paid for the food given to the dogs. No evidence has come to light that drovers returned from the South by boat, and it would seem that a possible alternative explanation is that the dogs belonged to drovers who had remained in the South through the autumn for the harvest when the dogs would not be needed.

The second explanation seems unconvincing, as whereas a dog would follow its master home and would be capable of retracing the original route, no dog could be persuaded to leave its master and take its journey home without the prospect of finding him at the end of it. Miss Stewart Mackenzie's parents could have been wrong that the drovers had returned to Scotland by boat. Had they gone by coach or train, the dogs could still have been left to make their own way home.

14 Ibid., p. 24.
15 I.F. Grant, *Highland Folk Ways*, pp. 78–9.
16 Ibid., p. 80.
17 Grant and Cheape, p. 22. The authors allude to the 'Song of Cael', in which the house of Cael's beloved is described as having a roof thatched with blue and yellow birds' wings. Possibly the feather effect of thatch enshrined this poetic memory, as well as creating a watertight roof.
18 Grant, *Highland Folk Ways*, p. 156.
19 Grant, *Along a Highland Road*, p. 53.
20 Youngson, *After the Forty-Five*, p. 161.
21 David Hamilton, *The Healers*, p. 96.
22 Samuel Johnson, *A Journey to the Western Isles*, p. 63. Perhaps the other eighty inhabitants of Muck had been reluctant or unable to pay. Dr Johnson also recorded an amusing detail concerning the Laird himself: 'This gentleman whose name is, I think, MacLean, should be regularly called Muck; but the appelation which he thinks too coarse for his Island, he would still less like for himself, and he is therefore regularly addressed by the title Isle of Muck' (Ibid.). The custom was to address a laird by his territorial designation – in this instance 'Muck'. The laird had tried to rename his island 'Monk', but as no one complied in this, he settled for being addressed as 'Isle of Muck'.
23 Youngson, *After the Forty-Five*, pp. 164–5.
24 Martin Martin, *Description of the Western Isles*, p. 99.
25 Revd John Grant (1750), cited in Michael Brander, *Making of the Highlands*, p. 134.

26 Kelp and Barilla were very similar. Barilla was the Spanish name for the ash of a fleshy plant, salsola soda, grown on the coasts of the Mediterranean.

27 William Marshall, *General View of the Agriculture of the Central Highlands* (1794), cited in Grant and Cheape, *Periods in Highland History*, p. 231.

28 Ibid., p. 230.

29 Youngson, *After the Forty-Five*, p. 173.

30 Ibid.

31 Eric Richards, *The Leviathan of Wealth*, p. 12. The title of this study of the uses of his fortune is taken from the sobriquet bestowed by Greville on the first Duke of Sutherland.

32 Ibid., p. 284.

33 The title *Gloomy Memories* was chosen as a rebuttal to *Sunny Memories of Foreign Lands* by the novelist and anti-slavery pioneer, Harriet Beecher Stowe, in which she had given a fulsome description of her reception at Dunrobin Castle, Sutherland. Perhaps her head had been a little turned by the adulation she had received in Scotland. The following song was sung at a banquet given in her honour in Edinburgh, 20 April 1853:

> Come, Scotland, tune your stock and horn,
> And hail with song this joyous morn,
> When on Love's eagle pinions borne,
>   Harriet Beecher Stowe's come . . .
>
> A woman's arm Truth's falchion bears,
> A sweet low voice stern Conscience fears,
> And stony hearts dissolve in tears:
>   Harriet Beecher Stowe's come . . .
>
> Chorus: Freedom's angel now's come,
>   Mercy's sister now's come,
>   Grim Oppression drees his doom:
>   Harriet Beecher Stowe's come.
>
> (James Ballantine, 'Welcome to Harriet Beecher Stowe',
>   20 April 1853).

34 Cited in Brander, p. 151.

35 Youngson, p. 190.

36 Gordon Donaldson, *Scotland: The Shaping of a Nation*, p. 171.

37 James Boswell, p. 346

38 'Selkirk settlement is now represented by the flourishing province of Manitoba, in which his name is highly revered and his memory perpetuated by the town and county of Selkirk, both so called after him' (Miller Christy, 'Thomas Douglas, fifth Earl of Selkirk', *Dictionary of National Biography*).

39 T. M. Murchison in *Companion to Gaelic Scotland*, p. 68.

Notes and References

CHAPTER EIGHT: THE HIGHLANDS DISCOVERED

1 A letter by Karl Klingemann, Mendelssohn's companion in Scotland, quoted in Sebastian Hensel, *The Mendelssohn Family, from Letters and Journals*, 2 vols, 1881, vol. 1, p. 205. Cited in Roger Fiske *Scotland in Music*, p. 137.

2 Martin Martin, *Description of the Western Isles*, preface, p. viii.

3 Stuart Piggott, *The Druids*, p. 135, quotes a letter from Lluyd to an unnamed correspondent: 'I conjecture they were places of sacrifice and other religious Rites in the Times of Paganism, seeing the Druid were our antient heathen Priests.'

4 Dr Johnson gave the following account of 'Second Sight':

> The Second Sight is an impression made either by the mind upon the eye, or by the eye upon the mind, by which things distant or future are perceived, and seen as if they were present. A man a journey far from home falls from his horse, another, who is perhaps at work about the house, sees him bleeding on the ground, commonly with a landscape of the place where the accident befalls him. Another seer, driving home his cattle, or wandering in idleness, or musing in the sunshine, is suddenly surprised by the appearance of a bridal ceremony, or funeral procession, and counts the mourners or attendants, of whom, if he knows them, he relates the names, if he knows them not, he can describe the dresses. Things distant are seen at the instant when they happen. Of things future I know not that there is any rule for determining the time between the Sight and the event . . . This receptive faculty, for power it cannot be called, is neither voluntary nor constant. The appearances have no dependence upon choice: they cannot be summoned, detained, or recalled. The impression is sudden, and the effect often painful . . . By pretension to Second Sight, no profit was ever sought or gained. It is an involuntary affection, in which neither hope nor fear are known to have any part. Those who profess to feel it, do not boast of it as a privilege, nor are considered by others as advantageously distinguished. They have no temptation to feign; and their hearers have no motive to encourage the imposture. (Samuel Johnson, *A Journey to the Western Isles*, pp. 97–8, 99–100.

5 *The Poems of Ossian etc, Containing the poetical works of James MacPherson with notes and illustrations by Malcolm Laing*, 2 vols, Edinburgh, 1805, 'Fingal', book 1, vol i, pp. 13, 14.

6 Roger Fiske, *Scotland in Music*, pp. 48–9.

7 Sir Walter Scott, *The Lord of the Isles*, canto iv, verse x.

8 James Boswell, *Journal of a Tour to the Hebrides*, p. 322.
9 Samuel Johnson, p. 107:

> I asked a very learned Minister in Sky [sic] who had used all arts to make me believe the genuineness of the book, whether at last he believed it himself? but he would not answer. He wished me to be deceived, for the honour of his country; but would not directly or formally deceive me. Yet this man's testimony has been publicly produced as of one that held Fingal to be the work of Ossian.

Dr John Mackenzie (1803–1886) wrote in his memoirs:

> Mentioning the Bard [his family's bard and historian 'Allister Buy'] reminds me that one of our summer evening amusements was getting him to the dining-room after dinner where, well dined below stairs and primed by a bumper of port wine, he would stand up, and with really grand action and eloquence, give us poem after poem of Ossian (in Gaelic), word for word exactly as translated by McPherson not long before then, and stupidly believed by many to be MacPherson's own composition; though had Allister heard anyone hinting such nonsense, his stick would soon have made the heretic 'sensible'. Allister could not read, and only understood Gaelic, and these poems came down to him through generations numberless, as repeated by his ancestors round their winter evening fires. (Christine Byam Shaw (ed.), *Pigeon Holes of Memory: The Life and Times of Dr John Mackenzie, 1803–1886*, pp. 41–2).

10 Alan Cunningham, *The Life of Sir David Wilkie*, 3 vols, 1843, vol. ii, p. 83, and J.G. Lockhart, *Memoirs of Sir Walter Scott*, (7 vols, 1837–38), vol. v, p. 191, both cited in Gerald Finley, *Turner and George IV*, p. 10.
11 J. Telfer Dunbar, *History of Highland Dress*, chapter eleven, 'Tartan Pattern Books', *passim*.
12 Queen Victoria, *Our Life in the Highlands*, p. 21 (entry for Wednesday, 7 September 1842).
13 Ibid., p. 172.
14 The full dedication was:

To
MY LOYAL HIGHLANDERS
and especially
to the memory of
my devoted personal attendant
and faithful friend

JOHN BROWN
These records of my widowed life
in Scotland
are
gratefully dedicated

VICTORIA R. I.

Queen Victoria's attachment to John Brown was mercilessly satirized in *Punch*, and the rumour was current that they were secretly married. This rumour was satisfactorily disposed of by Queen Victoria's biographer Elizabeth Longford, *Victoria R.I.*, pp. 327–8

15 Cited in Michael Brander, *The Making of the Highlands*, p. 167.

16 An amusing satirical poem on the subject appears in Donald and Catherine Carswell (eds.), *The Scots Week-End and Caledonian Vade-Mecum for Host, Guest and Wayfarer*, 1936, pp. 112–13:

THE BEST-DRESSED HIGHLANDER

['A Prize of £5 to be awarded to the best-dressed Highlander at his own expense' – Programme of any Highland Gathering.]

My name is John Macleod – from Chiefs descended
　　Distinguished for their courage and their size.
A Highland gathering lately I attended,
　　Because I saw there was to be a prize
　　　　For the best-dressed Highlander,
　　　　The best-dressed Highlander,
The best-dressed Highlander at his own expense.

My kilt and tartan stockings I was wearing,
　　My claymore and my dirk and skian-dhu,
And when I sallied forth with manly bearing
　　I heard admiring whispers not a few –
　　　　'He's the best-dressed Highlander,
　　　　The best-dressed Highlander,
The best-dressed Highlander at his own expense.' . . .

The world has many shining paths of glory,
　　And I have chosen out this path for me –
That John Macleod, until he's old and hoary,
　　Will always and incomparably be
　　　　Quite the best-dressed Highlander,
　　　　The best-dressed Highlander,
The best-dressed Highlander, at his own expense.

Chorus: At his own expense,

> At his OWN expense,
> THE BEST-DRESSED HIGHLANDER AT HIS OWN
> EXPENSE.
>
> D.M. McKay

17 Grant and Cheape state:

> There is a very strong tradition that the old schools of piping used a
> syllabic notation to preserve their music and to pass it on to their pupils.
> Known as *canntaireachd*, it has survived in three forms, differing
> slightly from each other, MacCrimmon *canntaireachd*, MacArthur
> *canntaireachd* and Campbell or Nether Lorn *canntaireachd*. The last
> has survived in sufficient bulk in manuscript, for it was written out in the
> 1790s, to allow a reasonably complete system of notation to be
> reconstructed and to be published through the work of the Piobair-
> eachd Society in our own day . . . The principle of the vocal notation is
> the same for all sources. The notes of the melody are represented
> mainly by vowels, such that the vowel can have a specific pitch
> meaning, and the grace notes by consonants. (*Periods in Highland
> History*, pp. 133–4).

18 John MacInnes, Derick Thomson (ed.), *Companion to Gaelic Scotland*, p. 59.
19 Christian Hesketh, *Tartans*, p. 126.
20 Grant and Cheape, p. 282.
21 Ibid., p. 260.
22 *Carmina Gadelica*, vol. III (Edinburgh, 1940), p. 114.
23 John MacInnes, in Derick Thomson (ed.), *Companion to Gaelic Scotland*, p. 35.
24 Albert Mackie, *Scottish Pageantry*, 1967, pp. 240–41.
25 Grant and Cheape, p. 252.
26 Gordon Donaldson, *Scotland: The Shaping of a Nation* pp. 171–2.
27 Ibid., p. 172.
28 I.F. Grant, *Along a Highland Road*, p. 178.
29 Ibid., p. 96.
30 Ibid., pp. 105, 106.
31 Michael Brander, pp. 221–2.
32 Hugh Sutherland, in Derick Thomson (ed.), *Companion to Gaelic Scotland*, p. 214.
33 Grant and Cheape, p. 284.
34 Michael Brander, pp. 192–3.

SELECT BIBLIOGRAPHY

ANDERSON, ALAN ORR, *Early Sources of Scottish History, vol. 1 AD 500 to 1286* (Oliver and Boyd, 1922)

ANDERSON, MARJORIE O., *Kings and Kingship in Early Scotland* (Scottish Academic Press, 1973)

BAILEY, PATRICK, *Orkney* (David and Charles, 1971)

BANNERMAN, JOHN, 'The Lordship of the Isles', in Jennifer M. Brown (ed.), *Scottish Society in the Fifteenth Century*

BARROW, G.W.S., *Kingship and Unity: Scotland 1000–1306* (Edward Arnold, 1981)

BLAIR, ANNA, *Croft and Creel, A Century of Coastal Memories* (Shepheard-Walwyn, 1987)

BOSWELL, JAMES, *Journal of a Tour to the Hebrides with Samuel Johnson LLD* ed. R.W. Chapman (Oxford University Press, 1924, reprint 1979, in one volume with Johnson's *Journey to the Western Isles of Scotland*)

BRANDER, MICHAEL, *The Making of the Highlands* (Constable, 1980)

BROCK, WILLIAM R. AND DR C. HELEN BROCK, *Scotus Americanus: A Survey of the Sources for Links between Scotland and America in the Eighteenth Century* (Edinburgh University Press, 1982)

BROWN, A.L., 'The Cistercian Abbey of Saddell, Kintyre', *Innes Review*, 20 (1969)

BROWN, JENNIFER M. (ED.), *Scottish Society in the Fifteenth Century* (Edward Arnold, 1977)

BUTT, JOHN AND PONTING, KENNETH, *Scottish Textile History* (Aberdeen University Press, 1987)

CHILDE, GORDON V., *Scotland Before the Scots: being the Rhind Lectures for 1944* (Methuen, 1946)

CLAPPERTON, CHALMERS M. (ED.), *Scotland: a New Study* (David and Charles, 1983)

CREGEEN, ERIC, *Recollections of an Argyllshire Drover*, *Scottish Studies*, 3 (1959)

DARLING, F. FRASER AND J. MORTON BOYD, *The Highlands and Islands* (Collins, 'Fontana New Naturalist', 1964, revised ed. 1969)

DARLING, F. FRASER (ED.), *West Highland Survey: An Essay in Human Ecology* (Oxford University Press, 1955)

DILLON, MYLES, AND CHADWICK, NORA K., *The Celtic Realms* (Weidenfeld and Nicolson, 1967)

DODGHSON, R.A., 'Pretense of Blude and Place of thair Duelling: The Nature of Scottish Clans, 1500–1745' in R.A. Houston and I.D. Whyte (eds.), *Scottish Society 1500–1800* (Cambridge University Press, 1989)

DONALDSON, GORDON, *Common Errors in Scottish History* (Historical Association, 1956)

DONALDSON, GORDON (ED.), *Scotland: James V to James VII, The Edinburgh History of Scotland Vol. III* (Oliver and Boyd, 1965)

– *Scotland: The Shaping of a Nation* (David and Charles, 1974)

– *Scottish Historical Documents* (Scottish Academic Press, 1970)

DONALDSON, WILLIAM, *The Jacobite Song: Political Myth and National Identity* (Aberdeen University Press, 1988)

DUNBAR, JOHN TELFER, *History of Highland Dress* (B.T. Batsford, 1962, 2nd edition 1978)

FEACHEM, RICHARD, *Guide to Prehistoric Scotland* (B.T. Batsford, 1963, reprint 1980)

FENTON, ALEXANDER, *Country Life in Scotland: Our Rural Past* (John Donald, 1987)

FINLEY, GERALD, *Turner and George IV in Edinburgh, 1822* (The Tate Gallery, in association with Edinburgh University Press 1981)

FISKE, ROGER, *Scotland in Music: A European Enthusiasm* (Cambridge University Press, 1983)

FRASER, LADY ANTONIA, *Mary Queen of Scots* (Weidenfeld and Nicolson, 1969)

GILLIES, WILLIAM, 'Courtly and Satiric Poems in the Book of the Dean of Lismore', *Scottish Studies*, 21, (1977)

GRANT, I.F., *Along a Highland Road* (Shepheard-Walwyn, 1980)

– *Every-day Life on an Old Highland Farm, 1769–1782* (Longmans, Green and Co, 1924, revised edition Shepheard-Walwyn, 1981)

– *Highland Folk Ways* (Routledge and Kegan Paul, 1961)

– *The Lordship of the Isles: Wanderings in the Lost Lordship* (The Moray Press, 1935)

GRANT, I.F. AND CHEAPE, HUGH, *Periods in Highland History* (Shepheard-Walwyn, 1987)

GRIMBLE, IAN, *Highland Man* (Highlands and Islands Development Board, 1980)

HALDANE, A.R.B., *The Drove Roads of Scotland* (Thomas Nelson and Sons, 1952)

HAMILTON, DAVID, *The Healers: A History of Medicine in Scotland* (Canongate, 1981)

HENDERSON, DIANA M., *Highland Soldier: A Social Study of the Highland Regiments, 1820–1920* (John Donald, 1989)

HESKETH, CHRISTIAN, *Tartans* (Weidenfeld and Nicolson, 1961, second impression, 1970)

HOBSBAWM, ERIC, AND RANGER, TERENCE (EDS.), *The Invention of Tradition* (Cambridge University Press, 1983)

HOPKINS, PAUL, *Glencoe and the end of the Highland War* (John Donald, 1986)

HOUSTON, R.A. AND WHYTE, I.D. (EDS.), *Scottish Society, 1500–1800* (Cambridge University Press, 1989)

HUGHES, KATHLEEN, *Celtic Britain in the Early Middle Ages: Studies in Scottish and Welsh Sources* ed. David Dumville (The Boydell Press, Bowman and Littlefield, 1980)

JACKSON, ANTHONY, 'Pictish Social Structure and Symbol Stones: an Anthropological Assessment', *Scottish Studies*, 15 (1971)

JACKSON, KENNETH H., 'The Duan Albanach', *Scottish Historical Review*, 36 (1957)

– *A Celtic Miscellany: Translations from the Celtic Literatures* (Routledge and Kegan Paul, 1951, revised edn, 1971)

JOHNSON, SAMUEL, *A Journey to the Western Isles of Scotland* ed. R.W. Chapman (Oxford University Press, 1924, reprinted 1979 in one volume with Boswell's *Journal of a Tour to the Hebrides*)

KERMACK, W.R., *The Scottish Highlands: A Short History* (W. and A.K. Johnston and G.W. Bacon, 1957, reprinted, 1967)

LAING, LLOYD, *Celtic Britain* (Routledge and Kegan Paul 1979)

LENMAN, BRUCE, *The Jacobite Clans of the Great Glen, 1650–1784* (Methuen, 1984)

LEVEY, MICHAEL, *Painting at Court* [for Chapter Six, 'At Home at Court' on Queen Victoria and Landseer] (Weidenfeld and Nicolson, 1971)

MCGREGOR, SIR JAMES, *The Dean of Lismore's Book, a Selection of Ancient Gaelic Poetry*, editor and translator Revd Thomas McLauchlan, additional introduction by William F. Skene (Edmonston and Douglas, 1862)

MACINNES, JOHN, 'The Oral Tradition in Scottish Gaelic Poetry', *Scottish Studies*, 12 (1968)

MACKENZIE, OSGOOD HANBURY, *A Hundred Years in the Highlands* (Edward Arnold, 1921, new edition Geoffrey Bles, 1965)

MCKERRAL, ANDREW, *Kintyre in Seventeenth Century* (Oliver and Boyd, 1948)

MCLEOD, DONALD, *Gloomy Memories of the Highlands of Scotland: versus Mrs Harriet Beecher Stowe's Sunny Memories . . .* (Archibald Sinclair, Glasgow; John Grant, Edinburgh; John Noble, Inverness; Hugh MacDonald, Oban, 1892)

MCLYNN, FRANK, *The Jacobites* (Routledge and Kegan Paul, 1985)

MACPHAIL, J.R.N. (ED.), *Highland Papers* 'History of the MacDonalds', vol. 1 (Scottish History Society, 2nd Series, 1914)

– *Highland Papers* 'MacKenzies, Campbells, The Lews', vol. II (Scottish History Society, 2nd Series, 1916)

MACPHERSON, JAMES, *see* Ossian

MAJOR, JOHN, *A History of Greater Britain* (1521), editor and translator Archibald Constable (Scottish History Society, 1892)

MARTIN, MARTIN, *A Description of the Western Isles of Scotland* (Facsmile of second edition, 1716, James Thin, 1981)

MENZIES, GORDON (ED.), *Who Are The Scots?* (British Broadcasting Corporation, 1971)

MILLER, M., 'The Last Century of Pictish Succession', *Scottish Studies*, 23 (1979)

MILLMAN, R.N., *The Making of the Scottish Landscape* (B.T. Batsford, 1975)

MITCHISON, ROSALIND, *Lordship to Patronage: Scotland 1603–1745, The New History of Scotland volume V* (Edward Arnold, 1983)

MUNRO, R.W., *Kinsmen and Clansmen* (Johnson and Bacon, 1971)

MURRAY, W.H., *The Islands of Western Scotland: The Inner and Outer Hebrides* (Eyre Methuen, 1973)

NICHOLSON, RANALD, *Scotland: The Later Middle Ages, The Edinburgh History of Scotland volume II* (Oliver and Boyd, 1974)

NICOLSON, JAMES R., *Shetland* (David and Charles, 1972)

O'CONNOR, ANNE AND CLARKE, D.V., *From the Stone Age to the Forty-Five: Studies presented to R.B.K. Stevenson* (John Donald, 1983)

'OSSIAN', *The Poems of Ossian etc. Containing the Poetical Works of James MacPherson, with notes and illustrations by Malcolm Laing*, two volumes (Edinburgh, 1805)

PIGGOTT, STUART, *The Druids* (Thames and Hudson, 1968, new edition, 1987)
 – *Scotland Before History: with a Gazetteer of Ancient Monuments by Graham Ritchie* (Edinburgh University Press, 1982)

POWELL, T.G.E., *The Celts* (Thames and Hudson, 1958, new edition, 1980)

RENFREW, COLIN (ED.), *The Prehistory of Orkney* (Edinburgh University Press, 1985)

RITCHIE, GRAHAM AND HARMAN, MARY, *Exploring Scotland's Heritage: Argyll and the Western Isles*, The Royal Commission on the Ancient and Historical Monuments of Scotland (H.M.S.O. Edinburgh, 1985)

SELLAR, W.D.H., 'The Earliest Campbells – Norman, Briton or Gael?' *Scottish Studies*, 17 (1973)
 – 'The Origins and Ancestry of Somerled', *Scottish Historical Review*, 45 (1966)

SHAW, CHRISTINA BYAM (ED.), *Pigeon Holes of Memory: The Life and Times of Dr John MacKenzie (1803–1886)* (Constable, 1988)

SHEPHERD, IAN A.G., *Exploring Scotland's Heritage: Grampian*, The Royal Commission on the Ancient and Historical Monuments of Scotland (H.M.S.O. Edinburgh, 1986)

SMYTH, ALFRED P., *Warlords and Holy Men, The New History of Scotland, vol. I* (Edward Arnold, 1984)

STEER, K.A. AND BANNERMAN, J.W.M., *Late Medieval Monumental Sculpture in the West Highlands*, The Royal Commission on the Ancient and Historical Monuments of Scotland (1977)

STEVENSON, DAVID, *Alasdair MacColla and the Highland Problem in the Seventeenth Century* (John Donald, 1980)

THOMAS, CHARLES, *Celtic Britain* (Thames and Hudson, 1986)

THOMSON, DERICK S. (ED.), *The Companion to Gaelic Scotland* (Blackwell Reference, 1983)

THOMSON, DERICK, *An Introduction to Gaelic Poetry* (Victor Gollancz, 1974)
   – 'The Harlaw Brosnachadh' in J. Carney and D. Green (eds.), *Celtic Studies: Essays in Memory of Angus Matheson* (New York, 1968)

TREVOR ROPER, HUGH, 'The Highland Tradition of Scotland', in E. Hobsbawm and T. Ranger (eds.), *The Invention of Tradition* (Cambridge University Press, 1983)

VICTORIA, QUEEN, *Our Life in the Highlands*. Compilation from the two volumes of Queen Victoria's Journals: *Leaves from the Journal of Our Life in the Highlands*, 1868, and *More Leaves from the Journal of A Life in the Highlands*, 1884 (William KImber, 1968, reprint, 1972)

YOUNGSON, A.J., *After the Forty-Five: The Economic Impact on the Scottish Highlands* (Edinburgh University Press, 1973)

INDEX

Index